Loyal till Death

Indians

and the North-West Rebellion

Loyal till Death

Blair Stonechild
Bill Waiser

FIFTH
HOUSE
PUBLISHERS

Published by
Fifth House Ltd.
A Fitzhenry & Whiteside Company
195 Allstate Parkway
Markham, ON L3R 4T8
www.fifthhousepublishers.ca

Cover design by Jamie Tucker.
Cover photograph Mistahi maskwa (Big Bear), vers 1825-1888, un chef cri des
Plaines, courtesy O.B. Buell / Bibliothèque et Archives Canada / C-001873.
Cover photograph Poundmaker (vers 1842 1886), également appelé "The
Drummer", chef cri, plus tard adopté par Crowfoot de la nation des Pieds Noirs,
courtesy O.B. Buell / Bibliothèque et Archives Canada / C-001875

Printed and bound in Canada.

1 3 5 7 9 10 8 6 4 2

Library and Archives Canada Cataloguing in Publication

Stonechild, Blair
Loyal till death : Indians and the North-West
Rebellion / Blair Stonechild and Bill Waiser.
Includes bibliographical references and index.
ISBN 978-1-897252-73-4
1. Riel Rebellion, 1885—Participation, Indian.
2. Indians of North America—Saskatchewan—History.
I. Waiser, W. A . II. Title.
FC3215.S85 2010   971.05'4   C2010-902502-4

Fifth House Ltd. gratefully acknowledges the support of the Canada Council for
the Arts and the Department of Canadian Heritage. We acknowledge the financial
support of the Government of Canada through the Book Publishing Industry
Development Program (BPIDP) for our publishing program.

Canada Council   Conseil des Arts
for the Arts   du Canada

contents

preface and acknowledgements

THE AUTHORS OF *LOYAL TILL DEATH* came to the project from different backgrounds and perspectives. Blair Stonechild, a member of the Muscowpetung band in southern Saskatchewan and currently executive director of planning and development for the Saskatchewan Indian Federated College, heard stories from elders about how the First Nations had remained faithful to their treaty promises during the North-West Rebellion. This information did not correspond to the official version of events—that the Indians had been rebels in 1885—and prompted Stonechild to undertake his own investigation of the rebellion story and prepare a Master's thesis that proposed an alternative explanation for Indian behaviour. Bill Waiser, on the other hand, a former historian with the Canadian Parks Service and now head of the Department of History at the University of Saskatchewan, was influenced by a small volume of scholarly literature, appearing around the time of the rebellion centennial, that persuasively argued that there was no Indian rebellion in 1885. The validity of this interpretation was confirmed when Waiser toured the rebellion sites in northwestern Saskatchewan in the fall of 1991 and learned firsthand how any Cree involvement was spontaneous, isolated, and defensive.

In the spring of 1992, Walter Hildebrandt, formerly of the prairie and northern regional office, Canadian Parks Service, organized a meeting in Saskatoon to work out the details for a new project to incorporate the Indian point of view in interpretative materials at rebellion sites in Saskatchewan. Waiser, Rick Stuart of the Winnipeg Parks office, and Mariam Robinson, then superintendent of Fort Battleford National Historic Park, attended the meeting. It was agreed that Waiser and Stonechild would undertake the project, on the understanding that Indian communities would be involved in the collection of historical material, that the Parks Service would provide funding for the oral history program, and that the resulting manuscript could be used for future site interpretation. Stonechild and Waiser, with the assistance of Mariam Robinson, launched the oral history program in the fall of 1992 by visiting some ten reserves in central Saskatchewan and securing the cooperation and endorsement of the chiefs and/or councils. All reserves agreed to participate in the project; several regretted that the information had not been collected a generation earlier.

Aboriginal research assistants from the various reserves conducted the interview program over a two-year period (1992-94). These research assistants, recommended by the band offices, would visit elders, present them with traditional gifts, and then explain the nature and purpose of the project; if the elder agreed to participate, stories about the rebellion were recorded—in most instances, in the Native language. Stonechild and Waiser, in the meantime, conducted a thorough examination of the archival records of several government departments and political figures. Collectively, the two sources of information demonstrated that the Indians of western Canada had their own concerns and strategies in 1885; their findings also helped explain why some Indians resisted during the rebellion, and equally important, why the majority chose not to participate.

Loyal till Death benefited greatly from the assistance of several individuals and organizations. Walter Hildebrandt, Rick Stuart, and especially Mariam Robinson provided support and encouragement for the project during its initial stages. John Bird, Winnie Eagle, Wallace Fox, Brenda Gardipy, Jeff Kahmakoostayo, Rod King, Alma and Simon Kytwayhat, Norman Paul, Clarence Swimmer, Tyrone Tootoosis, Glenda Wahobin, and Alice Wuttunnee collected interviews from elders or made suggestions for the oral history component of the manuscript; the authors are also greatly indebted to the elders who willingly told their stories. Diane Payment graciously shared her knowledge of the history of the Saskatchewan Métis community. Susan Kooyman of the Glenbow Archives, Anne Morton of the Hudson's Bay Company Archives, and Lorraine Gadoury of the National Archives of Canada recommended possible primary sources. Jim Miller, Gerry Friesen, and Hugh Dempsey read the manuscript at various stages and gave expert feedback and reaction; naturally, any possible errors of interpretation or fact are our own.

James Smith of the John Smith reserve prepared a series of new sketches of rebellion events, while George Duff drew the maps. Jean Horosko, Kathryn Drake, and Jessica Waiser helped with the preparation of the appendices, photograph cutlines, and index. Finally, a special thank-you is owed to the descendants of Canadian Indians who made our visit to Montana in the fall of 1994 a memorable one.

Financial assistance for the research, preparation, and production of *Loyal till Death* was secured from a variety of sources: the Canadian Parks Service, the University of Saskatchewan President's SSHRCC Fund, the publication fund at the Saskatchewan Indian Federated College and the University of Saskatchewan, and the Association for Canadian Studies. This generous funding is gratefully acknowledged.

Fifth House Publishers expressed an interest in the manuscript in its early stages. Charlene Dobmeier supplied insightful editorial advice and direction throughout the preparation of the manuscript, while Nora Russell designed yet another attractive book. Fifth House's dedication to western Canadian history merits greater recognition.

Loyal till Death is dedicated to the First Nations of western Canada who stood by the Queen during the troubles of 1885 and yet were deliberately tarred with the brush of rebellion. May their loyalty to the country be finally recognized.

BLAIR STONECHILD   BILL WAISER

The executions of the Indians . . . ought to
convince the Red Man that the White Man governs.

John A. Macdonald
20 November 1885

Lifting a Blanket

O N 30 APRIL 1885, Charles Tupper, the Canadian high commissioner to the United Kingdom, frantically cabled Prime Minister John A. Macdonald about a London news story claiming there had been an "indian rising" in western Canada.[1] The report was a gross exaggeration. In fact, in the weeks immediately following Métis leader Louis Riel's declaration of a provisional government, several Indian leaders across the West came forward and solemnly affirmed their allegiance to Queen Victoria and to the spirit of the treaties they had signed in the 1870s. Canadian officials, however, chose to ignore these declarations of loyalty in favour of portraying the 1885 North-West Rebellion as a concerted, yet futile, attempt by the Indians and Métis to wrest control of the region away from the Canadian state. They were all traitors, united in an evil cause, and political figures like Tupper and Macdonald had good reason to worry about their seditious behaviour.

This idea of an Indian-Métis uprising has evolved into one of western Canada's most persistent myths. And it has been expressed in many forms. In his 1910 history of the force, *Riders of the Plains*, mounted police historian A.L. Haydon observed that "both half-breeds and Indians [had been] taught a severe lesson" in 1885. "There had been war—red war, with its opportunities for fighting, for revenge, and for many other outlets of energy so dear to the primitive mind. These instincts are hard to eradicate."[2] The idea also spilled over into fiction. In *The Patrol of the Sun Dance Trail*, minister-turned-novelist Charles Gordon (Ralph Connor) had a handful of resolute mounties facing the prospect of an Indian war in 1885. It was a prospect "so serious, so terrible, that the oldest officer of the force spoke of it with face growing grave and voice growing lowered."[3]

The most influential expression of the Indian-Métis conspiracy theory has been historian George Stanley's 1936 book, *The Birth of Western Canada*. In trying to make sense of the 1885 rebellion, Stanley attributed the outbreak to a clash of cultures between primitive and more advanced peoples. "The gravest problem presented to the Dominion of Canada by the acquisition and settlement of Rupert's Land and the North-West," he observed, "was the impact of a superior civilization upon the native Indian tribes." He went on to explain how the First Nations were bewildered and frustrated by the momentous changes occurring around them, and not knowing how to respond, fell under the influence of Louis Riel and the Métis. The Indians, according to Stanley, were "rebels" in 1885, and the only reason things did not turn out worse was because "the demands of savage democracy rendered them incapable of rapid decision." In the end, though, despite their treasonous acts, the Indians suffered less than the Métis for their involvement; they were "punished" and rightly so, "but not with vindictive severity."[4]

Seductive in its simplicity, *The Birth of Western Canada* is widely regarded as the classic work on the rebellion.[5] And though Stanley's sixty-year-old interpretation has been challenged, if not altogether dismissed by several prominent scholars working in the field,[6] it continues to cast a long shadow over writing on the topic. Many of the newer general histories of Canada, for example, insist that Plains Cree leaders, driven by broken promises and incredible hardship, joined Louis Riel in armed struggle against the Canadian government in the spring of 1885.[7] This argument is not only misleading, but it also negates the work of western Canadian historians over the last decade to bring about a better understanding and appreciation of the Indian role in the 1885 troubles, especially the motivations underlying Indian behaviour. Indians, in the public eye, are generally regarded as confused, angry allies who played a secondary, supporting role in the rebellion.

This popular image is confirmed by the official record, which suggests that First Nations were anything but innocent. Twenty-eight reserves were identified as disloyal in 1885, while over fifty Indians were convicted of rebellion-related crimes.[8] Those sentenced included Chiefs Big Bear and Poundmaker, two prominent Cree leaders at the time, and eight warriors who dropped to their deaths simultaneously at Battleford on 27 November 1885 in Canada's largest mass hanging. The notion of an Indian uprising has also become ingrained in the western Canadian conscience—thanks, in no small part, to how the events have been interpreted. The commemorative bronze plaques at rebellion sites such as Battleford and Frenchman Butte, erected before the new scholarship was available, create the distinct impression that Indians were full and willing participants.[9] This apparent involvement in the rebellion was also one of several factors that delayed the resolution of long-standing aboriginal grievances. It was not until the mid-1970s, for example, that the question of treaty land entitlement went forward in Saskatchewan.[10]

Indian elders, on the other hand, tell a much different story. Over the last few years, especially since the centenary of the rebellion, they have quietly, though resolutely, asserted that their ancestors were not rebels and that they were not as involved in the troubles as history has portrayed them. According to the late John B. Tootoosis, former head of the provincial chapter of the League of Indians of Canada and later president of the Federation of Saskatchewan Indians, the Cree were determined to remain loyal in 1885. "When the Métis people were preparing to have this uprising," Tootoosis recounted on the Poundmaker reserve in November 1984, "they [the Indian people] all said no. We can't support you. We signed an agreement with the Crown not to fight any more; they were to live in peace with these people. We signed a treaty, we have to live up to this treaty."[11]

Getting at these oral accounts in order to understand what actually happened in 1885 was difficult until recently. Many elders were reluctant to share their stories outside their home communities because they feared retribution—one hundred years later! Others worried about bringing shame to their families or possibly implicating someone else. A few were concerned about offending the dead. "It is like when something is covered with a blanket and held down on all four sides," explained Mrs. Florence Paul of the One Arrow reserve when asked about the reluctance to speak out. "They talked about it in parts only—not the whole story. And they got nervous telling it. They were afraid of another uprising and more trouble. And they were also afraid of getting the young people into trouble."[12]

Over the last decade, however, many elders have agreed to tell what they know about the North-West Rebellion by recounting stories that had been passed down through the generations in the traditional manner.[13] And when this historical information was combined with a thorough review of the primary government records,[14] it became apparent that the First Nations role in the troubles has been sadly misrepresented or grossly misunderstood—despite the recent efforts of historians working in the area. The material not only cast a different light on many of the events of 1885, but also provided insight into the political strategy of the various Indian leaders and their relationship with the Métis and the Canadian government. Above all, it indicated the need for a new account of the rebellion from the Indian point of view.

Loyal till Death argues that the Indians of western Canada had their own strategies for dealing with their situation in the 1880s and that these strategies did not include open rebellion. It also explains why some individuals or groups resisted in 1885, and equally important, why the majority of the bands chose not to participate in the troubles. Building on the recent work of several specialists in Indian-White relations, it examines the events of the rebellion from the First Nations perspective and demonstrates that Indian involvement was isolated and sporadic, not part of a grand alliance with the Métis. Finally, the book describes how the Canadian government deliberately portrayed Indians as rebels in order to justify a number of restrictive and repressive measures and how the punishment meted out to the bands in the aftermath of the troubles has been generally ignored—what one historian has called the "great amnesia."[15]

Loyal till Death brings a different but equally vital perspective to the North-West Rebellion, and in doing so, provides a more balanced understanding of the events of 1885. It also offers an alternative explanation for Indian behaviour at the time: that they knew how to respond to change, that they looked to their own leaders for direction, and that they remained loyal to the Queen. And it calls into question the treatment of Indian peoples in the weeks and months after the rebellion, especially the imprisonment of Cree leaders for treason-felony. Reconsideration of the rebellion story has an important bearing on the First Nations legacy today. To use Florence Paul's analogy, it is time to lift the blanket.

chapter one

Accepting the Queen's Hand

MISTAWASIS AND AHTAHKAKOOP anxiously awaited the arrival of the other delegates. The two Cree chiefs and their followers had been among the first to arrive at Fort Carlton in August 1876 in anticipation of the Queen's treaty commissioners. Although both men had been seeking such a meeting for several years, they did not want to hurry into an agreement they would later regret, especially since several of the other Indian leaders had not yet arrived. The chiefs looked upon the forthcoming negotiations with mixed emotions. Until recent memory, the Plains Cree were masters of their territory, which included much of present-day central Saskatchewan and Alberta. With guns and horses acquired through trade, they had driven the Blackfoot and Gros Ventres to the west and south, occupying the rich buffalo-hunting lands of the prairie-parkland. Other nations held them in fear. But the glory won by their warriors was gradually slipping away. Decades of intertribal warfare had taken a heavy toll. So too had diseases such as smallpox, scarlet fever, and whooping cough—invisible foes that killed indiscriminately. The cruellest blow, however, was the rapid decline of the buffalo, the mainstay of their lives. These animals, once numbering in the millions, were now rarely seen north of the North Saskatchewan River. And with their sudden disappearance, leaders like Mistawasis and Ahtahkakoop realized that the Cree had reached a crucial turning point in their nation's history—the future seemed bleak—and that their plight would only worsen unless they reached an agreement with the British Crown to help them adapt to a new agricultural way of life. The negotiations at Fort Carlton were therefore a solemn undertaking for the Indian participants that went beyond the simple transfer of land. Indeed, the talks were comparable to the passionate, at times acrimonious, confederation debates that had charted a new future for the Canadian colonies a decade earlier.

Mistawasis and other prominent Cree chiefs had been asking to meet with Canadian representatives since 1870, following the transfer of Rupert's Land and the Northwestern Territory from the Hudson's Bay Company to the young dominion. The Indians were upset by rumours about the apparent sale of their lands and wanted to ensure that settlement did not proceed until their own interests and needs had been dealt with. Ottawa, however, had no immediate plans to negotiate treaties with those groups living west of the new province of Manitoba and had to be forced to deal with the Cree. In 1875, on Mistawasis's orders, his men stopped a construction crew from building a telegraph line through their territory; they also turned back a Geological Survey of Canada party that was working in the area.[1] The Cree resented these incursions and were determined, in the words of Methodist missionary George McDougall, "to oppose the running of lines, or the making of roads through their country, until a settlement between the Government and them had been effected."[2] Canada had no choice. If it wanted to guarantee the peaceful, orderly settlement of the region, Ottawa had to reach an agreement with the Cree for their lands. Finally, in the fall of 1875, Reverend McDougall brought the promising news that Alexander Morris, the lieutenant governor of Manitoba, would meet with them the following August.

In making treaties with the western Indians, Canada was following a British tradition that had been established by the Royal Proclamation of 1763. In recognition of the important role that First Nations had played as allies in the military struggle between Great Britain and France, the British promised not to allow agricultural settlement of Indian territory until title had been surrendered to the Crown by means of treaties. This policy of negotiating through the Crown for

Assiniboine camp, late summer 1874. The First Nations presence in the plains-parkland area was a testimony to their resourcefulness and resiliency. *National Archives of Canada C81793*

Indian lands had been followed, albeit imperfectly, in the late eighteenth and early nineteenth centuries and had become well-entrenched by the time Canada acquired its North-West empire in 1870.[3] The motives underlying the process, though, had changed. Whereas British military officials had been anxious to secure and maintain Indian allies in their struggle with an aggressive, expansionary United States, Canadian civil authorities now wanted to avoid costly Indian wars over western lands. In other words, negotiation was the cheaper course of action. This was clearly borne out by the experience south of the border, where the United States spent more money fighting Indian wars in 1870 than the entire Canadian budget for that year.[4] The young dominion feared that the First Nations, as "savage" races, could explode with violence if not handled delicately; in particular, Ottawa was determined to avoid a repetition of the troubles at Red River in 1869–70. The process was also imbued by an imperialist ideology that held that the Indian would inevitably vanish as a distinct race in the face of the white man's "superior" civilization and that it was Canada's duty to remake them into loyal subjects of the Crown. Alexander Morris neatly summed up this thinking in his closing remarks to his 1880 book on the treaties. "Let us have Christianity and civilization to leaven the mass of heathenism and paganism among the Indian tribes," he invoked. "Let us have a wise and paternal

Government . . . doing its utmost to help and elevate the Indian population, who have been cast upon our care."[5]

This notion that First Nations faced certain extinction unless saved by Canadian humanitarian efforts was completely at odds with the real situation in western Canada at the time. Although the Cree faced a number of difficulties in the 1870s, in particular the loss of the buffalo, they were not a defeated or doomed people. They had not only developed a richly vibrant society and culture, but practised what one author has described as an "opportunity-based economy,"[6] using every available resource. They were also an extremely dynamic, resilient people who had faced similar challenges in the past and adapted accordingly; their very presence in the prairie-parkland area was a testimony to their resourcefulness and innovation. Above all, they were a proud, self-governing community that was not about to step aside without protest when some foreign country tried to claim their territory. The Cree saw themselves as equals in their dealings with Canada and were prepared to negotiate in order to guarantee their future security and well-being in the region as an independent nation. They had no interest in or need for a Canadian crutch. They recognized, though, that the demise of the buffalo placed a severe, if not unbearable, strain on the remaining resources of the region and that they had to convert to agriculture in order to compete with the newcomers.[7]

Another important aspect of the western treaty process is that the Indians had a tradition of negotiating treaties or agreements. The Cree had formed beneficial alliances with the Assiniboine and Saulteaux in their westward push to the plains and had once served as powerful middlemen for the British-based Hudson's Bay Company in the western Canadian fur trade. In fact, the Indians regularly renewed their alliance with the English by means of pre-trading ceremonies that included expressions of kinship and the exchange of gifts.[8] It now appeared that the Queen, through the Canadian government, was willing to enter into a similar relationship. When several Cree chiefs, in particular the venerable Sweetgrass, requested help in becoming farmers in 1871, they were told that the Queen would "protect you and do you justice"[9] when the time arrived to conclude a treaty. And in August 1874, HBC trader William McKay of Fort Pitt visited the Plains Cree camps along the North Saskatchewan to advise them that the North-West Mounted Police—the Queen's soldiers— had been sent into the region to protect them from unscrupulous

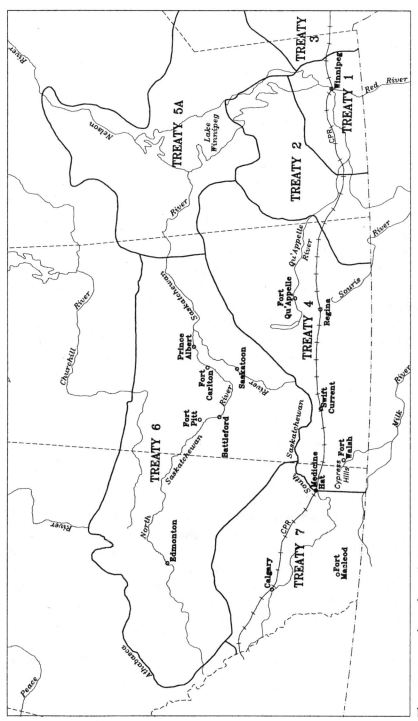

The seven numbered treaties.

American traders and the whisky they peddled; as a symbol of the Queen's goodwill, McKay also distributed presents.[10] These assurances suggested to the Cree that the Crown was genuinely concerned about their welfare and that an alliance offered the best hope of restructuring their economy.[11] But they were equally determined to leave nothing to chance. When Mistawasis and Ahtahkakoop learned of the impending arrival of the treaty commissioners, they decided to hire the best interpreter in the North-West and invited Peter Erasmus, a mixed-blood they knew only by reputation, to serve as their translator.

The agreement to be negotiated at Fort Carlton in August 1876 was the sixth of seven western treaties that were signed between 1871 and 1877. The deliberations proved to be a long, at times protracted, process because Indian negotiators insisted on better terms than those offered in the formal treaty. They also tried to build on the concessions that had been won in previous agreements. The treaty commissioners, in turn, were under strict orders to concede as little as possible to the Indians and not make any additional or "outside" promises to the original terms. In his later account of the Treaty Six proceedings, Peter Erasmus compared the dominion government stance to "a boxer sent into the ring with his hands tied."[12] But like a prize fight, there was much at stake. The proposed treaty area covered some 120,000 square miles in present-day central Saskatchewan and Alberta—lands crucial to Prime Minister John A. Macdonald's national policy of western expansion.

On the afternoon of 27 July 1876, the Hon. Alexander Morris and his treaty party left Fort Garry (present-day Winnipeg) and headed northwest along the Carlton trail towards the HBC post of the same name. Two and a half weeks later, at Gabriel's crossing on the South Saskatchewan River, Morris was greeted by a young messenger and handed a letter of welcome to Cree territory. The gesture was more than a symbolic act. Several members of Yellow Quill's Saulteaux band who were unhappy with Treaty Four had tried to convince the Cree to prevent Morris from crossing the river. Aware of the potential for trouble, Mistawasis had sent the messenger ahead to escort Morris's party the remaining distance. The discontented Saulteaux would later appear at Fort Carlton to argue that Treaty Four had been a bad bargain and that the Cree should not accept any agreement unless the terms were significantly better.[13]

Once across the river, the treaty commission was one day's

Alexander Morris, lieutenant governor of the North-West Territories, negotiated Treaty Six on behalf of the Canadian government. *Alexander Morris Collection 3/Provincial Archives of Manitoba*

journey from its objective. But as the party neared Duck Lake, it was intercepted by Chief Beardy, leader of the Willow Cree, a group of Parkland People who inhabited the area along the river south of Prince Albert. Beardy invited the entourage to his nearby campsite where an impressive display awaited Morris. The riders held their right arms to the skies, thanking the Creator for the fine day and invoking His blessing. Beardy, or Kamiyistowesit, a man known to possess spiritual powers, then revealed that he had received a vision urging him to sign the treaty at the top of a local hill, rather than at the planned meeting place. Not wanting to compromise his prearranged meeting with the other Cree chiefs, Morris refused Beardy's request and continued on to Carlton. The incident, however, would be grossly misunderstood. Although the Willow Cree were anxious to negotiate an agreement in keeping with Beardy's vision, Morris would later describe them as "an obstacle to the progress of the treaty,"[14] especially for their decision to remain at their encampment during the Carlton deliberations.

That evening, Tuesday 15 August, Mistawasis and Ahtahkakoop, the two senior chiefs of the Carlton Indians, officially welcomed Morris to their country. Mistawasis, whose name meant "Big Child," was actually quite small in stature, but had a forceful personality and was revered by his fellow chiefs. Ahtahkakoop, named after a "star blanket" or night sky, was a tall, muscular, dignified-looking man, yet very reserved; he was more likely to be seen in European clothes than traditional Cree dress. Both chiefs had developed close ties with the Hudson's Bay Company, had been influenced by Christianity, and had tried their hand at growing root crops. Their followers, who made up more than half the assembled lodges at the Carlton meeting, were sometimes known as the House People, because of their adoption of the white man's style of accommodation.[15]

On 16 August, the Indians notified Commissioner Morris that they wished to confer among themselves. Although the assembled chiefs favoured a treaty and had brought together some 250 lodges, they were reluctant to proceed when several other leaders, such as Little Pine and Lucky Man, were absent. They also wanted Beardy and his Willow People to join the meeting. When no other chiefs had appeared by the next day, Morris insisted on getting started the following morning. The other potential stumbling block was the Cree's determination to have their own interpreter. When Morris heard that Mistawasis and Ahtahkakoop had hired Peter Erasmus to translate for them, he claimed it was an unnecessary expense. The government had already secured the services of two official interpreters: the Reverend John McKay, who spoke a Swampy Cree dialect rarely used on the plains, and the mixed-blood Peter Ballendine, who knew Assiniboine well but whose proficiency in Cree was questionable. Morris eventually relented, but only after Mistawasis threatened to cancel the meeting. "If you do not want the arrangement there will be no talks," he heatedly told the Queen's representative. "We did not send for you, you sent for us."[16]

The negotiations finally got underway on Friday 18 August at a traditional camping area, known to the Cree as "pehonanik" or the waiting place, about a mile and a half from the fort.

Mistawasis (seated right) and Ahtahkakoop (seated left), the two senior chiefs of the Carlton Indians, were prepared to accept the Queen's hand of friendship. *Saskatoon Archives Board R–B2837*

The Cree were determined to have their own interpreter at the Treaty Six negotiations and hired mixed-blood Peter Erasmus to translate for them. *Provincial Archives of Alberta A1821*

With hills and woods forming a backdrop and surrounded by marshes and small lakes, the slightly elevated meeting ground was an impressive sight. At exactly 10:30 A.M., Governor Morris, in a gold-braided uniform and cocked hat, left the fort in a carriage for the Indian encampment, accompanied by a band and about one hundred mounted policemen in their scarlet tunics. The importance of having the Queen's "warriors" present was not lost on the commissioners, for the Indians viewed them as potential allies to be befriended, rather than a hostile force called upon to intimidate them. Erasmus suggested in his account of the negotiations that "the great prestige of the Governor was somewhat overshadowed by the smart appearance of his escort."[17]

Once Morris had arrived at his tent, set on a slight rise overlooking the grounds, and the Union Jack had been hoisted, the two thousand Indians came together, beating drums, singing, dancing, and discharging guns. They then advanced slowly in a large semicircle, led by some two dozen riders on horseback who rode in circles while performing intricate feats. Within fifty yards of the governor's tent, all fell silent as the sacred pipe-stem bundle was unwrapped.[18] This ceremony—described by Morris as most "peculiar"[19]—was an invitation to the Creator to witness the proceedings and provide guidance. It also signified that the Cree approached the negotiations with considerable thought and commitment. Chief Strike-Him-on-the-Back carried the large, beautifully adorned pipe-stem to the front of the semicircle where blankets and robes had been spread for the Indian chiefs and headmen. Strike-Him-on-the-Back had received his name from a coup he had counted by striking the enemy on the back during a horse raid. His bravery gave him the honour of serving as bearer of the pipe-stem at this important occasion. Chanting, he raised the pipe-stem towards the heavens, turning it to the north, south, east, and west, acknowledging all of creation. He then returned to the seated leaders, and together, the whole body once again moved forward to greet the Queen's representatives and formally present them with the pipe-stem. Morris stroked the sacred object a few times, then passed it to his fellow commissioners, William Christie, a long-time servant of the Hudson's Bay Company, and James McKay, a former company guide.

Treaty Six negotiations were held at a traditional camping area, known to the Cree as the "waiting place," near Fort Carlton. *RCMP Museum*

After the Cree had set the tone for the meeting, Governor Morris began his address. But as his words were translated, the shortcomings of the two official interpreters soon became apparent, and the Indians grew increasingly frustrated by the resulting confusion. Eventually, the objections became so loud that Mistawasis stood up, ordered silence, and then warned the commissioners that they were breaking their word about providing clear understanding. He demanded to be addressed in his own Plains Cree dialect. Wanting to avoid further trouble, Morris turned to the Indians' interpreter, Peter Erasmus, and asked him to take over translation duties for both sides. This turn of events was not only a moral victory for the chiefs, but suggested that the exact meaning of the governor's words was just as important as what he said.[20]

Uncomfortable with the bad start, Morris tried his best to soothe his ruffled audience. "My Indian brothers . . . I have shaken hands with a few of you, I shake hands with all of you in my heart," he stated. "God has given us a good day, I trust his eye is upon us and that what we do will be for the benefit of his children . . . You are, like me and my friends who are with me, children of the Queen. We are of the same blood, the same God made us, and the same Queen rules over us."[21] He then explained how the government was genuinely concerned about their welfare and that Indians elsewhere, particularly those in southern Ontario, were happily living under the benevolence of the Queen, the so-called "Great Mother." He ended his opening remarks by imploring the Indians to take his words seriously and to think of the future: " . . . what I will promise, and what I believe and hope you will take, is to last as long as that sun shines and yonder river flows."[22]

At the request of the Indian leaders, the discussions were recessed until the following morning—this time with a representative from the Willow Cree in attendance. After the chiefs and headmen had been formally introduced, Morris proceeded to elaborate on the terms of the treaty. He first reassured the Indians that the Queen had no intention of interfering with their traditional form of making a living by hunting, fishing, and gathering. Such activities would be guaranteed for future generations. He pointed out, however, that the wild game was disappearing and that the Indians would have to learn how to grow food from the soil if they were to provide for their children and their children's children. To facilitate this transition to farming, the Canadian government would set aside reserve lands for each band based on the formula of one square mile for every family of five. This suggestion that land would be given to the Cree sparked a stinging rebuke from Poundmaker, one of the bolder young men. "This is our land!" he protested loudly. "It isn't a piece of pemmican to be cut off and given in little pieces back to us. It is ours and we will take what we want."[23] Momentarily stunned by the outburst, Morris advised the Indians that thousands of prospective homesteaders would soon invade the country and that the reserves would be held in trust by the Queen. "[I]t is your own," he counselled them, "and no one will interfere with you . . . no one can take [your] homes."[24] He then listed the specific agricultural items—from tools and implements to animals and seed—that would be given to the bands to help them become farmers. He also emphasized the cash payment that every man, woman, and child could expect to receive for the life of the

Poundmaker and one of his wives. An eloquent and forceful speaker, he was concerned that the treaty provide adequate assistance, especially in times of famine. *Saskatoon Archives Board R-B8776*

treaty. And he promised special gifts for the chiefs and headmen; these presents included symbols of the new order: treaty uniforms, silver medals, and a British flag. "I hold out my hand to you full of the Queen's bounty," Morris concluded, "and I hope you will not put it back . . . act for the good of your people."[25]

In response, Mistawasis stepped forward, clasped the governor's hand, and remarked, "We have heard all he has told us, but I want to tell him how it is with us as well; when a thing is thought of quietly, probably that is the best way. I ask this much from him this day that we go and think of his words."[26] To many chiefs, the promises of friendship and aid sounded good, especially when weighed against the circumstances they now faced. But others were suspicious. There was more than just land and money at issue. Some feared that their people could lose their independence and find themselves at the mercy of the white man. Others questioned the wisdom of placing all their trust in a treaty. Chief Beardy's representative, for example, urged the chiefs to rent the land rather than sell it forever, while the handful of Saulteaux Indians from the Treaty Four area called for the outright refusal of the treaty. A minority of younger leaders, meanwhile, doubted whether the Cree could actually make a decent living from farming. Wisely, the chiefs decided to adjourn the formal discussions until Monday.

The next day being Sunday, religious services were held in the fort square and, at the request of some of the Indians, at the encampment.

There, some two hundred Cree worshippers heard missionaries John McKay (Church of England) and Constantine Scollen (Roman Catholic) promote the advantages of accepting the treaty. On Monday morning, Mistawasis sent a message to Morris indicating that the chiefs had not yet met in council and that they needed another day for deliberations. The Indian leaders wanted to ensure that all concerns were voiced, and, equally important, reach a consensus on how to proceed with the treaty—no easy goal given the variety of opinions being expressed.

The council members decided to listen first to the concerns of the objectors—a process, according to Erasmus, that took up most of the day. Poundmaker, an eloquent and forceful speaker from Red Pheasant's band, together with The Badger, from the John Smith band, acknowledged the hardship caused by the disappearance of the buffalo, but placed little faith in agriculture. The Cree were first and foremost skilled hunters and feared warriors. The detractors also lamented the loss of pride and dignity if their people signed the treaty. For almost two centuries, the Cree, Assiniboine, and Saulteaux had held a monopoly over European trade goods and weaponry entering the western interior. Together, they had created an "iron alliance" that enabled them to expand across the northern plains. They still controlled this territory; to trade their land for an uncertain future would be an admission of defeat.

Mistawasis, who listened patiently to the speakers, finally rose in the late afternoon and directly challenged those who opposed the treaty. "Have you anything better to offer our people?" he demanded of Poundmaker and The Badger. "I ask, again, can you suggest anything that will bring these things back for tomorrow and all the tomorrows that face our people?"[27] He went on to argue that the buffalo would disappear before many snows had fallen and that the treaty offered protection against the twin threats of starvation and misery. He also asserted that the Great Queen Mother had their best interests at heart, recounting the sorry impact of the American whisky trade on the Blackfoot and how the Queen had sent her red-coated police to drive the evil men out of the country. Perhaps his most persuasive argument came when he admitted candidly that past glory would not feed his people and that his days of fighting were over. "The prairies have not been darkened by the blood of our white brothers in our time," he concluded. "Let this always be so. I for one will take the hand that is offered."[28]

A profound silence enveloped the council in the wake of Mistawasis's passionate speech, and it was several minutes before Ahtahkakoop rose and voiced his support. Like his fellow chief, he drew attention to the Cree's weakened state—how they were power-less to keep the white man from entering the region—and warned that they had to choose a different road from the one travelled in the past. "Let us not think of ourselves but of our children's children," Ahtahkakoop implored. "Let us show our wisdom by choosing the right path now while we yet have a choice."[29] This right path, according to the Cree leader, was the adoption of agriculture. He noted how mother earth had always provided grass for the great buffalo herds. There was no reason that the Indians could not make a living from the soil, especially when the Queen's representatives promised assistance and instruction. The Cree could be strong once again.

These two speeches, capping a long day of intense debate, had the desired effect. One by one, chiefs and councillors endorsed the treaty, either by raising their hand or uttering a few words of approval. This support did not mean, though, that the Cree were simply resigned to accepting what the Canadian government had offered. At the council's conclusion, Mistawasis told the gathering they would proceed at their own pace and there would be an opportunity to question the commissioners directly about specific matters. He also indicated that they would be presenting a list of counterdemands.[30]

On Tuesday, when the negotiations finally resumed, Lieutenant Governor Morris greeted the Indians with a warning that his time there was limited. Poundmaker then stepped forward and broached the subject of famine relief. In his mid-thirties, Poundmaker, the son of an Assiniboine father and mixed-blood mother, had the mark of a future great chief; he was intelligent, dignified, and eloquent. He was also related to key Indian leaders. His uncle was Mistawasis, and his brother-in-law was Ermineskin of the Beaver Hills Indians. More significant, his adoption by Chief Crowfoot had consummated the ties between two powerful Plains Indian foes, the Cree and Blackfoot. He had the potential to generate considerable political influence. Speaking on behalf of the chiefs, Poundmaker stated that while his people were anxious to make a living for themselves, he wanted assurances that they would receive adequate help when needed.

This request clearly went against government thinking at the

During Treaty Six negotiations, the Cree presented a list of counterdemands designed to smooth the transition to an agricultural way of life. *National Archives of Canada C64741*

time. Morris knew that any commitment to provide rations would conflict with the Victorian philosophy that held that every man should make a living for himself. Besides, it was generally assumed that Indians would be able to learn how to farm fairly rapidly and that the buffalo would be around long enough to smooth the transition to agriculture. Time would quickly prove the government wrong on both counts. Morris consequently refused and insinuated that the real problem was Indians' laziness. "I cannot promise . . . that the Government will feed and support all the Indians," he replied. "You are many, and if we were to try to do it, it would take a great deal of money, and some of you would never do anything for yourselves."[31] The Badger then attempted to clarify their motives: "We want to think of our children; we do not want to be greedy; when we commence to settle down on the reserves that we select, it is there we want your aid, when we cannot help ourselves and in case of troubles seen and unforeseen in the future."[32] When Morris countered that the Cree had to trust the Queen's generosity, The Badger's tone changed markedly. "I do not want you to feed me every day," he asserted bluntly. "You must not understand that from what I have said. When we commence to settle down on the ground to make there our own living, it is then we want your help."[33]

Mistawasis, disturbed that the commissioners were dismissing the seriousness of their concerns about provisions, waded into the debate.

"[I]t is in case of any extremity, and from the ignorance of the Indian in commencing to settle that we thus speak," he advised Morris, recalling his words that the agreement was to last forever. "[T]his is not a trivial matter for us."[34] The chiefs then asked that the meeting be adjourned for the day to allow them to hold another council. Morris acquiesced, but he warned the Cree leaders not to make unreasonable demands. It was obvious to him that those chiefs who supported the treaty were as concerned about the famine as those leaders who opposed it. He also recognized that the negotiations were in danger of collapse.

When the meeting reconvened on Wednesday 23 August, the chiefs asked their interpreter, Peter Erasmus, to read their list of counterdemands. These included additional tools, implements, and livestock; a supply of medicines free of charge; exemption from war service; the banning of alcohol; and schools and teachers on the reserve. The list also insisted that traditional hunting practices be guaranteed and repeated the earlier request for provisions during the transition to farming and to guard against famine. When Erasmus finished reading the document, Chief Strike-Him-on-the-Back cried out: "Pity the voice of the Indian, if you grant what we request the sound will echo through the land; open the way. I speak for the children that they may be glad . . . let us now stand in the light of day to see our way on this earth."[35]

After consulting with his fellow commissioners, Morris granted most of the new demands. He agreed, for example, to give additional agricultural help to those Indians cultivating the soil on their reserves—but for three years only. He also promised that a medicine chest would be kept at the house of each Indian agent. And he vowed, albeit reluctantly, to add a clause to the treaty providing famine assistance. The Alexander Mackenzie administration would criticize these terms for being too generous, and they would later return to haunt the Canadian government. But it is difficult to deny that the treaty, which settled Indian claims to several thousand square miles of rich agricultural land, was a good bargain for Ottawa. Unrest in Indian ranks also continued. Although the sceptics had extracted a number of concessions from Morris, some, such as Poundmaker, remained unconvinced. "From what I can hear and see now," he told the gathering, "I cannot understand that I shall be able to clothe my children and feed them as long as the sun shines and water runs."[36] The majority of the Cree chiefs and headmen, on the other hand, were prepared to accept the treaty, believing it was the best strategy for survival. They realized they had to adjust to the new conditions and deliberately chose to enter into an agreement with the Queen. After all, they had been constantly assured that the Great Mother and her representatives would keep a "watchful eye and sympathetic hand"[37] on them. So when Morris called on the Cree to take what was being offered and sign the revised draft, some fifty men, led by Mistawasis and Ahtahkakoop, came forward and affixed their mark to the document after the commissioners' signatures.

The next morning, the governor presented the principal chiefs with their uniforms, medals, and flags. He also delivered a short lecture, reminding the Cree leaders that they were now the Queen's representatives and to remain faithful to the terms of the new agreement.[38] Morris then turned and confronted the group of non-treaty Saulteaux who had been quietly speaking against the agreement and accused them of trying to disrupt the negotiations. Their leader rose to the challenge and charged that the treaty was a bad deal and that the government was cheating the Indians. This nasty exchange did not ruin the mood of celebration and was quickly followed by the commencement of treaty payments—a process that took two full days because of the numbers involved.[39] Morris used the time to send a message to the Willow Cree, along with tobacco and provisions, inviting them to meet with the treaty commissioners at a site halfway between Fort Carlton and Duck Lake on 28 August. The governor was determined to get Beardy and his fellow chiefs to sign the settlement that had just been reached with their House and Parkland cousins. When he learned that the Indians were still willing to enter negotiations, he bid farewell to his Cree hosts in a brief ceremony in the fort square—including three cheers for the Queen—and headed for the rendezvous site.[40]

Concern about the demise of the buffalo dominated this second meeting with the Willow Cree. The Creator had made this "ally" for the Indian, an ally that provided every conceivable need, from meat and clothing to cooking utensils and fuel. But the herds that once roamed the prairie as far as the eye could see were now a mere shadow of their former greatness. Beardy used the disappearance of the buffalo to complain that the assistance promised at Carlton would prove inadequate. He also suggested that special steps be taken to preserve and manage the remaining animals so that all could share equally. "I do not want very much more that what has been promised, only a little thing," Beardy pleaded with the commissioners, "on account of the buffalo I am getting anxious."[41]

Morris did not share this sense of crisis. Instead, he told Beardy that the Willow Cree would receive the same farming assistance that had been promised at Carlton and that any special help would be restricted to times of famine or sickness. He also indicated that the preservation of the buffalo was a matter for the North-West Territories council and that he could not predict what, if anything, would be done; he did, however, promise that any new game laws would be printed in Cree, as well as in English and French. While Morris's response probably did little to ease Beardy's concerns, the governor's repeated assurances that the Queen wanted to enter into a lasting relationship with the Indians and that the Canadian government would assist their conversion to agriculture sounded convincing. Like their counterparts at Carlton, the Willow Cree had to change the basis of their economy, and the agreement being offered by the Queen's representatives appeared to be the best, perhaps the only, alternative. Beardy, together with fellow chiefs Cutnose and One Arrow, signed Treaty Six, believing that their new ties with Canada would provide a more secure future.[42] A special request that they be given blue uniforms instead of the traditional red was rejected by Morris. So too was their attempt to have the treaty payments made at the site envisaged in Beardy's dream. Morris had been inconvenienced by the Willow Cree's refusal to attend the Carlton meeting, and he was not about to accommodate them. Nor did he understand the importance of fulfilling the vision—although he himself spoke in prophetic terms at times—and dismissed it as mere superstition.[43]

The treaty commission's next stop was Fort Pitt, a Hudson's Bay Company post some 150 miles farther west on the North Saskatchewan River and midway between Forts Carlton and Edmonton. The northern Plains Cree who lived in this area were known as the River People, and unlike the followers of Mistawasis and Ahtahkakoop, many had not tried their hand at agriculture nor been converted to Christianity. When Morris and his entourage arrived at Pitt on 5 September, ten days earlier than expected, many of the Plains Cree were away hunting buffalo. The chiefs of the eight hundred Indians already assembled, mostly Woods Cree and Dene from the region north of the river, immediately requested that the talks be delayed. On the advice of one of the missionaries in his party, however, Morris had taken the precaution of sending a messenger ahead from Carlton to retrieve Sweetgrass, the acknowledged leader of the River People and a Christianized Indian. And when the chief arrived at the fort the following day, negotiations went ahead—even though other influential leaders, such as Big Bear and Little Pine, and their sizeable bands were still away on the hunt.[44]

Before the Indians met with Morris, they held a brief caucus to learn what had transpired at Carlton. Little Hunter, a Plains Cree chief who had observed the negotiations, gave a favourable account of the agreement. So, too, did Peter Erasmus, who was now being paid by the treaty commission. Erasmus reviewed the arguments for and against the treaty and the concessions made by the commissioner; he also described the dramatic speeches of Mistawasis and Ahtahkakoop and how their moving words had influenced the assembly to take the Queen's hand. These same arguments now figured in the Pitt proceedings. No sooner had Erasmus completed his summary when Sweetgrass rose and addressed the council: "Mistawasis and Ahtahkakoop I consider far wiser than I am; therefore if they have accepted this treaty for their people after many days of talk and careful thought, then I am prepared to accept for my people."[45] The other chiefs concurred. Before the Indians and Morris even came face to face, then, Sweetgrass was ready to lead the group into the treaty.

At 10:00 A.M. on Thursday 7 September, the treaty commissioners proceeded to the negotiation tent, located on a high plateau overlooking the fort, accompanied by a mounted police escort and band. The Indians, in turn, formed themselves into a large semicircle, and led by

Pakan or James Seenum, a Woods Cree leader, expected a larger reserve than that allowed for under the treaty. Despite his dispute with the government, he would remain loyal during the rebellion. *Provincial Archives of Alberta B1056*

performing horsemen, advanced forward to the meeting spot. Four sacred pipe-stems were then ritually presented to the Creator, while the police band played "God Save the Queen." Morris told the assembly that he had come at the Indians' request—an obvious reference to Sweetgrass's earlier message that he wanted a treaty. He then explained in a lengthy, at times rambling, speech how other Indians were content under the Queen and that they too could enjoy her protective care. "I see the Queen's councillors taking the Indian by the hand saying we are brothers." Morris forecast, "We will lift you up, we will teach you . . . the cunning of the white man."[46] He concluded by offering the same terms agreed upon at Carlton.

The chiefs and headmen spent the following day in deliberation—mostly reviewing what the governor had said. A few voiced additional demands, such as James Seenum, a Woods Cree leader from White-fish Lake, who wanted a larger reserve than that allowed for under the treaty. Any dissent, though, was limited and promptly defused by Erasmus and the missionaries in attendance, who spoke in favour of the terms at every opportunity.[47] As a result, when the two sides reconvened on 9 September, Morris's request for comments elicited only silence—a perplexing reaction given his previous experience at Carlton.[48] Eventually, Sweetgrass came forward and acknowledged that the days of the buffalo hunt were numbered and that he was prepared to turn to farming. "I am thankful," he said in reference to the treaty. "May this earth here never see the white man's blood spilt on it." He continued, "When I hold your hands and touch your heart, as I do now . . . let us be as one. Use your utmost to help me and help my children, so that they may prosper."[49] The other chiefs voiced their agreement with shouts of "hau." Morris praised the apparent unanimity and promised that the same terms would apply to the absent chiefs and their followers. He then called on the Indian leaders and their councillors to affix their mark on the document, to be followed by the presentation of the medals and flags. Before signing, most of the leaders expressed their thankfulness for the treaty and hoped that the Creator would look favourably on them. Seekaskootch's comments, however, hinted at what the Indians expected from their new relationship with Canada. "I recognize now that this that I once dreaded most," he confessed, "is coming to my aid and doing for me what I could not do for myself."[50]

On 12 August, as the commissioners were about to continue westward, Big Bear, one of the leading chiefs among the buffalo-

Sweetgrass was the acknowledged leader of the River People in the Fort Pitt area. He was killed accidentally by the gun he had received as a special treaty gift. *Glenbow Archives NA47-26*

hunting bands of the northern Plains Cree, arrived at Fort Pitt and asked to see Morris. The diminutive, wiry Big Bear, whose face had been disfigured by smallpox, told the governor he had not been notified about the early start of the meeting and he was there to represent the Plains Cree and Assiniboine who were out hunting on the prairies. Morris agreed to stay an additional day to hear Big Bear, but the fact that the treaty had already been concluded placed the Cree leader in an awkward situation. Big Bear had come to Pitt to express the concerns of several bands, such as the need to preserve the buffalo, and was duty-bound to discharge this responsibility. At the same time, those leaders present, in particular his mentor Sweetgrass, were urging him to accept the treaty—as is. "Say yes, and take his hand," they told him.[51] This pressure only stiffened Big Bear's resistance, and he spoke out in his defence. "Stop, stop, my friends . . . I heard the Governor was going to come and I said I shall see him; when I see him I will make a request that he will save me from what I most dread, that is: the rope to be about my neck."[52]

The way this statement was translated to Morris changed the tone and nature of the meeting; one of Big Bear's biographers suggests that it affected the course of history.[53] Peter Erasmus had left once the official ceremonies ended, leaving the less competent Reverend John McKay to do the translating. He apparently confused "rope . . . about my neck," a metaphor Big Bear used in pleading that Indians not lose their freedom like tethered animals, with a literal meaning, suggesting that Big Bear feared hanging as a punishment. This apparent request that Indians not be punished for serious crimes shocked Morris, and he replied, "No good Indian has the rope around his neck."[54] Big Bear, somewhat confused by the response, raised the need for further talks, then returned to his concern about independence—again translated as hanging. Morris countered, "What you ask will not be granted, why are you so anxious about bad men?"[55] By this point, further discussion seemed futile, and Morris ended the meeting with the assurance that other leaders, including Big Bear, would have the opportunity to join the treaty agreement the following year. Once the other chiefs had said their goodbyes, Big Bear made one last attempt to explain his position. "I am not an undutiful child, I do not throw back your hand," he told Morris, "but as my people are not here, I do not sign. I will tell them what I have heard and next year I will come."[56] But the damage had been done. Big Bear henceforth acquired a reputation in official circles as an obstinate, possibly evil, chief.

Lieutenant Governor Morris returned to Fort Garry in the late fall, pleased with what had been accomplished during the treaty commission. In his report to the Mackenzie government, however, he cautioned that even though the Indians were willing, if not anxious, to embark on an agricultural way of life, it was essential that they receive adequate assistance and instruction as soon as possible. This advice, coming from the man who had served as the Queen's personal negotiator, could not be taken lightly. The Cree who agreed to Treaty Six at Carlton and Pitt had made a conscious decision to give up the hunt and become farmers—on the understanding that Canada would be there with a helping hand. Those who remained outside the treaty, meanwhile, were upset that they had not been consulted before the settlement had been reached and would have to be convinced of the merits of the new relationship before accepting the Queen's hand. How the dominion government discharged its obligations over the next few years was therefore critical. And it appeared, almost immediately, that the Cree had made a grievous mistake. A few months after the Pitt meeting, Sweetgrass died at the hands of his best friend, who shot him, by accident, with the gun the chief had received as a special treaty gift.[57] It remained to be seen whether it was a bad omen.

chapter two

Feed Them
or Fight Them

W AR CRIES SOUNDED and guns blazed as Poundmaker's young men circled their Fort Walsh camp in anger in August 1881. It was now five years since the signing of the treaty. Their first efforts at farming in the Battleford area had failed miserably, and with famine stalking the band, Chief Poundmaker had led his people south to the Cypress Hills, near the international border, where large game could still be secured. Here, up to three thousand other Cree and Assiniboine, many of them still unwilling to take treaty, had gathered around Fort Walsh, the government's main supply depot. The summer had produced a great shock—for the first time in living memory, the buffalo had failed to appear north of the boundary! Once other local food resources were depleted, the refugees found themselves at the mercy of an unsympathetic Indian Affairs department and its stingy rations policy. In fact, the Macdonald government was prepared to use the widespread hunger to subjugate the First Nations.[1] When local authorities at the fort refused to pay the Poundmaker band members their annuities or provide them with rations, the young men responded with the threatening show of protest. Poundmaker, who had emerged as a leading critic of government

By the end of the 1870s, Poundmaker had emerged as one of the leading critics of federal Indian policy; Ottawa considered him a trouble-maker. *Saskatchewan Archives Board R-B8775*

policies, did not wish to risk further trouble, and encouraged his band to return to its reserve on the understanding that aid would be given there. The alternative was starvation.

In signing Treaty Six, the Cree chiefs did more than grant access to their territory, or signal that they had chosen farming as their best route to survival. Their motivation, what mattered above all else during the negotiations, was the belief that they were establishing a special relationship with the Canadian government, consisting of two equal parties who stood to benefit mutually from the agreement.[2] Once the treaty had been concluded, then, several chiefs were prepared to select reserves in the expectation that Ottawa would fulfil its responsibilities and help them make the transition to the new agricultural economy and a more secure future. They were wrong. The Canadian government did little to assist the Cree in the first few years after the treaty, believing that the Indians could fend for themselves. Ottawa also had other, more important priorities in western Canada, such as the building of a transcontinental railway to the Pacific. When Ottawa did turn its attention to the First Nations, it deliberately chose to interpret its treaty obligations in the narrowest possible terms—or ignore them. This policy of neglect might have been excusable if the buffalo had continued to provide sustenance. But the almost overnight disappearance of the great herds, combined with the failure to establish a flourishing agricultural base on the reserves, reduced the Indian population on the prairies to a state of wretchedness that has had no equal in modern Canadian history.[3] For those chiefs and their followers who chose treaty, the Queen's hand was often empty, when not shaped in a fist.

Two of the first Cree leaders to ask for their treaty lands were Mistawasis and Ahtahkakoop, the joint spokesmen at the Carlton negotiations. Ahtahkakoop wanted his reserve located at Sandy Lake, near the North Saskatchewan River, where his band already cultivated gardens. Mistawasis chose land in the Snake Plains area on the advice of Reverend John Hines, a local missionary who was active among the House People.[4] These reserve selections were a necessary first step to securing agricultural assistance: once a reserve had been surveyed, then—and only then—would the band receive the animals, implements, seed, and other farm items specified in the treaty. But the government surveyors did not arrive to stake out the reserves for another two years, in part because Ottawa believed that the treaty commissioners had exceeded their mandate and promised too much at the negotiations. And when goods and supplies arrived in 1878, they were not only inadequate, but came too late in the season to begin cultivation. The two bands would have starved that year if not for the distribution of rations by the local North-West Mounted Police.[5]

Chief Beardy of the Willow Cree also had trouble getting the government to recognize his reserve—because of where he wanted it. During the winter of 1876–77, Beardy built a house near the shores of Duck Lake and had about two acres in garden by the following summer. This good start soon soured, though, when the chief made his reserve selection; he asked for all the land within a two-mile radius of Duck Lake and from there across the South Saskatchewan River some fifty miles south to Caswell Hill (in present-day Saskatoon). The proposed reserve, comprising nearly one thousand square miles, suggests that Beardy expected to receive enough treaty land for both farming and hunting. Any misunderstanding about the size of his allotment might have been resolved if the government had been able to assign the land around the lake to the Willow Cree, especially since Beardy's father was buried there.[6] But this area had also been claimed by the Métis, a predominantly French-speaking, Roman Catholic mixed-blood population. They had migrated into the so-called South Branch district in steadily increasing numbers in the 1860s and 1870s, particularly after the Red River Resistance, and settled along the banks of the river in the traditional river-lot land-holding system. As early as 1871, in an effort to establish a permanent land base, the Métis had embarked on a campaign to have Ottawa set aside a large, self-contained colony that straddled both the South Saskatchewan River and the Carlton trail, including the flourishing village of Duck Lake.[7]

To resolve these competing claims, both the Indians and the Métis turned to the Queen's representatives. On 28 January 1878, Beardy petitioned the governor general of Canada to have the Duck Lake region confirmed as his band's reserve; otherwise, he threatened to suspend any farm work.[8] The Métis, meanwhile, called on David Laird, the new lieutenant governor of the North-West Territories, not to allow "Beardy's reserve to surround their claims or encroach upon their lands."[9] Ottawa was not prepared to stir up the Métis, let alone hand them another cause for complaint, and consequently told Beardy that his reserve could include only the western portion of the land around the lake. The chief, however, refused the offer and instructed his band not to accept their treaty annuities that summer. He also suggested that the Métis now living at Duck Lake would be required to pay one-half their crops in return for the use of the land.[10] This stalemate made for a miserable winter for the band—so much so that Beardy agreed to the proposed reserve, but not before some of his men had threatened to break into a local store for rations.[11] Yet when a surveyor arrived in the spring of 1879 to stake out the reserve, Beardy once again asserted his claim to all of the land around Duck Lake. At this point, persuasion gave way to coercion. Threatened with the possible loss of treaty entitlement, Beardy had no alternative in 1880 but to accept a reserve that excluded any land occupied by the Métis or continue to see his band suffer.[12] The Battleford-based *Saskatchewan Herald* sarcastically summed up his predicament: "The Beardy, Duck Lake chief, promised, as he usually does when he is hungry, that he would have his reserve surveyed, and in return for his pledge, the agent gave him some flour. Whether he will adhere to his promise is another thing."[13]

The situation in the Battleford district was little better—but not for lack of trying by the local Indians. Initially, the bands that settled in this area were dubious of the treaty agreement. Wuttunee, for example, the leader of a group of River People, had so little faith in the negotiations that he stepped aside at Carlton and had his brother, Red Pheasant, sign on behalf of the band as their new chief.[14] In 1878, Red Pheasant selected a reserve in the Eagle Hills, south of the new

In 1878 Red Pheasant selected a reserve in the Eagle Hills, south of the territorial capital at Battleford. *Saskatchewan Archives Board R–A5669*

territorial capital. This decision prompted Poundmaker, an outspoken critic of the treaty, to leave the band with a group of his followers and remain out on the plains hunting. The following year, the scarcity of game forced Poundmaker to return to Battleford and choose his own reserve some forty miles to the northwest at the junction of the Battle River and Cut Knife Creek. These hunters-turned-farmers were doubly handicapped in their new endeavour. Unlike the House People in the Carlton district, they lacked any practical agricultural experience. Nor was their reserve land ideal for raising crops; the chiefs had shown a decided preference for rolling, heavily wooded terrain that was better suited for more traditional pursuits such as hunting and gathering. Still, they toiled "like trojans,"[15] breaking and seeding the prairie sod and building crude log houses. Their efforts were a testament to their resiliency—the same resiliency that had made them undisputed masters of the buffalo hunt. But in the end, their first few crops failed and they came face to face with the harsh reality that large-scale farming in the North-West was anything but certain in the late nineteenth century. It would take several years of failure and experimentation, by both white farmers and Indians alike, before the prairie wilderness could be made over into the kind of agricultural eden prophesied by Canadian expansionists.[16]

In retrospect, these kinds of problems were unavoidable, if not inevitable, in the first few years after the treaties. Canada had increased seven times in size with the acquisition of Rupert's Land

and the Northwestern Territory and faced a formidable challenge in overseeing the development and integration of the region; it was an empire more in keeping with an established world power, not a dominion less than a decade old. Mistakes or delays were bound to happen, especially since policy makers in Ottawa were far removed from the western interior and had little practical knowledge of the region and its peculiarities. It also did not help that politicians grossly underestimated the task at hand and were initially caught up in the euphoria of seeing the country reach the shores of not one, but two oceans. But what made the situation worse for First Nations was the prevailing attitude in official circles that Indians were not only an irrelevant minority, but a beggarlike race more interested in government handouts than fending for themselves.[17] They were deadbeats, standing in the way of progress and a greater future. Any expenditure on Indian matters—even if it was part of western treaty obligations— was viewed as a questionable drain on the public purse, all the more so since the country was mired in a deep recession in the mid-1870s and headed by a Liberal prime minister, Alexander Mackenzie, who believed that economy was a virtue.

The Canadian government's reluctance to assume the responsibilities that had been solemnly promised during the negotiations and specified in the actual treaty text can best be illustrated by the administrative framework for handling Indian matters in the western interior. In 1877, Ottawa created the North-West Superintendency to oversee the interests of some seventeen thousand treaty Indians living in a two-hundred-thousand-square-mile area from the present-day Manitoba border to the Rocky Mountains (roughly the boundaries of Treaties Four, Six, and Seven). David Laird, a former federal minister of the Interior living in the new territorial capital at Battleford, was named Indian superintendent in addition to his other official duties as lieutenant governor for the Territories. He had two assistants: M.G. Dickieson, a former recording secretary at treaty negotiations, who now doubled as assistant Indian superintendent and Indian agent for Treaty Six; and ex-military officer Allan McDonald, who served as Indian agent for Treaty Four. These three men were to dispense treaty annuities, provide instruction in farming, and generally have a "civilizing" influence on the Indians.[18] The sheer enormity of the workload and the vast distances involved quickly made a mockery of these duties. The two agents had little time for anything beyond the distribution of treaty payments. They also came to recognize that the federal government's insistence on economy, of keeping costs down to a bare minimum, was making things harder for the Indians; it was as if they were being asked to tend their fields and gardens with one arm behind their back. It also became clear that the adoption of agriculture on the reserves was not going to be an overnight success and that the Indians would never succeed as farmers unless they received practical, on-site instruction and assistance.[19]

Laird, himself the son of a farmer, shared these concerns and in December 1879 advised Ottawa to give provisions to the Indians during seeding time and engage experienced farmers to help them put in their first crops. These were reasonable suggestions. After all, how could Indians be expected to tend to their fields if they had to worry about their next meal? And what good was a plough if they did not know how to use it? But the government remained convinced that it had done more than enough for the Indians; any extra help beyond that specified in the treaties would promote laziness, if not dependency.[20] In short, the Indians had to take the initiative and bring their reserve lands under crop—or face the consequences. This line of reasoning provoked a somewhat heated response from Agent Dickieson. "As I think we are on the eve of an Indian outbreak which will be caused principally by starvation,"

Lieutenant Governor David Laird was responsible for some seventeen thousand treaty Indians living in a two-hundred - thousand - square-mile area in western Canada.
Saskatchewan Archives Board R-A1

he warned a senior Ottawa bureaucrat, "it does not do to scan the exact lines of a treaty too closely."[21] Laird was blunter. He told the minister of the Interior that the government had three choices: "to help the Indians to farm and raise stock, to feed them, or to fight them."[22]

Violence seemed a real possibility as the summer of 1878 unfolded. Game was so scarce that once-mighty bands were reduced to eating gophers, dogs, and even their horses in a desperate attempt to avoid starvation. Many others sought temporary refuge at the nearest HBC post in the hope that rations might be distributed. The Canadian government denied any responsibility for these wretched conditions. Afraid that adverse publicity would give the region a black eye and scare off prospective settlers, Ottawa attributed any hardship to the Indians' own failings.[23] The simple truth is that the government did as little to save the buffalo from extinction as it did to promote Indian agriculture. Despite repeated warnings to the contrary, it chose to believe that the buffalo would survive long enough to ease the transition to agriculture.[24] When the great herds failed to appear on the Canadian plains as they had done each season for countless generations, it precipitated a crisis—both for the First Nations and the federal government. The Plains Indians, having lost their major source of sustenance, faced a future of uncertainty, hardship, and starvation. These were the very things they had sought to avoid by taking treaty. The government, meanwhile, scrambled to ease the famine by providing ten thousand dollars in temporary relief in March 1879 to those bands in the Battleford, Duck Lake, and Qu'Appelle districts.[25] It was evident, however, that unless Ottawa was prepared to incur large annual expenditures to feed the Indians, it would have to provide meaningful agricultural assistance. The one consolation was that the Indians remained peaceful, patiently waiting for the government to honour its treaty pledges.

Ottawa launched its new reserve farm-instruction program in the spring of 1879 with the appointment of a new federal Indian commissioner. A disillusioned Laird had resigned this part of his official duties in March. He was replaced two months later by Edgar Dewdney, an engineer-turned-politician, selected to spearhead the new initiative because of his ties to the prime minister, not because of any special qualifications. A large, hulking figure, best known for his affable manner and trademark mutton-chop whiskers, Dewdney was to oversee a system of "home" farms, where resident farm

Edgar Dewdney and wife. Dewdney, a friend of the prime minister, was named Indian commissioner in 1879 and given the task of overseeing the new reserve farm-instruction program. *Glenbow Archives NA-3205-1*

instructors, with the assistance of the local band, would raise grain and vegetables to feed themselves and their charges. If time permitted, the farm instructors were also to teach the Indians—in most cases, by example—how to manage their own lands and care for their crops and animals. However, the distribution of food from on-reserve supply depots soon became their most important duty. These relief provisions were intended to help the Indians survive the famine conditions until reserve lands could be cultivated. But they were not to be given freely. Government authorities believed that Indian idleness—and not the loss of the buffalo—had caused their sorry state. Obviously, easy access to food was not in the best interests of the First Nations. Some form of labour, no matter how menial or degrading, had to be performed before they were fed.[26] Many chiefs would later question whether such work was intended under the treaty; the Queen was supposed to help them, not vice versa.

The home farm system was designed to put the Indians on the

road to self-sufficiency in only a few years, thereby ending the need for further government assistance. Although many Ottawa politicians and bureaucrats expected, in the words of one commentator, "immediate, miraculous results,"[27] their optimism was shortsighted, if not completely unwarranted. Not only was prairie agriculture still in the experimental stage, but the men hired as farm instructors and Indian agents were patronage appointees who had little understanding or sympathy for the Indians and the dramatic changes they faced. Their general unsuitability for the task at hand, often bordering on incompetence, led to a high turnover rate.[28] Those who were singled out for commendation and promotion, on the other hand, tended to be hard-nosed disciplinarians who believed that their first and only duty was to establish their authority over the Indians. Hayter Reed, a Manitoba lawyer and former militia officer who quickly ascended to the position of Indian commissioner, perhaps best embodied this attitude. Soon after he assumed the post of Indian agent at Battleford in the spring of 1881, local bands began referring to him as "Iron Heart."[29] The feeling was mutual. Twelve years later, in looking back upon his early career with the department, Reed confided in a private letter to a cabinet minister that the Battleford Indians were the "scum of the Plains."[30]

Despite these obstacles, the Indians made a genuine effort to adapt to their new life as pioneer farmers. The Mosquito band was a good case in point. When the Assiniboine reluctantly signed an adhesion to Treaty Six at Battleford in August 1878, they were dismissed by Edgar Dewdney in his annual report as "a wild devil-may-care lot."[31] But before long, he and his officials in the field were marvelling at the band's industry and commitment. Although the Assiniboine had settled on marginal land immediately west of the Red Pheasant reserve, they had cleared thirty acres within two years—mostly by using grub hoes and axes! The band population, in the meantime, almost tripled in size, as starving groups straggled in from the open plains and sought refuge on the reserve. Like groups elsewhere in the region, though, the Assiniboine were thwarted by unpredictable weather, little or no equipment, and government inertia. In the end, they had little to show for their backbreaking labour except empty stomachs.[32] The situation at nearby Poundmaker's reserve was equally frustrating. Here, the Cree faced the ironic situation of enjoying a rare good harvest but going hungry because there was no local grist mill to grind the grain into flour.[33]

This sense of futility produced a ground swell of discontent, even among the most cooperative chiefs. Mistawasis and Ahtahkakoop complained to Commissioner Dewdney that their appeals for assistance had been ignored—"as if they were thrown into the water."[34] Poundmaker was more direct, and in a letter prepared for him by the reserve missionary, challenged Ottawa to live up to its promises, perceptively noting "we are as anxious to be independent as the Government are [sic] to get rid of the burden of supporting us."[35] The newly elected Conservative government, like its predecessor, was more interested in reducing Indian expenditures than providing a helping hand. Agents and instructors consequently encouraged hungry Indians to leave their reserves whenever possible to hunt, even if it meant abandoning farming operations. They also insisted on strict adherence to the "work for rations" policy—a mean-spirited act since the amount of food provided was not only well below daily caloric needs but sometimes unfit for human consumption.[36] The economic strategy of the new Macdonald administration concerning its Indian obligations was ruthlessly simple: it was more important to save money than lives.

Many of the treaty Indians responded by adopting more assertive tactics. Never one to accept a subordinate position in his dealings with Ottawa, Chief Beardy erected a toll gate across the Carlton trail in the summer of 1880 to affirm the band's control over its territory. He also sent men to the local home farm to slaughter cattle for his starving people. This last act enraged Indian Affairs officials, so much so that all three

Hayter Reed, who began his government career in 1881 as the Indian agent at Battleford, was known to the local bands as "Iron Heart." *Notman Photographic Archives, McCord Museum of Canadian History 106454–BII*

Willow Cree chiefs were rounded up for destroying government property and spent several weeks in mounted police custody.[37] There was also trouble in the Battleford area. Hungry, disillusioned, and growing more exasperated with each passing day, the local bands refused to work their fields in the spring of 1881 unless they received the promised assistance. And when the newly appointed agent, Hayter Reed, countered by suspending the distribution of rations, Chief Poundmaker threatened to butcher government cattle. This standoff ended peacefully when several of the bands, under Poundmaker's leadership, defiantly abandoned their reserves and headed south to the Cypress Hills in search of buffalo and a friendlier environment. Reed used their departure as evidence of their unwillingness, if not inability, to abandon their nomadic ways and settle down and become hard-working farmers. He also vilified Poundmaker as a troublemaker and source of Indian unrest—and in doing so, deflected any blame from the government and its niggardly ways.[38] *Saskatchewan Herald* editor P.G. Laurie, who seldom had a kind word for the local bands, agreed with this assessment and warned that the failure to take a hard line with the Indians "is making them quite saucy and independent."[39]

Nontreaty Indians, in particular Big Bear, followed these developments in the Saskatchewan country with great interest. With the death of Sweetgrass, Big Bear emerged as the leading chief of the Fort Pitt Cree—a position he used to try to secure better treaty terms. It was not that he was unwilling to accept the Queen's hand of friendship, but he questioned the compensation the government was offering for Indian lands, especially since the buffalo were rapidly disappearing from their traditional range. Big Bear tried twice in the two years immediately after Treaty Six to secure more favourable concessions for his people and save them from possible starvation. Each time, though, the official sent to deal with him had no power to alter the terms of the Carlton agreement, and in a pique of frustration, he announced in 1878 that he would wait four years for Ottawa to fulfil it duties.[40] This rock-solid determination to hold out, to put the government's sincerity to the test, made Big Bear a kind of magnet for the disgruntled and the distrustful. By 1879, he had some four hundred lodges in his camp, including several treaty Indians and their leaders. Many Cree saw him as the one leader with the diplomatic ability and spiritual prowess to set things straight and avoid a confrontation.

Government officials and white settlers were not as impressed by Big Bear or his motives. His massive following, together with his seeming intransigence, confirmed his unwarranted reputation as an evil, potentially dangerous leader. Former Governor Morris, for example, had predicted "exaggerated demands" from the wayward chief, while the residents of Battleford feared trouble from him at any moment.[41] Commissioner Dewdney was equally wary, but for a completely different reason. When the new Indian commissioner first encountered the feared chief at Fort Walsh in early July 1879, he was struck by the Cree leader's speaking ability and sense of purpose. Standing a mere four feet, five inches and bearing the ravages of a lifetime on the open plains, Big Bear, reported Dewdney, "is of a very independent character, self-reliant, and appears to know how to make his own living without begging from the Government."[42] Unfortunately, this grudging respect did not mean that the new commissioner was prepared to listen to Big Bear's entreaties and offer a better deal. Now that the last of the major western treaties had been signed with the Blackfoot Confederacy in 1877, Dewdney's principal task was to consolidate government control over all the Indians of the region—on his terms, of course.

Big Bear's four-year wait proved one of the most challenging, costly periods of his chieftainship. Because of the size of his following and the absence of buffalo from traditional hunting areas, he had to take his people south to the Cypress Hills, where small herds could still be found. The region had become a haven of last resort for other, equally desperate groups—other Cree, Assiniboine, Blackfoot, and several hundred American refugee Sioux and Nez Perce who had fled north into Canadian territory after bloody incidents in the United States. It was not long, then, before the food resources of the area were severely strained, if not completely wiped out in some places. Dewdney's determination to use the hunger to crush any nontreaty opposition only made things worse. With calculated coolness, he refused to give rations to those Indians who had not taken treaty or had left their reserves. He also offered, in an effort to undermine Big Bear's leadership, to recognize as chief any headman who could marshal one hundred followers and bring them into treaty. The Indian commissioner was convinced that the lure of rations and treaty money would prove irresistible—he would simply starve the holdouts into submission.[43]

Dewdney's tactics had the desired effect. In July 1879, Little Pine,

Lucky Man, and Thunderchild—all River People leaders—broke away from Big Bear's camp and entered Treaty Six at Fort Walsh with almost five hundred followers. Their departure was a disappointing blow, especially the loss of Little Pine, a veteran warrior and non-Christian chief who had refused to attend the Carlton negotiations in 1876. Hunger and a growing fear for their children's future now drove them into Dewdney's waiting arms. The desertions left Big Bear with those most opposed to dealing with the Canadian government, including several who favoured a more aggressive strategy, such as his war chief, Wandering Spirit, and his own son, Imasees. These men were still willing to listen to the chief's counsel, but it was only a matter of time before their empty stomachs dictated other action—only a matter of time before Dewdney's dangerous game became a deadly one.

With the buffalo effectively gone from the Canadian prairies, Big Bear moved his band south of the international border in the fall of 1879 to the Milk River district of Montana. They spent the next three years in temporary exile, crossing back and forth over the line whenever the buffalo wandered north or when driven out by American authorities. It was as if they had no home. Neither country wanted them, let alone cared about them; they were, in Dewdney's words, "worthless and troublesome."[44] Big Bear did his best under the circumstances to hold his band together. But many fell prey to local whisky traders who dispensed debauchery and violence with each barrel. Others slipped away quietly and joined bands that had taken treaty and qualified for rations. The greatest challenge to Big Bear's leadership, however, came from the Métis leader Louis Riel. The driving force behind the 1869–70 Red River Resistance, Riel had been forced to flee to the United States by a vengeful Canadian government before he was able to secure his rightful place as Manitoba's father of confederation. After a decade-long odyssey, including election to the House of Commons, a clandestine meeting with American President Ulysses Grant, and a spell in two Québec insane asylums, he moved to Montana and fell in with a small group of Métis hunters and traders. From this new base, Riel tried to win over the Canadian Indians to his latest scheme—an invasion of the Canadian North-West by a combined Indian-Métis force. He believed that if the various tribes united under his divine leadership, he could sweep north in lightning fashion, reclaim the region from Ottawa, and establish a separate Native republic.[45]

Big Bear's camp near Maple Creek, Saskatchewan. His six-year odyssey outside Treaty Six often took him to the United States in search of buffalo. *National Archives of Canada PA50749*

Riel pushed his insurrection through the winter of 1879–80 by telling the nearby Cree bands that the North-West rightfully belonged to the aboriginal peoples, not the white invaders. He also ridiculed the treaties between the First Nations and the Queen; at one meeting, he took the document that Little Pine had recently signed at Fort Walsh and ground it under his foot.[46] These campfire theatrics secured a handful of devotees, some of whom Riel called upon during the subsequent troubles in 1885.[47] But his general appeal for a Native confederacy floundered because the chiefs and headmen were committed to pursuing their own nonviolent solution to their problems; they had no faith, or interest, in Riel's agenda. Big Bear made this point perfectly clear when he reluctantly accepted an invitation to visit the Métis leader at his camp on the Milk River. "We should not fight the Queen with guns," he chastised the gathering. "We should fight her with her own laws."[48] This strategy would remain the backbone of Big Bear's diplomatic initiative until the outbreak of the North-West Rebellion six years later. Riel's antics that winter greatly disturbed the Cree chief, and he experienced a terrible vision: "I saw a spring shooting up out of the ground. I covered it with my hand, trying to smother it, but it spurted up between my fingers and ran over the back of my hand. It was a spring of blood."[49]

In the spring of 1881, when hundreds of Indians from the

Saskatchewan country, including those from the Battleford region, headed south to the Cypress Hills, violence seemed imminent. They were driven there by frustration and hunger. By August, it was estimated that there were over three thousand Cree and Assiniboine camped in the vicinity of Fort Walsh. This concentration of Indians alarmed Canadian authorities; not only was it impossible to control such a large gathering, but it included many treaty bands who had defiantly abandoned their new reserves as part of a growing campaign to revise the treaty agreements.[50] The tension escalated when local police refused to pay Poundmaker's followers their annuities unless they returned to their reserve. Fortunately, the near riot subsided when a buffalo herd appeared in the area and the Indians set off in pursuit. This turn of events prompted the federal minister of the Interior to remark that "The Buffalo are our best allies"[51]—a comment that revealed the government's appalling ignorance of the situation on the prairies. The minister hoped that the timely appearance of the buffalo would lessen the demand for rations and thereby save the government money. The other reason that the Indians dispersed was that they heard that the governor general, the Marquis of Lorne, planned to tour the North-West. The protesting bands looked upon this visit as an ideal opportunity to voice their complaints over the nonfulfilment of treaty promises and hurried back to their reserves to prepare for the arrival of the Queen's representative.[52]

Lorne arrived at Battleford by steamer on the last day of August 1881, and despite a hectic social schedule during his brief stay in the territorial capital, found time to meet with a number of Treaty Six chiefs. He had apparently been forewarned about the recent unrest on the reserves, for he advised the leaders in his opening remarks, "I have not come to alter the treaties but to meet the red children of the Great Queen and to see how by keeping the treaties I can help them to live."[53] The chiefs, who keenly appreciated Lorne's stature, especially since he was also the Queen's son-in-law, responded with equal candour. Acknowledging that farming was the only way that Indians could make a living now that the buffalo were gone, Mistawasis complained about the lack of implements and animals. "At the time of the treaties," he reminded the governor general, "it was mentioned that while the sun rose and set and the water ran the faith in the treaties was to be kept." He continued, "I was always peaceful as a child with the whites and am anxious to be friendly with those now coming."[54] Beardy, who had been something of a thorn in the government's side, echoed these concerns. "If I have done anything wrong yesterday," he admitted readily, "today I am trying to do what is right. Everything that was promised at the treaty I want fulfilled now."[55] Poundmaker also spoke with Lorne, but on a less formal basis. Because he was the adopted son of the powerful Blackfoot chief Crowfoot, Poundmaker was asked to guide the governor general and his entourage, including Indian Commissioner Dewdney, through Blackfoot territory to Calgary. It was an odd request, since the chief had been accused of seditious activity only a few months earlier. His daily conversations with Lorne on the trail, however, provided a much different portrait of the Cree leader—that he wanted to live in peace and learn agriculture, but urgently needed assistance to help his people make the transition.[56]

Although Lorne did little more than listen politely to Indian concerns, Poundmaker returned to his reserve that fall determined to try his hand at farming a second time. And by the following summer, the once troublesome chief had become a model farmer. The band's progress even impressed the unsympathetic editor of the *Saskatchewan Herald*. "Their chief, dressed as becomes a Canadian farmer, with sleeves turned up, was busy, fork in hand, in securing his excellent crop of wheat," Laurie reported enthusiastically on his visit to the reserve. "He seemed to take great pleasure in showing visitors around his extensive, well fenced and neatly kept field."[57] But once again, despite the best efforts, the crops failed, not only there but throughout the region. Promises of government help, in the meantime, remained just that—promises. Even much-needed rations were withheld in favour of sending the bands roving around the country in search of game. It seemed the Canadian government wanted to make things worse, not better, for the First Nations.

Big Bear and his band fared little better in Montana. Although the Cree had reached an understanding with their traditional enemies, the Blackfoot, who were also hunting south of the border, American authorities viewed the Indians as unwelcome interlopers and treated them with contempt. In one incident, a detachment of soldiers surrounded some of Big Bear's men as they were butchering buffalo and confiscated their horses. Some of the warriors were anxious for revenge, but Big Bear counselled restraint and travelled to Fort Assiniboine to try to have the horses returned. His request offended the commanding officer, who responded flatly, "You are thieves from another land and you should be shot like dogs!"[58] This tension simmered until the spring of 1882, when the U.S. army, in response to complaints from local ranchers about missing cattle, mounted the Milk River Expedition to drive the Canadian intruders—dead or alive—from American territory. Luckily, Big Bear's camp had been warned of the approaching force, and under the able leadership of the war chief, Wandering Spirit, the band skilfully avoided detection and reached Fort Walsh safely in April 1882.[59]

Big Bear's return to Canada brought the Cree leader one step closer to accepting treaty. Once willing to wait for better terms at almost any cost, he now realized painfully that continued resistance might jeopardize his people's very existence. Dewdney's policy of withholding rations from nontreaty Indians would see to that, as evidenced by a report prepared by Dr. Augustus Jukes, the mounted police surgeon at Walsh. Inspecting Big Bear's camp, now numbering about three hundred, in mid-October 1882, he found to his horror that the Indians were "literally in a starving condition and destitute of the commonest necessities of life."[60] They had little or no food, scanty clothing, and inadequate tents—all because of the disappearance of the buffalo. "I saw little children, at this inclement season, snow having fallen," he shockingly related, "who had scarcely rags to cover them." Dewdney probably regarded this "extreme wretchedness" as a necessary evil, for it meant that the influential Big Bear might finally be forced to enter the treaty. He ruthlessly pushed ahead with his no-treaty no-rations stance, confident that his war of wills with the chief was almost over. Not even questioning by the prime minister caused him to reconsider his starvation policy.[61]

Big Bear held out as long as he could. But the more he delayed taking treaty, the more he risked breaking up his band and losing his chieftainship. As winter tightened its cold grip over the region, several of his followers could no longer resist the lure of rations and abandoned their leader. The more warlike members of his band, meanwhile, became openly critical of Big Bear's position: whereas they had once advocated fighting, they were now more concerned with their day-to-day survival and that of their children. Finally, on the cold morning of 8 December, Big Bear met the Indian agent at Fort Walsh to sign an adhesion to Treaty Six. But before he put his mark on the two copies, he made one last futile attempt to secure improvements. He wanted guarantees that the government would quickly deliver what they had promised and assurances that his people would not simply be ignored and allowed to slowly starve once settled on reserves. His four-hour speech, like his efforts over the past four years, did nothing to change Ottawa's position. And at the urging of his own headmen, Big Bear entered treaty. His struggle was far from over though. It merely entered a new phase.

chapter three

Anything Short of War

W E WERE ONCE a proud and independent people and now we . . . can get neither food nor clothing, nor the means necessary to make a living for ourselves . . . the treaty is a farce enacted to kill us quietly . . . let us die at once."[1] That is how several chiefs in the Fort Edmonton district dramatically summed up their plight to the federal minister of the Interior in early January 1883. It was a revealing letter. Even though most First Nations people on the prairies had now entered treaty, either willingly or by force of circumstance, they refused to accept anything less than what had been faithfully promised, and worked actively to force the Canadian government to honour its obligations. "The conditions were mutually agreed to," the Edmonton chiefs reminded the minister. "We understood them to be inviolable and in the presence of the Great Spirit reciprocally binding; that neither party could be guilty of a breach with impunity." Yet in order to secure the equipment, seed grain, animals, and other assistance that had been offered in the name of the Queen Mother, the Indians realized that they had to appeal directly to Ottawa as a collective group. It was brutally apparent from their "dire poverty, our utter destitution" that the Indian agents, who were supposed to watch over their well-being on the reserves, effectively had their hands tied and could offer "little or no help, and . . . less sympathy."

Even under these grim circumstances, even though "our very existence is involved" and the government's behaviour amounted to "an
outrageous breach of good faith," the seven bands represented in the
letter continued to look upon their agreement with the Crown as a
sacred undertaking, not to be broken by violence. If anyone had
breached the treaties, it was "the white man [who] has indirectly
doomed us to annihilation little by little."

These were damning words. But they made little, if any, impression on the Conservative administration. Part of the problem for First
Nations was that Prime Minister John A. Macdonald doubled as his
own minister of the Interior and superintendent general of Indian
Affairs. The Tory leader was the most senior Indian official in the
country for a nine-year period from 1878 to 1887.[2] These additional
responsibilities did not mean, however, that Macdonald took an
abiding interest in the Indians of western Canada or their welfare.
The "old chieftain," as he was ironically known, had other, more
pressing concerns in the early 1880s, in particular the passage of a new
federal franchise bill and the construction of the Pacific railroad. He
left Indian matters to his deputy superintendent and family friend,
Lawrence Vankoughnet, an unimaginative, tight-fisted civil servant—
the Toronto *Mail* once called him an imbecile[3]—who ran the department as his own little fiefdom. Far from benefiting from Macdonald's
influence, then, Indian-government relations could not have been
much worse in the years leading up to the North-West Rebellion.
Vankoughnet, along with Indian Commissioner Edgar Dewdney in
Regina, was not only contemptuous of Indian complaints, but believed he and Dewdney knew what was best for First Nations. Together, they were prepared to get their way by any means, including
violating the treaties.

The Canadian government's determination to bring the Plains
Indians under its thumb can best be seen in how it dealt with the
bands in the Cypress Hills area. In 1879, in one of the more creative
solutions to their situation, Cree Chiefs Little Pine and Piapot and
several Assiniboine leaders requested contiguous reserves in a six-
teen-hundred-square-mile area stretching from Medicine Hat to the
Cypress Hills. This Indian territory would have allowed the bands to
continue hunting the area's remaining buffalo, as well as make a start
at agriculture. Edgar Dewdney, who had only recently assumed his
duties as Indian commissioner, readily agreed, probably in the belief
that he would have a stronger hand once troublesome leaders had

entered treaty and were permanently settled. He had good reason to want chiefs such as Piapot to select a reserve. Piapot, an extremely influential leader with an estimated one thousand followers, claimed that he had entered Treaty Four in 1875 under different terms than those agreed upon at the Qu'Appelle negotiations a year earlier, and that until these terms were recognized, he did not have a treaty with the government.[4] Although Dewdney had hoped to neutralize influential Indian leaders, he soon realized that a concentration of the Plains Cree nation in the Cypress Hills region would not be as easy to control as bands on isolated reserves. And if Canadian Indians continued to pursue the remnants of the great buffalo herds south of the border, it could also lead to an ugly international incident.[5] The rerouting of the Canadian Pacific Railway main line across the southern prairies further complicated matters; the vital transportation link, Macdonald's so-called national dream, would have skirted the proposed Indian territory. The Indian commissioner decided to renege on his promise to the Cree chiefs—even though it was a breach of the treaty agreement with the Queen—and told Piapot in the spring of 1882 that a reserve had been selected for him at Indian Head, while Little Pine had to move north to Saskatchewan country. To back up his new stance, Dewdney refused to dispense rations unless the Indians agreed to leave.[6]

The Cree, for their part, were not so easily evicted from their last refuge on the Canadian prairies. By summer's end, an angry Piapot had returned to the Cypress Hills, complaining that the government's fine promises had not been fulfilled at Indian Head and that many of his followers had become ill and eventually died from their steady diet of salty bacon. This news stiffened Cree resistance to the Indian department's policy of removal, and they insisted on their treaty right to choose their own reserves—where they wanted. Dewdney's predicament only worsened when the recalcitrant Big Bear and his band returned from the United States and set up camp near Fort Walsh; Big Bear, Little Pine, and Piapot—the leaders of the last major Cree war effort against the Blackfoot—were together once again.[7] Not foolish enough to risk an armed confrontation with the trio, Dewdney chose to continue denying aid to any band, treaty or nontreaty, that refused to go north. This strategy may have been less bloody, but it still exacted a terrible human toll, as a letter from Fred White, the mounted police commander at Fort Walsh, revealed. "They are very stubborn on the northern reserve question," he advised the Indian

Piapot was forced to leave the Cypress Hills district in the spring of 1882 and move to a reserve selected for him near Indian Head. He would later attempt to bring together the southern bands to protest government policy. *National Archives of Canada C3863*

commissioner in the fall of 1882, "still to allow them to starve here w[oul]d be a scandal."[8] In the spring, unmoved by White's warning, Dewdney took the next logical step in his exploitation of Indian hunger and closed Fort Walsh, thereby eliminating the only source of provisions and one of the last inducements for remaining in the Cypress Hills. With local game resources exhausted, and the clear probability of a hostile reception across the border, the Cree and Assiniboine had no choice but to accept the government offer—sweetened by the lure of rations—and leave for their new homes under police escort.[9]

The dispersal of the Fort Walsh refugees to different parts of the North-West was part of what could best be termed a divide-and-conquer policy; powerful Indian leaders would hopefully be more manageable, if not compliant, if they were separated by several hundred miles of prairie wilderness. But this forced move did not mean that the Cree chiefs had abandoned their struggle for greater autonomy— or were prepared to cooperate.[10] Instead of returning quietly to the Qu'Appelle district as expected, Piapot tried to bring about a new concentration of Indians by taking up residence near a group of reserves at Qu'Appelle. A similar plan was being hatched at Battleford. Little Pine had no sooner arrived from the south than he asked for a reserve near the Poundmaker and Sweetgrass reserves. This request brought the local Indian population to two thousand. It would have been even higher if Big Bear had had his way.

At Walsh, Dewdney informed the Plains Cree leader that a reserve had been selected for his band at Frog Lake, a hamlet just northeast of Fort Pitt, near the present-day Saskatchewan-Alberta boundary. But western Canada's newest treaty chief refused to go into exile voluntarily, and—against the wishes of his Indian department escort—led his beleaguered band to Battleford instead. Here, he conferred with Poundmaker about reserve life and then met with John Rae, the new Indian agent for the district and cousin of the prime minister. At the mid-July council, Big Bear spoke at length, stabbing the air with his hand for extra emphasis, about Dewdney's many unfulfilled promises and how his people were weak and destitute from hunger and the arduous trip north. The corpulent Rae, who sat impassively throughout the harangue as if seated on a throne, brusquely responded that he was to "carry out instructions to the letter"[11] and that there would be no food unless they left for their new reserve. He also threatened to jail anyone who killed government livestock.[12] An angry Big Bear vowed to stay put, but within a few weeks, the growing threat of starvation forced him to take his five hundred followers westward as far as Fort Pitt, where he planned to spend the winter near his friend, HBC trader William McKay. He steadfastly refused, though, to accept the reserve set aside for him at Frog Lake.

Other treaty bands in the Battleford Indian agency fared little better that summer. During his meeting with Big Bear, a disillusioned Poundmaker complained that the Canadian government was not providing the farming assistance promised during the Carlton negotiations, let alone honouring its special pledge to supply food during times of crisis—the so-called famine clause. It was as if his initial predictions about entering treaty were coming true—with horrible consequences for his followers. "I saw gaunt children, dying of hunger, come to my place to be instructed," recounted Father Louis Cochin, the Poundmaker schoolteacher. "[T]heir bodies were scarcely covered with torn rags . . . It was a pity to see them."[13] The suffering was probably worse on the nearby Assiniboine reserve. In June 1882, the Grizzly Bear's Head and Lean Man bands[14] were driven north to Battleford, as part of Dewdney's effort to clear the Cypress Hills of Indians. Although both leaders had signed Treaty Four and

Father Louis Cochin, the Poundmaker schoolteacher, was appalled by the Indian starvation in the Battleford district. *Provincial Archives of Alberta OB2797*

had been living with fellow Assiniboine in southern Assiniboia, they were forced to settle in Treaty Six territory with Chief Mosquito until their own reserves could be set aside. The addition of the two new bands—numbering 266 in October 1882—quickly overwhelmed the already strained resources of the area, and they became even more dependent on government support for their existence. Local authorities, meanwhile, did not seem to realize that much of the hardship could be blamed on the decision to place all three Assiniboine groups on the same reserve; they insisted that the Indians, no matter how weak or sickly, work for their rations. As a result, the Cypress Hills refugees endured yet another winter of starvation, and with it, growing frustration, to the point where Lean Man threatened to shoot the farm instructor for forcibly evicting several begging Indians from his house.[15] By the time the last of the snow in the Eagle Hills had melted, a whopping one-fifth of the newcomers had perished, while an almost equal number had slipped away, sensing that their chances for survival were probably better elsewhere.[16]

The Canadian government knew of this misery and death—from official inspection reports, if not directly from the Indians themselves. But officials chose to dismiss the conditions on the reserves as either fabricated or misunderstood. When the Edmonton chiefs' letter was read aloud in the House of Commons in early May 1883, for example, Prime Minister Macdonald stoutly defended his administration's Indian policy by depicting the complainants as chronic whiners who would rather be fed at government expense than work. "The Indians will always grumble," he remarked, as if it were some natural trait, "they will never profess to be satisfied."[17] Sir John also denied that Ottawa had ignored its treaty commitments. "We have kept faith with them," he maintained adamantly, "and they have received large supplies . . . if there is an error, it is in an excessive supply being furnished to the Indians."

This image of First Nations as pampered idlers would be used regularly into the twentieth century to cover up government neglect and indifference. But it assumed particular importance in 1883, when the Canadian economy began to sputter and stall. Faced with a serious deficit, the Macdonald government needed to slash spending in order to continue to help underwrite construction of the more difficult sections of the transcontinental railway. The Indian rations program became an obvious target for cutbacks. In his report for the fiscal year ending in June 1883, Canada's auditor general drew special attention in his opening remarks to the large sums being spent on supplies for destitute Indians in Manitoba and the North-West Territories.[18] Nearly one-half million dollars was going to feed First Nations; this amount represented almost two-thirds of all spending on Indian matters in western Canada and was more than twice the expenditures in all other parts of the country.[19] Nor was the auditor general singling out this assistance on his own initiative. His investigation of the Indian feeding program was spurred by growing criticism in the House, especially from the Liberal Opposition benches, about the amount being spent to keep a dying race alive.[20]

Deputy Superintendent General Vankoughnet responded to the auditor general's probe by arguing that such generous distribution of rations had been necessary to remove the Indians from the Cypress Hills district. Now that the Cree and Assiniboine had taken up their new homes, such levels of support would no longer be necessary.[21] What he did not say is that large numbers of Indians had to be fed because the reserve agricultural program failed dismally. The federal government was more concerned with economy than ensuring that fledgling Indian farmers received a helping hand, especially during the critical first years when prairie agriculture was still in the experimental stage. The size of the rations expenditure, moreover, was not at all extravagant, considering that four out of five Indians in the region had no other means of support because of the sudden loss of the buffalo. If anything, the cost was modest; according to Dewdney's own calculations for 1881-82, the government was feeding an estimated eighteen thousand Indians in Treaties Four, Six, and Seven for less than eight cents a day per person.[22]

The Conservative government had grudgingly absorbed these expenditures for essentially practical reasons—it was the easiest and cheapest way to deal with the Indian famine. But any humanitarian spirit or sense of treaty obligation quickly evaporated when the economy slid into recession. Forced to choose between the railway and the Indians, the prime minister opted for his sacred iron horse and instructed Commissioner Dewdney in September 1883 to cut Indian expenditures wherever possible.[23] He also sent his deputy, Lawrence Vankoughnet, on an inspection tour of the North-West that fall, to look for further reductions. The penny-pinching Vankoughnet arrived in the region just as the crops were maturing, and there seemed every reason to believe that the Indians would soon become self-sufficient farmers. He consequently ordered that rations be reduced, as well as dismissed a number of agency or reserve employees. To ensure that he gained effective control over department spending, he centralized all decision-making power in Ottawa; even the most minor purchase now had to be approved by his office. Perhaps the most telling example of the new regime's autocracy, however, was when Vankoughnet met Big Bear at Fort Pitt. Angered to learn that the chief still had not taken up his reserve, the senior Indian bureaucrat delivered an ultimatum: Big Bear either moved there by the beginning of November or his entire band would have to fend for itself over the coming winter.[24]

These retrenchment measures would prove painful on their own. But they were compounded by two other stinging developments that fall: the loss of the promising grain crop to a killing frost, and the beginning of an unusually severe winter. At a time, then, when the First Nations needed the Queen's helping hand more than ever, the Canadian government decidedly turned its back on its Indian responsibilities.[25] And it was not long before the cutbacks provoked a reaction. On the Crooked Lake reserves, about one hundred miles east of Regina, the Indian Affairs department had dismissed the popular farm instructor for being too generous in his distribution of rations and directed his replacement, Hilton Keith, to feed only the aged and infirm. On the Sakimay reserve, Assistant Indian Commissioner Hayter Reed took the reductions even one step further and

Lawrence Vankoughnet, the deputy superintendent general of Indian Affairs, was determined to reduce Indian expenditures as much as possible in the early 1880s—regardless of the consequences. *National Archives of Canada PA6695*

decided that the entire band could survive the punishing winter on local game and fish resources alone. These instructions may have saved the department money, but they also led to incredible hardship.

On 18 February 1884, Yellow Calf had had enough. He and about twenty-five armed young men knocked an uncooperative Keith aside and raided the government storehouse. When a mounted police party reached the reserve a few days later to apprehend the culprits, they found the Indians barricaded in a house, prepared to defend the food with their lives if necessary. Tense negotiations followed, during which Yellow Calf claimed that his band was starving, that his people had been forced to help themselves to the provisions because of Keith's repeated refusals, and that they were taking only what rightfully belonged to them. "If . . . the provisions were not intended to be eaten by the Indians," Yellow Calf reportedly asked, "why were they stored on our reserve?"[26] In the end, Reed relented and reinstated the rations policy; nothing was said, however, about hunger being the cause of the trouble or how bloodshed had been narrowly averted because of Indian restraint.

The Yellow Calf incident may have been an isolated event, but it did not mean that all was well on other reserves in the Assiniboia district. Sickness and disease, in the form of scurvy and tuberculosis,

prowled hand-in-hand that winter, generating a mortality rate that
even Edgar Dewdney found alarming during his spring inspection
tour.[27] A subsequent investigation attributed much of the illness to
salty rations, something the Indians already knew. Chief Long Lodge
told the department doctor that he wanted "medicine that walks . . .
give fresh meat to my people and they will get better."[28] Piapot,
meanwhile, decided to abandon his Indian Head reserve in mid-May
1884 because of the growing number of deaths and seek a new home.
He sent runners to nearby bands and invited them to join him at
Pasquah's reserve, where he intended to hold a sun dance and discuss
treaty promises. These latest moves greatly annoyed Indian Affairs
officials, especially since Piapot seemed to be attracting several bands
to his cause. Initially, Dewdney decided that the Indian leader must
be stopped—short of violence—and not allowed to abandon his reserve. Discretion soon dictated, however, that it would be best to
grant Piapot the land he wanted next to the Muscowpetung reserve
on the Qu'Appelle River. The alternatives were to make him the focus
of discontent in the south and bring about a coalition of Treaty Four
chiefs or force him to move north, as he once threatened, to be near
his old friends, Big Bear and Little Pine.[29]

The situation on the northern reserves was equally bleak that
winter. Yet instead of blindly lashing out against the government and
its empty promises, the Cree were determined to bring about change
by peaceful means. They had solemnly pledged in the presence of the
Creator to honour their treaty pledges and remain loyal to the
Queen. And they were not prepared to break their vow and plunge
the region into war, even if Ottawa was violating both the spirit and
terms of the agreement with such horrendous consequences. The
Cree hoped to force Canadian officials to revise the treaty so that it
provided more adequate support and assistance. Big Bear had called
repeatedly for these changes during his six-year odyssey outside
Treaty Six, and it became his main strategy during the winter of
1883–84 for relieving his people's misery after their forced return to
the Fort Pitt district. This time, though, he planned to carry on his
campaign for better terms by building a broad-based Indian political
movement that spoke with a single, strong voice. His discussions with
other chiefs that winter convinced him that this was probably the best
time to try to put the idea into effect. Poundmaker, for example, had
decided that a return to political activity held the most hope of
securing more aid for his followers.[30]

Big Bear launched his diplomatic offensive in late spring 1884 by sending messengers to disgruntled bands, announcing his intention to sponsor a thirst dance on the Poundmaker reserve in mid-June. The traditional spring ritual, representing renewal and cooperation, proved an ideal vehicle for Big Bear's strategy. In the councils leading up to the ceremony, he managed to convince the other chiefs to recognize him as their spokesman on treaty grievances; the next step was to meet with Piapot about his organizing efforts in the south and then travel to Ottawa to deal directly with that otherwise faceless person in charge of Indian policy.[31] Unfortunately, Big Bear's promising plans were tempered by problems of his own. Arriving early in the Battleford area, the old chief had met with Commissioner Dewdney and once again asked about a possible reserve next to Poundmaker. When the request landed on Vankoughnet's desk, he vehemently rejected it, claiming that it threatened to re-create another Fort Walsh situation—"namely, a big camp composed of all the idle Indians in the country being fed at large expense."[32] The department's position remained brutally simple: there would be no rations for Big Bear's band as long as he refused to select a new home in the Pitt district. This punishment may have been the unavoidable price of continued resistance, but it ultimately worked against Big Bear's leadership by strengthening the influence of dissidents, including his own son, Imasees, who were dismayed with the chief's seemingly endless manoeuvrings and wanted him to take up his reserve. Eventually, they would lose all patience with their leader's strategy.

The meeting on the Poundmaker reserve also did little to enhance the Cree's reputation among white settlers and government officials. Already wary of the large number of Indians living in the district, Battleford residents looked upon the thirst dance, with its emotionally charged atmosphere, as the warm-up to an eventual Indian rebellion.[33] These fears seemed justified when two of Lucky Man's sons assaulted John Craig, the Little Pine farm instructor, in a heated scuffle on 18 June over the sudden withdrawal of rations. Although Craig was not seriously hurt—Kahweechatwaymat had whacked him on the arm with an axe handle—the local mounted police detachment used the incident as an excuse to disperse the Indians and attempted to arrest the two brothers the next day. Their interruption of the sacred ceremony, however, amounted to a grievous insult, and the police found themselves face to face with several armed, angry warriors spoiling for a fight. Only the most strenuous efforts of the leaders—especially Big Bear and Poundmaker, who offered to give themselves up in place of the two young men—prevented the tense showdown from reaching a bloody conclusion, and the dispute was resolved peaceably to the apparent surprise of both sides.[34] But the Craig incident, as it became known, had been costly. The near violence suggested that Big Bear and Poundmaker were "bad" Indians, even though they had both counselled restraint; they would perform a similar role as peacekeepers during the rebellion—that, once again, would be misinterpreted. Doubts also arose about the sincerity of the new Cree diplomatic initiative. NWMP Superintendent Leif Crozier, the commander at Fort Battleford, interpreted the incident as a stark warning of how the Cree might behave in the future. "I unhesitantly state," he told Ottawa, oblivious to the spiritual violation that his men had committed, "that never since the occupation of the Country by the Police, was there anything like such a determination shewn by any Indians anywhere in the Territory, as there was by those to resist the authority of the Government."[35]

Cree activities would continue to be misunderstood over the next few months, thanks in no small part to the arrival of Métis leader Louis Riel in the Saskatchewan country on Dominion Day 1884. Throughout the early 1880s, the Métis of the South Branch communities had been trying unsuccessfully to get the federal government to deal with a number of problems. They, like several of the local white farmers, had suffered through a series of bad harvests. They also lost a vital transportation link when the CPR abandoned the North Saskatchewan route for the railway in 1882 in favour of one across the southern prairies. Their most urgent concern, though, now that the buffalo were gone, was compensation for the loss of their aboriginal title and formal recognition of their existing land holdings before development engulfed the region. When Ottawa failed repeatedly to respond to their petitions—the department of the Interior acted more like the department of indifference—the Métis summoned Louis Riel from Montana to take up their cause. As the successful leader of the 1869–70 Red River Resistance, Riel was a hero to the Métis. But the Riel who answered the call of his people in 1884 was fundamentally different from the Riel of Red River days. Although still a charismatic leader, he now regarded himself as God's personal emissary, whose mission was to create a homeland in the North-West for the Métis, Indians, and other oppressed peoples of the world in preparation for the day of judgement.[36] It was this religious mission that prompted Riel to return to Canada—the invitation to take up the Métis cause was the sign he had been waiting for. And his earlier plan to bring about a Native confederacy seemed assured. "Now, my dear cousin," read the letter carried by the delegation, "the closest union exists between the French and English [mixed-bloods] and the Indians, and we have good generals to foster it."[37]

Riel moved quickly to bring about his Indian-Métis alliance once he arrived in the Saskatchewan country, and this time it appeared that the Cree were willing to listen to his entreaties. Big Bear was leading his band back to Fort Pitt after the thirst dance when a messenger overtook him on the trail with news that Chief Beardy of the Willow Cree wanted him to take part in a special council on Indian grievances at the end of July. The chief's decision to turn around and head for Duck Lake was relayed immediately to the prime minister; according

to Edgar Dewdney's 26 July telegram, Big Bear was going to see Riel.[38] That some scheme was afoot and that Riel was at the heart of it seemed to be confirmed by Crozier. He reported that Riel had told the Indians in the Carlton district that they, like the Métis, had rights and "that he wished to be the means of having them redressed."[39] Crozier also suggested that the Indians would naturally sympathize with the Métis agitation—because

Louis Riel sought to bring about an Indian-Métis alliance following his return to Canada in the summer of 1884. *National Archives of Canada C18082*

of their aboriginal heritage—and that "precautionary measures should be taken." Ansdell Macrae, subagent at Carlton, was in full agreement. Knowing that Riel had taken up residence in the nearby St. Laurent parish and having watched Big Bear and Lucky Man arrive for the meeting, he panicked, pleading with Dewdney for the immediate dispatch of extra police to the region.[40]

The Duck Lake council did much to repair the damage the thirst dance standoff had done to the Indian diplomatic initiative. Although Beardy had tried in 1880 to bring the bands in the surrounding area together into one large camp, most of his efforts to assert his people's autonomy had been independent of other chiefs. His decision to host the Duck Lake meeting represented a marked change in strategy; like Big Bear, he now realized that First Nations must take collective action to secure redress for treaty grievances.[41] The council was also noteworthy for who was there. Several of the chiefs who accepted Beardy's invitation, most notably Mistawasis and Ahtahkakoop, were highly regarded by Indian Affairs officials for their cooperative spirit and accommodating nature. Their presence at the meeting was surprising, if not worrisome.[42] Riel, on the other hand, was essentially an outsider. Although granted a brief audience with the chiefs before the council, he did not participate in the formal deliberations nor associate with the leaders in another way. It was an Indian assembly, not the first step in some grand alliance with the Métis.

The council got underway at Beardy's on 31 July 1884, but relocated to Carlton ten days later when Subagent Macrae finally agreed to supply provisions to the visiting chiefs if the Indians held their meeting at the fort. This change of venue meant the twelve leaders could talk directly to a government representative—no matter how minor—and they spoke with the force of years of bitterness and frustration. Eighteen grievances were enumerated, from the lack of schools and health care to poor farming equipment, clothing, and rations. Most revealing, however, were the comments that accompanied the grievances, all dutifully recorded by Macrae. The chiefs complained that they had petitioned Ottawa "again and again without effect" and expressed relief that their young men had managed to keep their anger in check. "[I]t is almost too hard for them," Macrae noted, "to bear the treatment received at the hands of the Government after its 'sweet promises' made in order to get the country from them." They also affirmed their allegiance to the Queen, contending it was the Canadian government, not the Crown,

Chief Beardy of the Willow Cree hosted a council in the summer of 1884; it marked the beginning of collective action to secure redress for treaty grievances. *Saskatchewan Archives Board R-A5669*

who had created the current climate of ill will. "[H]ad the Treaty promises been carried out all would have been well," observed the chiefs. The council members warned Ottawa to expect some other action the following summer if the government continued to ignore its obligations. Big Bear reminded Macrae that while he had once stood alone in trying to realize better treaty terms, Indian leaders were now united in this cause. At the same time, he made it perfectly clear that the Cree chiefs shunned violence, citing his own recent efforts as a peacemaker during the thirst dance incident. Although the leaders were anxious to secure redress, the means never included war.[43]

Edgar Dewdney responded to the news of the Duck Lake council by sending his hard-nosed assistant, Hayter Reed, to investigate the attitude of the Indians in the region. In his subsequent report, dated 25 August 1884, Reed assured Dewdney that Indian dissension was greatly exaggerated and that "judicious management on our part" would make them forget their childish protest. "On my arrival," he wrote from Carlton, "I found the wildest rumours in circulation . . . but closest enquiry does not reveal that the Indians have any bad motives." Reed also claimed that Big Bear's visit had unsettled the local bands and that Riel's clandestine activities only added to the unrest.[44] This interpretation implied that the Duck Lake council had been largely Big Bear's doing, and that the Indians looked to the Métis leader to attend to their grievances as well. On the surface, this assessment of the situation seemed to make sense, especially after

Riel invited the Cree chief to a much-publicized private interview in Prince Albert following the council. This meeting, however, was more akin to a verbal sparring match; the two men spent most of their time sizing up each other and their respective strategies. Indeed, Big Bear had fought too long and too hard to bring about a First Nations alliance to abandon it just when the various bands seemed prepared to work together.[45] He also saw the Métis as competitors—he had once clashed with the Dumont family over the buffalo hunt[46]—and knew that Indian interests and concerns differed from those of the Métis. It was a profound misreading of the situation, then, to assume that the two leaders agreed to work cooperatively—something even the unsympathetic *Saskatchewan Herald* recognized. Commenting on Big Bear's mood as he made his way back to Pitt, the *Herald* editor gloated, "the old man does not seem to be favourably impressed by the prospects held out to him by Riel."[47]

The big question facing Dewdney was how to respond to the Indian diplomatic initiative. There was no shortage of advice. Indian Agent Rae and NWMP Superintendent Crozier cautioned that unless the Indian department adopted a more conciliatory, open-handed approach towards the Cree, Ottawa would have to fight them. "[I]t is nonsense to say to them that they must work or starve," a frustrated Rae lectured his cousin, the prime minister, in the aftermath of the Craig incident. "The thing must be brought about gradually . . . or trouble will surely follow. Of course if it is the intention of the Department to follow out their Cast Iron Rules then full preparations should be made for an Indian war."[48] Judge C.B. Rouleau of Battleford also called into question the wisdom of the department's new economy drive, following a judicial trip to Prince Albert in late August. Convinced that the Métis did not want to weaken their claims against the government by supporting the Indians' "supposed grievances," Rouleau argued that the most immediate threat to peace over the coming winter was the dire Indian need for "*food* and *clothing*." And he humbly urged Dewdney to spend some extra money on provisions in the interests of "the Government and the Country."[49]

Dewdney and Reed shared these concerns about Vankoughnet's new hard-line approach to Indian rationing. They believed that the senior bureaucrat's handling of Big Bear had aggravated the situation and made the chief even more reluctant to select his reserve.[50] But the two officials had made a startling discovery during their tour of western reserves that fall: Big Bear, Little Pine, and Piapot were succeeding in their campaign to bring the various Cree bands together for a special council the following summer that would collectively call for renegotiation of the treaties. This movement threatened to derail federal Indian policy in western Canada by making it impossible for Ottawa to maintain what little control it had enjoyed over First Nations since the late 1870s. Dewdney consequently adopted what one historian has described as a policy of "sheer compulsion" in order to smash the Cree diplomatic offensive.[51] Fully aware that the Indians were not "going to submit to be starved out,"[52] as seen by their behaviour over the past year, he decided that the best way to prevent the councils was to arrest the leaders, replace any chief who refused to cooperate, and make it difficult for band members to leave their reserves.[53] Sadly, Indian Affairs officials embraced this policy even though they knew that Cree intentions were peaceful; all they wanted was to reestablish a balance of power in their relationship with the federal government in keeping with the spirit of the treaties.[54]

Dewdney's first step that September was to beef up the mounted police presence in the region so that he had the necessary muscle to enforce his new Indian policy. Prime Minister Macdonald immediately instructed the head of the police to find another one hundred recruits. "It would appear that the situation is getting serious," Sir John confided. "I do not apprehend myself any rising, but with these warnings it would be criminal negligence not to take every precaution."[55] Dewdney also hired Peter Ballendine, the mixed-blood interpreter who had represented the government side during the Treaty Six negotiations at Carlton, to gather intelligence on Cree activities, especially Big Bear's plans. Ironically, his spying mission confirmed that the Cree leadership had its own agenda, separate from that of the Métis, and that Riel was the one trying to head an aboriginal alliance.[56] In Ballendine's secret report of 20 November 1884, he advised Dewdney that Ahtahkakoop had been visited recently by two messengers: one from Beardy inviting him to a gathering at Duck Lake the following summer, the other from Riel. The respected chief, however, refused to allow the Métis emissary to speak to his people, claiming that he had made a solemn promise to remain loyal and wanted no part of Riel's intrigues.[57]

While Dewdney prepared to decapitate the Cree leadership, the grand council idea was picking up momentum. Continued misery on the reserves and widespread disillusionment with government treaty promises contributed to the sense of urgency. In the Carlton district, for example, crop failures had left the local bands completely destitute,[58] while farther west, near Fort Edmonton, several of the chiefs had gathered at the Bear Hills in order to force Dewdney to deal with their grievances.[59] The other significant development—something that probably caused Dewdney to shake his head in disbelief—was the possible involvement of the Blackfoot of present-day Alberta. While Big Bear and Piapot worked on uniting the chiefs of Treaties Four and Six, Little Pine had been busy through the summer and into the fall trying to win over the Blackfoot, building on the friendship he had developed with Chief Crowfoot during his time hunting buffalo south of the border in the Milk River area. This initiative was stalled momentarily when the aged Little Pine developed temporary blindness—probably because of malnutrition—but when he recovered, he rode south to Blackfoot country and returned with a present of five horses, and more important, a request that a grand council of the two tribes be held at Blackfoot Crossing the following summer.[60]

This news only hardened Dewdney's resolve to crush the Indian resistance. And by the new year, his office had arrived at a strategy for justifying any future action against the Cree leadership—a strategy with little basis in reality. As Hayter Reed explained to the prime minister on 23 January 1885, ostensibly in response to the Duck Lake council petition, the government was faithfully keeping its treaty promises to the Indians; any complainants were dismissed as "ill-disposed and lazy . . . looking for extra aid." He also branded Big Bear as an "agitator" and claimed that Indian grievances had been deliberately exaggerated to promote unrest in the West and thereby force Ottawa to recognize their claims, however unrealistic. "Riel's movement has a great deal to do with the demands of the Indians," Reed argued, "and there is no possible doubt but that they as well as the Halfbreeds are beginning to look up to him as one who will be the means of curing all their ills and obtaining for them all they demand."[61] Dewdney planned to use this supposed alliance as the grounds for arresting Indian leaders. His reasoning was cleverly calculated: since Big Bear, Little Pine, and Piapot were inciting insurrection, they needed to be punished as an example. Macdonald, in his capacity as the senior Indian official in the country, concurred. But in blessing the policy in late February, the prime minister cautioned Dewdney to ensure that he had adequate police support to enforce any arrest and that any action be clearly defensible. He also recommended that he enlist the cooperation of local magistrates to impose long sentences.[62]

Dewdney planned to move against the Cree chiefs in the spring of 1885, confident that he could deal their diplomatic initiative a blow from which it would never recover. In his determination to sabotage the Indian councils, however, the Indian commissioner tended to discount two other critical developments. Throughout the fall of 1884, secret agent Ballendine reported that although Big Bear's intentions were peaceful, the old chief was losing control of his band and that some members, including his own son, were openly beginning to challenge his leadership. These internal divisions became even more pronounced during the winter because of Big Bear's continued refusal to select a reserve and thereby qualify for rations. The old man's penchant for thwarting the Canadian government at every opportunity was now causing his followers incredible suffering—only made worse by one of the harshest winters since meteorological records were kept. It would not take much provocation to give the disaffected reason to push Big Bear aside.[63] The other complicating factor was Louis Riel. While Dewdney chose to focus his energies on controlling the Cree, the Métis leader was busy trying to get the Indians to revoke their treaty pledges; he needed their numerical might in the event of a possible confrontation with the Canadian government. In fact, in late February 1885, at the very time that the Indian Affairs department was plotting against the Cree leadership, Riel had abandoned any pretence of peaceful negotiation with Ottawa and pushed his most militant followers in the direction of open rebellion. The ensuing war would prove doubly costly to the Indians of western Canada. Not only would the Cree diplomatic initiative die with the first bullets, but several bands would be implicated, if not blamed directly, for much of the turmoil over the next few troubled months. Dewdney could not have asked for a better outcome.

chapter four

Everything to Lose

SSIYIWIN WAS DISTURBED by the news.
The old man had no sooner arrived in Duck
Lake to visit a friend and buy a few supplies
when he heard that the mounted police and Métis appeared headed
for a bloody showdown.[1] The trouble had been simmering for a
week—since 19 March 1885—when Louis Riel formed a provisional
government at Batoche and called on the police forces at Carlton and
Battleford to surrender or "face a war of extermination."[2] The next
few days hung heavy with anticipation, as Riel and his council (or
Exovedate) rounded up as many men and arms as possible for their
cause, while an anxious Canadian government rushed police reinforcements to the area in an attempt to localize and crush the
fledgling movement. It was not until 26 March, however, that a clash
seemed imminent, when Riel learned that police at Fort Carlton
planned to confiscate the guns and ammunition from a Duck Lake
store. A small Métis party under Riel's adjutant general, the redoubt-
able Gabriel Dumont, mobilized quickly to intercept them.

Over the past few months, Assiyiwin, like many other Indians in
the Carlton Indian agency, had been wooed by the South Branch
Métis as a possible ally in their fight against an indifferent federal
government. In fact, on the same day that the provisional government
came into being at Batoche, the council drew up a list of Indian chiefs

considered sympathetic to the Métis and called on Albert Monkman to win them over.[3] Riel and his new regime were confident he would find willing recruits. Not only were many of the treaty Indians in the Duck Lake area of mixed ancestry, but a few of the local Métis had married Cree women and become part of their extended families. At least six Métis who fought during the spring of 1885, for example, had been on the pay lists of neighbouring reserves one year earlier.[4]

Riel also viewed his mission as part of a larger aboriginal struggle for recognition and rights and believed that the Indians, victimized by a decade of government parsimony and intransigence, would jump at the opportunity to exact revenge. But what the Métis leader and his devoted followers stubbornly refused to recognize was that Indian leaders had their own agenda for addressing their grievances and were pinning their hopes on a large intertribal council to be held at Duck Lake that summer. As a result, Chief Beardy, one of the prime movers behind this historic meeting, refused to be drawn into Riel's gambit. He deeply regretted the resort to arms—and what it might mean to Indian diplomatic efforts. He was equally worried about what might happen to his own people, especially since their reserve was strategically situated on the main route between Batoche and Carlton. All he could do, though, was counsel restraint and try to keep out any intruders.[5]

Assiyiwin, one of Beardy's four headmen, shared the chief's desire to remain aloof from the struggle and to preserve the sanctity of the reserve. When he learned that the Métis and police would probably meet outside Duck Lake, he tied his goods on his pony and started home on foot, hurrying as best he could despite his poor eyesight. The reserve was not far, and Assiyiwin soon heard excited voices, strained with emotion, but could not make out any figures. "Stop! Don't you know what is going on here?" a voice in Cree challenged the old man. It was "Gentleman Joe" McKay, the irascible police interpreter. "No, I am blind," replied Assiyiwin. "Tell me what is going on." The mixed-blood interpreter could hardly contain his annoyance with the old Indian. "There is going to be trouble here. Go back to where you came from."[6]

Assiyiwin had innocently walked into the middle of the unfolding drama. Earlier that morning, goaded into action by Carlton residents, Superintendent Leif Crozier, a veteran police officer, had set off rashly for Duck Lake with nearly one hundred police and civilian volunteers from the area to prevent a batch of guns and ammunition

Assiyiwin was mortally wounded when he tried to prevent the police and Métis from clashing on Beardy's reserve. *James Smith*

from falling into the hands of Riel's supporters. As the combined force headed southeast from the fort along the Carlton trail, they entered Beardy's reserve, where Crozier stopped briefly at the chief's home to question him. Beardy confirmed that he wanted no part of Riel's actions, but that he could not vouch for all of his young men.[7] He also complained that Métis patrols had been roaming in and around the reserve, and he told Crozier there were rumours of an impending fight.[8] Undeterred, Crozier's men continued towards Duck Lake about two miles distant. But before the force was able to leave the reserve, it spotted about twenty-five Métis horsemen led by Dumont and quickly assumed a defensive position. From the beginning of the troubles, the Métis strategy was to take hostages, make threats, and force the Canadian government to negotiate. Dumont consequently sent his brother, Isidore, forward to stall the police until further reinforcements arrived from Batoche.

By the time Isidore Dumont reached Assiyiwin and McKay, the pair was arguing. The old man was indignant that the police had intruded on the reserve and flatly told the interpreter, "If you are going to have a battle, if you are going to spill blood, you cannot do

"Gentleman Joe" McKay, mixed-blood interpreter for the mounted police, fired the first shot in what would become known as the Duck Lake battle. *RCMP Museum*

it on our reserve land." McKay once again ordered him to turn back to Duck Lake, but the unarmed though defiant Assiyiwin stood there with his horse and said, "No, I am going home." The interpreter then threatened Assiyiwin if he came closer, "Step over my coat ... I'll shoot you." Assiyiwin had once been a powerful warrior—one of his most prized possessions was a small box of Blackfoot scalps—and he was not about to back down from anyone. He grabbed McKay's rifle, and as the two men struggled, Isidore Dumont waved his hands frantically and shouted, "Don't shoot each other. We want to find a way to work this out peacefully. We don't want anyone killed." It was too late. Sensing that the parley was only a ruse for an ambush, McKay pulled out his revolver and shot Dumont in the head, killing him instantly. He then turned his gun on the unarmed Assiyiwin and mortally wounded him in the stomach.[9]

At the sound of gunfire, shooting erupted from both sides. The police and civilian volunteers had sought shelter behind their sleighs and a nearby clump of trees, while the Métis had taken over a log house, as well as occupied a shallow ditch along the north side of the trail. The casualties mounted by the minute, and it quickly became apparent that the Métis held the upper hand—especially once dozens of men, including Riel armed with only a crucifix, poured in from Batoche. Facing capture or possible annihilation, Superintendent

Crozier ordered a general retreat and then led his badly mauled force back to the relative safety of Fort Carlton. He left behind twelve dead, including nine civilians. The Métis lost four men. Assiyiwin was treated in Duck Lake for his wound, but died before sunrise the next morning.[10]

The Duck Lake fiasco cast the Métis resistance in an entirely different light. Neither side that morning had wanted to fire the first shot. But the blood-stained snow meant that they were now at war—a war that unfortunately appeared to involve the Indian people. Assiyiwin's death, the battle on Beardy's reserve, and the presence of a handful of Willow Cree among the Métis fighters pointed to an apparent Indian-Métis alliance—an assumption that the country's newspapers reached immediately, and that stubbornly persists to this day.[11] To suggest, however, that the Indians had joined the rebels is a shortsighted, if not blinkered, interpretation of events that prairie spring. The Canadian government and Riel and his council knew this at the time but chose to ignore it.

Indian Affairs officials had been aware for at least half a year that Riel, while living in Montana in the early 1880s, had tried to convince Big Bear and other Cree leaders to take up arms. A concerned Hayter Reed had reported this perfidious activity to Commissioner Dewdney in a wide-ranging, candid letter on Indian matters in early September 1884. He also advised Dewdney that Riel had continued to "work(s) upon the Indians" since his return to Canada and that trouble could be expected from the Métis, most likely in the coming spring.[12] This information, by itself, was extremely unsettling, for it suggested that the Indians were being targeted deliberately by Riel as likely allies in his agitation. But Indian Affairs also knew, thanks to Dewdney's special agent, the mixed-blood Peter Ballendine, that Cree leaders were not interested in Riel's behind-the-scene intrigues and were preoccupied with their own diplomatic efforts to bring about a workable alliance with the Blackfoot.[13] These overtures, moreover, were not for military purposes, but rather designed to give the Indians a stronger hand in negotiating with the federal government. First Nations leaders were fully aware that violence would bring about retribution and spoil any chance of getting Ottawa to honour the treaties. From the government's perspective, then, the situation with the Cree was bad, but it could have been much worse. Try as he might to seduce the Indians, Riel was still a lonely suitor at the altar.

Throughout the winter of 1884-85, Dewdney and his officials did what they could to undermine, if not prevent, the Duck Lake council. Although the commissioner publicly discounted the significance of the gathering, he was genuinely afraid that a Cree-Blackfoot alliance would thwart his policies of control and subjugation.[14] In the meantime, he continued to believe that any future unrest would be the handiwork of the Métis and that the Cree would remain peaceful—if left alone. He was convinced that the notion of an Indian-Métis union had little basis in reality. "If the Crees are looking to the Blackfeet to assist them," Dewdney reasoned in a February 1885 letter to Prime Minister Macdonald, "they can't be depending on the Half Breeds."[15] But, he asked himself, was it possible that Riel could provoke the Indians? The Métis leader certainly had not given up on securing their assistance; Métis messengers had continued to visit the reserves during the winter. One can only wonder whether the federal government's decision that January to create a commission to investigate Métis land claims was designed, in part, to deflect Riel's attention away from the Cree.[16]

By March 1885, the Cree-Métis equation took on new significance after Riel declared his intention to form a provisional government and try to wring concessions from Ottawa—by force, if necessary. Riel seemed determined to repeat the success of the earlier Red River Resistance, and Canadian officials were nervous that he might enlist the muscle of the Cree. Indian intentions were anything but clear, thanks to contradictory reports that Dewdney received about the deteriorating situation. On 13 March 1885, a somewhat frantic Superintendent Crozier had telegraphed

Superintendent Leif Crozier, a veteran police officer, had been dispatched to Fort Carlton to prevent Métis unrest; he resigned as a direct consequence of the Duck Lake clash. *Provincial Archives of Alberta B1964*

the commissioner of the North-West Mounted Police in Regina: "Half-breed rebellion liable to break out at any moment. Troops must be largely reinforced. If half-breeds rise, Indians will join them."[17] Crozier's assessment of the Carlton Cree's loyalty was noteworthy—some might say, reckless—considering he had just arrived from Battleford with reinforcements that same day and had not bothered to consult with the local bands. It was also squarely at odds with the opinion of Lawrence Clarke, long-time Hudson's Bay Company factor at Fort Carlton and arch opponent of the Métis agitation. On 14 March, the day after Crozier's plaintive plea, Clarke wired Dewdney from Fort Qu'Appelle: "Riel will not get Indian support."[18] He sent a similar message upon reaching Carlton three days later; he reported that Riel was interfering with the Indians but that he was unlikely to gain much support.[19] Crozier, by this point, had also regained his composure—perhaps, because of Clarke's influence—and telegraphed Regina: "No cause for alarm now."[20]

These assurances simply confirmed what Cree leaders had been telling government officials for several months—that they had no interest in Riel's machinations. But Dewdney took advantage of the situation to intimidate the Indians. On the morning of 18 March 1885, NWMP Commissioner A.G. Irvine left Regina with one hundred police reinforcements to deal with the Métis unrest while it was still in its infancy. It was probably no coincidence that Irvine's force camped on or near Indian reserves as it marched north to Carlton,[21] or that it would be stationed in the same area where the Duck Lake council was to be held. "I think it is better to have a good force in the north this summer," Dewdney confided to the commissioner of the Hudson's Bay Company following Irvine's departure, "it will assist us very materially in handling our Indians."[22] These men would be needed sooner than Dewdney expected, for the situation quickly took a turn for the worse. On 19 March, Superintendent Crozier sent another alarming message from Carlton: "All One Arrow's band of Crees joined the rebels this afternoon. Many of Beardies [sic] also joined them . . . My impression is that many of the Indian bands will rise."[23] Crozier's telegram might have been dismissed as the product of an overactive imagination if it had not coincided with the official formation of Riel's provisional government. Further, more bloody proof of what appeared to be Indian involvement came one week later when Crozier clashed with the Métis on Beardy's reserve and Assiyiwin was killed. It appeared the Cree said one thing, but did another.

NWMP Commissioner A.G. Irvine led a large force north from Regina in mid-March 1885 to intimidate Cree bands and prevent a possible alliance with the Métis. *Provincial Archives of Alberta B1961*

Crozier was technically correct when he claimed that the Indians of the Carlton area had joined Riel's forces. Members of both the Beardy and One Arrow bands were at Batoche in the days leading up to the Duck Lake encounter. But what is often ignored is how many Willow Cree were present and, more important, why they were there. Crozier himself provided the clue. On the evening of 18 March, the day before Riel proclaimed his provisional government, the police superintendent wired Dewdney that the local Indians were "being tampered with."[24] This brief comment did little to convey what was actually taking place; indeed, it was an incredible understatement, especially coming from someone who had been predicting grief from the Métis for weeks. On the same day as Crozier's telegram, J.B. Lash, the Indian agent for the Carlton district, and his interpreter, William Tompkins, visited the One Arrow reserve, located immediately east of Batoche, to ascertain the band's intentions. They did not anticipate any trouble, for Lash had just returned from an overnight visit to Duck Lake and found the Indians to be "all quiet."[25] The two officials secured a promise of loyalty from Chief One Arrow, but on their return to Carlton, they were taken captive by Gabriel Dumont, who was securing the area.[26] One Arrow's people suffered a similar fate the following day, 19 March, when the reserve farm instructor, Michel Dumas, ordered the Cree to slaughter their cattle and join the Métis. Dumont's presence with a contingent of armed horsemen ensured that the Indians complied.[27]

Gabriel Dumont, Riel's adjutant general, was prepared to involve local Indian bands in the Métis cause—by force if necessary. *National Archives of Canada C15282*

One Arrow's band may have had the distinction of being the first Indian group to enter the rebel camp, but it would be a mistake to assume that many of the Willow Cree supported Riel's cause. For one thing, One Arrow was an advocate of Indian rights, as seen by his attendance at the August 1884 Duck Lake council, at which government assistance was severely criticized. The Métis agitation was clearly at odds with this diplomatic initiative. His people also tended to identify more closely with the English and the Hudson's Bay Company; in fact, most of the Willow Cree, including One Arrow, were the mixed-blood progeny of George Sutherland, a Scottish HBC employee, and his three Cree wives.[28] The band, then, had limited historical ties with the Métis, most of whom were recent arrivals in the region. Band members were also somewhat bitter over how Ottawa had resolved a land dispute with the Métis. The One Arrow reserve originally included land along the South Saskatchewan River, but in 1884 a government surveyor relocated the western boundary so as not to disturb river-lot holdings at Batoche.[29] This revision left the Indians with poor quality farm land—and a good reason for not siding with the Métis.

The circumstances behind the band's presence at Batoche on 19 March are also revealing. By the time of the troubles, it is debatable whether the seventy-year-old One Arrow could have actively resisted the forced relocation of his band. He had already offered to resign his chieftainship because of his age. He was also a sickly man—so much so that he had been unable to stand and address Governor General Lorne during his 1881 tour of western Canada. What probably troubled him the most that March, however, was the recent death of one of his grandchildren.[30] These circumstances made One Arrow vulnerable to Gabriel Dumont's bullying tactics. It also did not help that Dumont's first cousin, Vital (Cayol), and his two oldest sons were members of the reserve and answered the call to arms.[31] The most significant player, though, was Michel Dumas, the One Arrow farm instructor who supervised the evacuation to Batoche. Dumas was no ordinary government appointee. An educated, acculturated Métis, he was one of the four delegates sent to retrieve Riel from the United States in June 1884 and would later serve as secretary to the Exovedate.[32] His presence at One Arrow virtually ensured that the band would "follow" Riel. An inspector of Indian reserves said as much almost a year later: "Surrounded by rebels and influenced by their own Instructor it was almost impossible to expect Indians to act differently to 'One Arrow's' Band."[33]

The other noteworthy aspect of the band's so-called participation in the rebellion is that no more than twenty men—many of them elderly—were at Batoche before the fighting erupted. The remainder of the band either hid along the river or fled eastward and took refuge in the Lake Lenore area.[34] It is also not clear how many One Arrow men took part in the Duck Lake battle. None of the former white hostages who testified at the subsequent rebellion trials actually witnessed the confrontation. This was painfully apparent at the hearing for Left Hand (Konahmahchee), the only One Arrow band member, besides the chief, to be tried for his part in the Duck Lake fight.[35]

Chief Beardy's case was similar to that of One Arrow. Beardy, also known in French as Barbu because of his long, wispy facial hair, was a shrewd, visionary leader, noted for his special spiritual powers. His persistent efforts on behalf of his people and their long-term interests, beginning with the signing of Treaty Six, had made him the undisputed chief spokesman for the Carlton district chiefs and their grievances; he had not only hosted the 1884 Duck Lake council but was busy helping organize a gathering of all the Plains Cree chiefs the following summer. It was obviously not in Beardy's interests to become involved with Riel and his political regime. Nor did it make sense in light of his relationship with the local Métis settlements. An aloof Beardy, for example, had steadfastly resisted the proselytizing efforts of the Roman Catholic clergy, which had established the Sacré-Coeur mission at Duck Lake in 1876 in a concerted effort to Christianize the local bands.[36] Like One Arrow, he had also wrangled with the Métis over land. Believing that his people would need a large land base to ease the transition to an agricultural way of life, Beardy had selected land around Duck Lake, along the west side of the South Saskatchewan River, and on both sides of the Carlton trail. But when the reserve was formally surveyed, much of the land he coveted was intentionally excluded to satisfy Métis interests in the area. The government ordered Beardy to accept the revised boundaries or face the possible loss of treaty provisions—something that the chief already considered inadequate.[37]

This uneasy relationship with Riel and the Métis prompted Beardy to remain neutral in March 1885. He was telling Superintendent Crozier the truth the day of the Duck Lake skirmish when he said he did not support rebellion—a position confirmed by a number of reserve elders to this day.[38] But clearly, other members of his band did ride with the Métis patrols once Riel had declared his plans. Who they were is a difficult question. Fearful of retribution, elders were careful not to talk openly about the events that March, and avoided mentioning the names of individuals who might have been involved with the Métis.[39] It is known, though,

Michel Dumas, the One Arrow farm instructor, served as secretary of Riel's governing council. His presence at One Arrow ensured that the band would "join" the Métis at Batoche. *Montana Historical Society 942-020*

that one was Boss Bull or Chicicum (alternatively known as Jaykeekum, Tchekikam, or Jack E. Cane). He had been one of Riel's customers in Montana during the winter of 1880-81 when the Métis leader was working for a trader in the Flat Willow Creek area.[40] Another was Charles Trottier, Jr. A mixed-blood by birth, he was a member of Beardy's reserve at the time of the troubles and was married to the daughter of Okemasis, the third Willow Cree chief in the area.[41] Several more had probably joined the Métis under duress. Hayter Reed had warned about this possibility in August 1884 when he observed that the "Halfbreeds could do any amount of Mischief with them and they are not idle even now. Indians at Duck Lake are surrounded by some of the worst Halfbreeds in the country."[42] Another official's comments were more circumspect. He reported in February 1886 that the local reserves had been under incredible pressure by armed gangs to join the Métis and that the government should have acted sooner to take the Indians across the river "out of danger."[43]

Beardy's attitude did not change after the 26 March battle. He was extremely upset that the police and Métis had used the reserve for a battleground and that Assiyiwin was brutally gunned down. He also realized that nearby Fort Carlton was virtually indefensible—the ramshackle stockade walls could be surmounted easily from horseback—and that Crozier could be made to pay for his transgression. He still refused, however, to support Riel's activities and counselled his people to do the same.[44] It was a sign of his status that Beardy was not compelled to go to Batoche, like One Arrow, but remained calmly on his reserve during the remainder of the hostilities. Most of his band followed his example, while a few took to the surrounding woods for safety; one elder remembers his grandmother recounting how they were continually running and hiding during the fighting.[45]

The Canadian government, unfortunately, chose to look at Duck Lake differently. It knew that the Cree had peaceful intentions. It was also fully aware that Riel was courting the bands with promises of food and aid. "Messengers have been among them . . . with presents," an exasperated Dewdney had told the prime minister only the day before Crozier's debacle. "Every reserve has been tampered with."[46] Lawrence Vankoughnet was equally sceptical that the Cree were acting on their own and was worried that if the government acted rashly it might drive the Indians into Riel's arms. "I do not see for my part what the Indians have to gain by joining the Halfbreeds in this movement," he advised Macdonald on 31 March. "On the other hand they have everything to lose."[47] Yet instead of sympathizing with their plight, Ottawa assumed that the Willow Cree in the Carlton district were hostile. How else could one explain the death of Assiyiwin and the twelve men that Crozier had left behind—dead—on Beardy's reserve? There was no attempt to try to understand their predicament, let alone give them the benefit of the doubt. As far as Indian Affairs officials were concerned, the Willow Cree chiefs had always been troublesome leaders—Prime Minister Macdonald had once taken steps to depose Beardy[48]—and their apparent involvement with the Métis insurgents was simply further evidence of their bad character. They had to be caught and punished. Macdonald went so far as to propose that a special Blackfoot corps be formed to spread panic among the Métis and especially their Cree allies.[49]

Louis Riel's activities also suggested that an Indian-Métis conspiracy was afoot. In fact, the Métis leader has often been heralded as a champion of aboriginal peoples who sacrificed his life for their cause. From his writing, however, a different portrait of Riel emerges, a portrait that suggests that First Nations were wise in keeping their distance from the Métis champion. Riel regarded Indians as a simple, primitive people, who should be made to work "as Pharaoh had made the Jews work."[50] He also assumed that the Métis, because of their mixed-blood parentage, could help solve the so-called Indian problem—in his words, "show them how to earn their living"[51]—by exercising a positive, uplifting influence on them. "The crees are the most civilized indians of the Canadian northwest because they have been . . . in constant communications with the halfbreeds," he wrote during his years in Montana. "The blackfeet and the bloods are nothing but savages. They are indians in the true sense of the word."[52] These "savages" were to have little or no place in Riel's brave new order, but were to be displaced by a Métis nation destined to arise on the prairies under Riel's messianic leadership—and, of course, God's divine inspiration. At the same time, the Métis needed the Indians' numerical might to vanquish the evil forces of Ottawa. They were to be Riel's foot soldiers—the means by which he would realize his mission and deliver his people. This is why Riel attempted to convince the Cree to rise up and sweep north while they were wintering in Montana in the early 1880s.[53] He would try again in 1885—this time in a more deadly game with the Canadian government.

In advancing the Métis cause in the Saskatchewan country, Riel followed a public and private agenda. On the one hand, he faithfully pursued traditional methods of protest by convening meetings, submitting petitions, and ranting against Ottawa and its lethargy. On the other, he quietly plotted to repeat the success of the Red River Resistance fifteen years earlier—only this time the Indians would assist. In late February 1885, Riel began to advocate more forceful measures and predicted that the United States and other nations would rush to the aid of the Métis; all he had to do was give the signal. He also started pushing for the creation of a provisional government, having first secured the allegiance of the most militant of the local Métis at a secret meeting at Norbert Delorme's home in early March.[54] His trump card, however, was an Indian-Métis alliance, something he pursued doggedly through the late winter of 1884–85, even though the Cree refused to play his game. He persistently told the local bands that their problems were his problems and that by joining with the Métis they could drive the white man from their lands and reclaim some of their former greatness.

These activities cost Riel the support of disaffected white settlers, the local Roman Catholic clergy, and even large segments of the local mixed-blood community. It was one thing for the Métis leader to become more bellicose in his demands, but to denounce the church, threaten Ottawa, and incite the Indians bordered on sheer madness. Father Alexis André of the Carlton-area clergy branded him a raving fanatic and disowned him. Such outright condemnation mattered little to Riel, the prophet, since he had surrounded himself with a small cadre of Métis disciples, ready to follow him wherever he led at whatever the cost.[55] He also seemed to believe that the Indians were undecided and that a miracle from God would bring the chiefs to his side; hence his claim, for example, that if the sun was "broken" on a particular day—the solar eclipse of 16 March—that it would be a sign from God.[56] Nothing would shake Riel from his determination to involve the Indians. If playing on their superstitious nature did not win him support, he was fully prepared to force the Cree to take up arms in violation of their treaty pledges. On 23 March 1885, in a letter appealing to the local English mixed-bloods for their support, he argued:

> As to the Indians, you know, gentlemen, that the Half-Breeds have great influence over them. If the bad management of indian affairs by the canadian government has been fifteen years without

resulting in an Outbreak, it is due only to the Half-breeds who have up to this time persuaded the Indians to keep quiet. Now that we ourselves are compelled to resort to arms, how can we tell them to keep quiet? We are sure that if the English and French Halfbreeds unite well in this time of crisis; not only can we control the indians: but we will also have them weigh on our side in the balance.[57]

Riel hoped that a combined force would effectively carry the day under God's watchful guidance. The English mixed-bloods, however, could not see the rightness of his cause—now that he had resorted to arms—and refused to budge from their neutral position. This rebuff during the heady days after the formation of his provisional government made Indian support all the more important, especially since the Métis could muster only about 250 men. Later, when one of Riel's prisoners chastised him for involving the Cree, he said that he had "called the Indians in ... because certain people had not joined him."[58]

This calling in of the Indians started in earnest on 24 March 1885. On that day, the Exovedate decided to send messengers—in all cases, a Métis and an Indian—to Battle River, Fort à la Corne, and Prairie Ronde.[59] Evidence presented at one of the subsequent trials suggests that Treaty Four Indians were targeted as well.[60] These messengers not only brought the latest news from Riel's headquarters, but carried with them letters explaining what was at stake and exhorting the mixed-blood population to recruit the local Indians and be ready at a moment's notice. "Dear Friends and Relatives, we advise you to be on the alert," read the note to the mixed-bloods living west along the North Saskatchewan.

> Be ready for anything. Take the Indians with you. Bring them together from all sides ... Murmur, protest and threaten. Stir up the Indians. Also render the police of Fort Pitt and Fort Battleford powerless ... Have confidence in Jesus Christ. Place yourselves under the protection of the Blessed Virgin.[61]

Clearly, the justness of his movement would prevail if they only placed their faith in God—and Riel's transmission of that will.

The routing of the police at Duck Lake less than forty-eight hours later provided Riel with further ammunition in his campaign to win

over the Indians. And he lost little time communicating the victory—
to the chagrin of government officials.[62] Emissaries immediately
fanned out across the North-West with news of the lopsided encounter. It was also the subject of a special letter, evidently prepared in
French and English versions the first week of April, in which Riel
called on potential supporters to assist him at Batoche.

> Dear Relatives, We have the pleasure to let you know that on the
> 26th of last month, God has given us a victory over the Mounted
> Police. Thirty Half-breeds and some five or six cree indians, have
> met one hundred and twenty policemen and volunteers. Thanks
> to God, we have defeated them. Yourselves, Dear relatives, be
> courageous. Do what you can. If it is not done, take the stores, the
> provisions and the munitions. And without delay, come this way;
> as many as it is possible. Send us news.[63]

The wording of the letter was important for a number of reasons. It
indicated that Riel would make his stand against government forces
at Batoche and desperately wanted reinforcements. It also suggested
that God was on the side of the Métis fighters that fateful morning
and that Riel's prophecies were coming true. Above all, it claimed
that the local Cree had thrown their lot in with the Métis and struck
a blow against the once invincible police. Riel did all he could in the
weeks immediately following the Duck Lake engagement to promote
the idea that the Indians were at his service. When, for example, three
Prince Albert men came to retrieve the bodies of the dead at Duck
Lake on 29 March, they were handed a letter warning that "the
struggle will grow, Indians will come in from all quarters, and many
people will cross the line [border] early this spring, and perhaps that
our difficulties will end in an American 4th July."[64]

The simple truth is that many of the Indians on neighbouring
reserves preferred to watch the struggle between the government and
the Métis from the sidelines. Those who did join the Métis in late
March—members of the Petequakey reserve, just northwest of
Batoche—were coerced into doing so, in much the same way as the
One Arrow people. A former chief of the Petequakey band was
Sounding with Flying Wings, more commonly known as Alexander
Cayen or Alexandre Cadieux. According to an 1871 census, Cayen was
living with his Métis cousins at the St. Laurent-de-Grandin mission;
five years later, he stepped forward as one of the signatories of Treaty

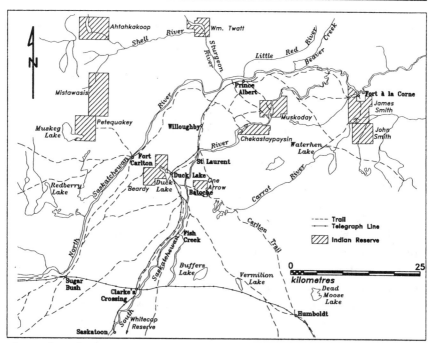

The Carlton district.

Six. He soon abandoned the reserve at Muskeg Lake, however, and surfaced again in 1885 as one of Riel's special emissaries—a position he used to bring the Petequakey band into Riel's camp.[65] Cayen was likely assisted by Augustin LaFramboise, a Métis militia captain who was married to a woman from the reserve.[66] That the Petequakey Cree were not willing participants was confirmed the following year when several Hudson's Bay Company employees appeared before the Rebellion Claims Commission in Prince Albert. George Robertson, a Carlton-area labourer, testified that he saw unarmed members of the band in the company of about forty Métis, led by Albert Monkman, at the fort in late March, and that they were being "taken to Duck Lake not of their own accord."[67]

The remainder of the Carlton-area Indians wanted nothing to do with Riel's chicanery. The reaction of Chief Mistawasis, a key figure at the Treaty Six negotiations, is a good example of this continued loyalty. On the afternoon of 26 March, a mounted policeman galloped onto the reserve from Fort Carlton. Mistawasis, who had asked the police to keep him informed, knew before the constable dismounted that something terrible had happened; what was especially frightening, though, is that the trouble had occurred less than twenty miles away. The chief immediately told his followers to get ready to move to the Sturgeon Lake area, north of Prince Albert, where the mounted police could protect them from the Métis. He also dispatched runners to the nearby Petequakey and Ahtahkakoop reserves with details of his plan. "We will flee from the war," Mistawasis announced. "We will not fight the Queen and we will not fight for her either. We will go our own way."[68]

Later that evening, the Mistawasis and Ahtahkakoop bands rendezvoused just east of present-day Shellbrook as previously arranged. Any hope of being safe was shattered, however, when two messengers rode into camp and told them to get ready for war and that fifty Métis would soon bolster their numbers. Mistawasis's cousin immediately jumped to his feet and shouted, "I came here to flee the war. I don't want to be involved. I want peace. I don't wish to leave our children behind and go help these half-breeds if they come for us. If I see them coming, I will fight them off." Ahtahkakoop's band felt much the same way. "It's not that I'm afraid," one of his headmen stated. "It's just that I want to hold the treaty we made with the Queen."[69] Sensing that they were unwelcome, Riel's messengers left after assuring the two senior chiefs that they would respect their desire to remain neutral. But the food and possessions the Indians had left on the reserve in their haste to get away were taken as war booty; many of their houses were destroyed as well.[70] The situation for the refugee House People would have been extremely bleak if Hayter Reed had not stepped in and ordered the emergency distribution of goods that had been evacuated from Carlton.[71]

The Touchwood Hills Cree were also unwilling to get mixed up with the Métis. On 18 March 1885, Antoine Rougeblanc, leader of the local mixed-blood population, called a meeting of the four reserves (Poor Man, Day Star, George Gordon, and Muskowekwan). It is not known what was said at the council, but Louis Couture, the farm instructor, later reported that all the chiefs had received letters from Riel warning "that the Government intended to take the indians to fight for them."[72] This disquieting news prompted the Indian agent for the Treaty Four district, Allan McDonald, to leave immediately for the Touchwood reserves, where he found the Indians "very much afraid and excited"—not only because they opposed Riel's actions, but because Colonel Irvine's one-hundred-man police column had passed through the region, unannounced, on its way to Fort Carlton.[73]

McDonald did what he could to calm the situation—in his view the agitation was strictly a Métis affair—and returned to Indian Head on 26 March with the assurance that the Indians would remain on their reserves. This pledge was tested the very next day when two men arrived from Batoche, fresh from the Duck Lake fight. The chiefs met again in council—this time late into the night—and sent a message the following day to Agent McDonald, expressing "their loyalty to their great mother the Queen . . . and disapproval of the course pursued by those at the head of the present struggle."[74]

When news of the Duck Lake battle reached eastern Canada, the Macdonald government quickly raised a large militia force to isolate and put down what it regarded as an Indian-Métis insurrection. *Saskatchewan Archives Board R-A458*

Riel's messenger fared little better at the Crooked Lake reserves, just north of Broadview, along the Canadian Pacific Railway main line. Once again, the initial reports from the area were worrisome; on 24 March, the Indians of the four contiguous reserves (Sakimay, Cowessess, Kahkewistahaw, and Ochapowace) were said to be "holding War Dances last two days."[75] Commissioner Dewdney, who was in Winnipeg at the time, decided to investigate the rumours on his way back to Regina and found that the Indians were more concerned with putting in that year's crop than joining the fray.[76] Dewdney was greatly relieved—no doubt, in part, because the railway, the government's main supply line, bordered the reserves for some twenty-five miles—and promised to supply the seed for all the land the Indians cleared. Things remained quiet until 29 March, when Riel's Ojibwa messenger, Keniswayweetung, arrived in Broadview and together with two local sympathizers tried to get the four reserves to assist the Métis. The Indians debated the matter all night, and in the end, several of the more prominent men, such as Alex Gaddie and Nepahpahness, convinced the others that only "misery and trouble would be brought about if they went north."[77] Chief Kahkewistahaw tersely summed up their thinking to Agent McDonald a few days later. "Agent, you remember the time I promised I would go to my reserve I also said that I and my young men's fighting days were over," he said in obvious reference to his treaty agreement. "I stick to those words no matter what may be done up north, we will remain on our reserves and attend to our work."[78]

Such statements of neutrality—if not outright loyalty—should have settled the question of a Cree-Métis alliance. Certainly, there had been a handful of Indians at the Duck Lake engagement and a larger number at Métis headquarters at Batoche. But the circumstances behind their presence, together with the reaction of other bands to the event, indicate that Indian support of the Métis cause was extremely limited. Neither Canadian officials nor the Métis provisional government seemed prepared to take the Indians at their word or let their actions, or lack of, speak for themselves. The Indians now faced a doubly ironic situation, in that both Ottawa and Riel saw them as potential allies of the Métis, despite considerable evidence to the contrary. In the days immediately following Duck Lake, although both sides were anxious to see what the Cree might do next, neither was willing to wait. When news of Crozier's fiasco and the subsequent abandonment and burning of Fort Carlton reached eastern Canada, the Macdonald government quickly raised a large militia force to isolate and put down the insurrection. Riel and his cohorts, on the other hand, redoubled their efforts to expand the resistance through the North-West and draw in as many Indians as possible. That Indian leaders were more determined than ever to honour their treaty promises seemed sadly irrelevant.

chapter five

Unnecessary Nervousness

T HE DUCK LAKE DEAD were still lying on the battlefield when word of the Métis victory reached Fort Battleford. The capture of the former territorial capital, situated at the junction of the North Saskatchewan and Battle Rivers, would go a long way in furthering Louis Riel's scheme to hold the North-West for ransom; Battleford was not only the largest settlement between Prince Albert and Edmonton, but served as divisional headquarters for almost one-fifth of the North-West Mounted Police force.[1] Taking the fort would also enhance Riel's leverage over the Indians, since the community served as agency headquarters for nine surrounding reserves and over two thousand Cree and Assiniboine.[2] The Métis desperately needed these Indian allies if they were to have any chance against the punitive force the Canadian government was hurriedly assembling to crush the rebellion. Battleford, then, was the key to broadening the Métis agitation beyond Batoche and increasing Indian support for the movement. And this is exactly what appeared to be happening when about one hundred Indians descended on the fort in the final days of March 1885.

On Friday 27 March, while visiting the Poundmaker reserve, some forty miles northwest of Battleford, Peter Ballendine, Edgar Dewdney's special agent, told the local Indians about the Duck Lake clash.[3] The news marked the beginning of an extremely troubled period for the chief and his band that would eventually see them blamed for fomenting rebellion in the Battleford area. For the time being, though, Chief Poundmaker was more concerned with turning the Métis unrest to the advantage of his people. He had no interest in joining Riel's movement—he had never even met the man. Nor was he game to attacking the nearby police post. He did rightly sense, however, that matters were at a critical stage and reasoned that if the chiefs made a special trip to Battleford to affirm their loyalty to the Queen, government authorities might reward them with increased rations. This plan certainly appealed to Chief Little Pine, for the old Cree leader was suffering from the debilitating effects of malnutrition. Several members of the Lucky Man band, who had taken up residence in the area following the deposition of their chief, also readily agreed to accompany Poundmaker to Battleford to plead for aid. But in order to ensure that their purpose was not misconstrued, they decided to send a messenger ahead to alert Battleford of their plans.[4]

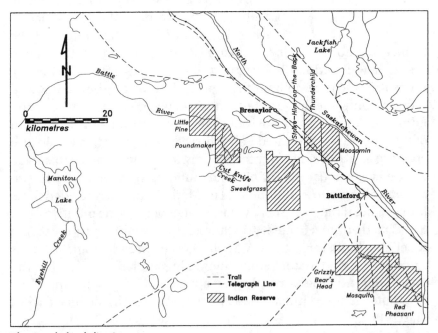

The Battleford district.

When word of the trip and its purpose spread through the two reserves, many of the residents decided that they wanted to go along—even though it meant a long, difficult trudge through the wet snow that had fallen over the past few days. Since first settling in the area, the Indians had developed a tradition of performing elaborate begging dances for the town's merchants in exchange for food.[5] These handouts never amounted to anything more than a few bags of flour and other provisions, but they could mean the difference between life or death, especially after a severe winter. The group that started for Battleford later that day numbered about sixty members from the three bands. It could not in any sense be regarded as a war party because of its general decrepit state and the presence of several women. If anything, it had more in common with the so-called hunger marches of the dismal 1930s.

By early evening, the procession had managed to reach the Sweetgrass reserve, and decided to camp there for the night and confer with Young Sweetgrass about Poundmaker's plan. These deliberations became strained when two of Riel's emissaries interrupted the council and tried to convince the Indians that they would be better served by supporting Riel and capturing the fort.[6] Little Pine, although precariously weak, did not like what he heard. He knew that violence would destroy any chance the Cree had of forming an effective alliance with the Blackfoot. He also probably realized that Riel's messengers were trying to hijack the trek for their own political needs—turning it into the first salvo in a war against the Canadian government. "No, do not do that. It will be useless," he pleaded with his young men. "You can defeat them here, but more will arrive . . . What ammunition do you have? Nothing. What food supply do you have? Nothing . . . The time will come when you will scatter and run, you will run in different directions. Go to work, do not fight."[7] Little Pine's impassioned words had the desired effect, but he was leaving nothing to chance. Riel's messengers had unsettled the group, and the old chief was worried that someone from outside his own band might try to provoke trouble. As a precaution, he instructed some of his followers to take their farm instructor, John Craig, who had accompanied the band on his own initiative, into protective custody;[8] this was the same government official who had nearly precipitated bloodshed in June 1884 by stubbornly refusing to dispense rations during the thirst dance on the Poundmaker reserve.

The next day, Sunday, the group resumed its slow march to

The Battleford-bound Cree held a council on the Sweetgrass reserve in late March 1885; the meeting was interrupted by two Métis messengers who wanted the Indians to capture the fort. *Glenbow Archives NA-1223-4*

Battleford, camping about eight miles from its goal that night. Young Sweetgrass, who sympathized with the delegation's purpose, had decided against joining the other chiefs, probably because he had little control over his band at this point; the reserve farm instructor, Joseph McKay, was robbed shortly after the council meeting.[9] This did not mean, however, that the purpose of the trip to Battleford had changed in any way. When Young Sweetgrass was asked about the plan to secure extra rations, he reportedly told Robert Jefferson, the Poundmaker farm instructor who had willingly come along with the Indians, that he did not "anticipate any trouble. They did not seek it."[10] John Craig later said much the same thing at Poundmaker's trial. The night before the group reached Battleford, Craig slept in Poundmaker's tent and was released—unmolested—the next morning; as he nervously slipped away, Chicoutis, one of Little Pine's counsellors, told him that nothing wrong was intended.[11] That neither Craig nor Jefferson was physically harmed—even though both were universally disliked[12]—confirmed the peaceful intentions of the Indians.

The several hundred residents of Battleford, on the other hand, had been anticipating trouble for at least ten days. On 20 March, the day after the establishment of Riel's provisional council, fifty Battleford civilians formed a home guard. Three days later, Lieutenant Governor Dewdney formally approved the creation of a militia corps, while three police deserters were released from confinement on the condition that they return to active duty. This paranoia increased with each passing day, as the townspeople waited anxiously for news from NWMP Superintendent Leif Crozier at Carlton; and when a messenger finally arrived the morning of 27 March with dispatches about the Duck Lake engagement, panic swept the settlement. The residents genuinely feared that they would be the next target and feverishly began to fortify the police stockade, including the erection of make-shift bastions.[13] Once this was done, the women and children were hustled into the post, which measured only five-hundred-feet square. By Sunday 29 March, some five hundred people from the town and surrounding countryside had abandoned their homes, farms, and stores and taken refuge inside the stockade walls.

Much of what the Battleford residents had done was based on wild speculation, as well as an irrational distrust of Indians. Many of the settlers, fresh from Ontario, were uneasy about the presence of so many Indians in the area—a mindset that Edgar Dewdney had ridiculed in his annual report for 1879 when he claimed that the inhabitants "have shown a great amount of unnecessary nervousness."[14] That local bands had not made their traditional visit to the settlement on New Year's Day also suggested to residents that something was amiss.[15] But to believe that the Indians would contemplate attacking the fort was sheer nonsense. And people in influential positions knew better. On 24 March, for example, Thomas Clarke, the Anglican principal of the Battleford Indian industrial school, visited three nearby reserves while searching for some runaway students and

Robert Jefferson, the Poundmaker farm instructor, willingly accompanied the Cree to Battleford. He later reported that their mission was a peaceful one—to affirm their allegiance to the Queen. *Saskatchewan Archives Board R-A25028*

noted in his diary, "The Indians appear to be well-disposed towards the white man."[16] P.G. Laurie, the publisher of the local newspaper, the *Saskatchewan Herald*, and member of the newly formed Battleford home guard, agreed with these sentiments; the day after learning about the Duck Lake fight, he telegraphed Winnipeg: "indians perfectly quiet notwithstanding contrary reports."[17]

What pushed the town over the brink, however, were incoming rumours that bands were assembling on Poundmaker's reserve before moving against Battleford. Any flickering hope that the settlement would be spared gave way to sheer, dark terror, prompting a mass evacuation to the police barracks. "Startling reports reached us abt 100 Inds on the road to raid the town," Clarke scribbled in his diary for 29 March. "Informed . . . that Inds . . . intended to burn all the houses . . . and take . . . Prisoners."[18] The sense of dread was perhaps best exemplified by Judge C.B. Rouleau, who hurriedly gathered up his family and set off for Swift Current. Less than a year earlier Rouleau had scoffed at the idea of an Indian-Métis uprising; now he was running for his life.

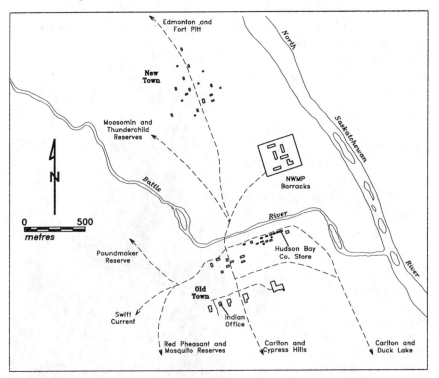

Fort Battleford.

By 29 March 1885, before the Cree delegation had reached Battleford, some five hundred people from the town and surrounding countryside had taken refuge within the fort. *RCMP Museum*

The situation might have been different had the settlement known why the Cree were coming. But the message that the chiefs had sent ahead—that the bands were coming to see the Indian agent for some tea and tobacco—was not taken seriously by Hudson's Bay Company Factor William McKay, the individual who first received the information.[19] Nor did Peter Ballendine help matters. He was the one who had informed Poundmaker about the outbreak of the Métis rebellion and undoubtedly knew that the Indians' intentions in going to Battleford were not hostile.[20] Why he kept quiet during those anxious days remains a mystery.

The reputation of the Cree leaders involved presented its own problems. Little Pine, as the key organizer of the proposed grand council of Cree and Blackfoot during the summer of 1885, was generally regarded by officials as a bad Indian. Poundmaker, because of his political activities, fared no better. Assistant Indian Commissioner Hayter Reed had described him as "one of the worst if not the worst moving spirit in the country,"[21] and he was being watched closely for any pretext to arrest him. It did not matter that the chief, like his uncle Mistawasis, had refused to meet with Riel's messenger in November 1884; or that Poundmaker had promised to keep his distance from any future trouble.[22] That the Cree leaders had left their reserves and were headed to Battleford seemed to confirm the wild rumours. Indian Agent John Rae certainly expected trouble. "Poundmaker and Little Pine band all camped within eight miles of here tonight and all are armed in war paint," he telegraphed Dewdney

Clinkskill's store at Battleford. Indians were regular visitors to the settlement and often held begging dances for extra food. *Saskatchewan Archives Board R-A7540*

from the overcrowded stockade. "Expect to attack tonight."[23]

On the morning of Monday 30 March, the Indians—now about 120 strong—reached the Battleford Indian office on the high south bank of the Battle River overlooking that part of the settlement known as old town. All of the townspeople—save for Arthur Dobbs, the cook at the Indian school, and some mixed-blood families camped near the junction of the two rivers or the "head"—were huddled nervously in the police barracks on the opposite bank, across the ice-choked river. Ballendine and McKay evidently volunteered to meet with the Cree leaders and see what they wanted. To the frightened occupants of the fort, this selfless action probably appeared courageous, but both men privately knew why the Indians had come to Battleford and that they would not molest them. Indian Agent Rae, for his part, was not so trusting. Known to be alarmist, indecisive, and volatile in times of crisis, he had told Commissioner Dewdney in July 1884 that never in his fourteen-year career had he seen the Indian situation so grave as it was following the thirst-dance incident on Poundmaker.[24] Then, in February 1885, little more than a month before Riel launched his rebellion, he warned that the Battleford bands were "quiet, too quiet."[25] Rae probably would have preferred to join his wife and run away with Judge Rouleau's party; as it was, he refused to leave the fort to meet the Indians.

Because Little Pine was so ill, Poundmaker spoke on behalf of the delegation. After exchanging greetings, he expressed surprise that the town had been deserted and that the police had fortified the barracks. He also said, according to McKay's subsequent trial testimony, that "he was sorry to hear that he was accused of coming down to create trouble in Battleford."[26] Poundmaker then innocently asked where Agent Rae was. Ballendine responded that he was across the river in the fort. This naturally led to another question—whether the chiefs' message had been received. Both Ballendine and McKay denied having heard anything.

Throughout these discussions, Poundmaker's demeanour remained friendly; there was no hint of annoyance, let alone hostility. Nor did he deviate from his mission. After asking Ballendine to recount the latest news, he said that he meant no harm and that he had simply come to Battleford to ask Agent Rae for supplies. It was obvious that Poundmaker would not be satisfied until he saw the agent to proclaim his continued allegiance to the Queen. Ballendine sensed his urgency and eventually agreed to send a note to Rae on behalf of the assembled chiefs. What he did not understand, however, is why the young men in the party were decorated and carried weapons, especially if their intentions were peaceful. He should have known from his own experience that Indians generally travelled armed and that the colours adorning their bodies were not war paints.

In the end, Ballendine dutifully recorded the chiefs' demands but secretly added his own postscript, warning Rae not to cross the river because the Indians were hostile.[27] Arthur Dobbs's experience proved the opposite as he busily fed a steady stream of appreciative customers at the Indian school until the food ran out.[28] McKay also did his part to ease tensions by distributing some tobacco and food from the HBC store. When some of the Indians asked for more, he testified a year later at the Rebellion Claims Commission hearings, he "refused them and told them to leave. They did so and I closed and locked up the shop."[29] That the group could easily have overpowered McKay and Ballendine yet chose not to, despite their hunger, spoke volumes about their intentions that day.

With Ballendine's note in hand, Agent Rae immediately sought the guidance of Commissioner Dewdney in Regina. "Indians willing to go back to reserve if their demands for clothing, sugar, tobacco, powder and shot are complied with," he wired over the still intact telegraph line. "Strongly urge you to give me full authority to deal with them, as we are not in a position at present to begin an Indian war."[30] The telegram was noteworthy, in that it suggested that trouble could be avoided if the government simply acceded to the Indian demands for rations and supplies—something officials had been under strict orders not to do. It also hinted that under different circumstances Rae would have preferred to fight and settle the so-called "Indian problem" once and for all. Dewdney, on the other hand, feared that the Métis rebellion would spread across the North-West. The best way to prevent this firestorm was to hold Indian loyalty

The Hudson's Bay Company store, Battleford. It would be burned during the so-called seige of the fort. *Saskatchewan Archives Board R-A7539*

at whatever cost. He decided to give Rae "full authority" to reach an agreement with the Indians gathered on the other side of the river. "Use discretion," he advised his agent, "and ask Poundmaker to meet me at Swift Current with copy of any agreement you make . . . I guarantee his safety."[31] Unfortunately, Poundmaker never received this message.

Dewdney's instructions placed Rae in an extremely awkward position. Although he had sought and received permission to distribute provisions to the Indians, Ballendine's warning had completely unnerved him, and he was not about to venture from the barracks unless absolutely necessary. Rae indicated initially that if the chiefs really wanted to see him he was prepared to meet them halfway, on the fort side of the Battle River. The Indians, however, refused to place themselves under the shadow of the fort's guns—they were not fools—and the stalemate dragged on. Dewdney, in the meantime, mistakenly assumed that the Indian demands were being settled favourably and notified Ottawa to that effect. He knew from Ballendine's secret reports the previous fall that Poundmaker did not support Riel. Surely, a generous gesture on the government's part would keep him loyal.

By late afternoon, with the Indians becoming increasingly restless, Rae screwed up his courage and decided to chance a meeting with Poundmaker. But just as he was about to step into a waiting scow to cross the Battle River, he abruptly turned back. There are two conflicting explanations for his behaviour. According to an internal Canadian Pacific Railway telegram, "Rae and two others started from barracks . . . and were fired on by breeds" on the other side of the river; this shooting incident was also reported in the police daily journal.[32] Factor William McKay tells a different story. In his reminiscences, he claims that a Métis woman, Mrs. Louis Flammond, came down to the far side of the river and shouted at Rae not to come across because the Indians planned to kill him.[33] Whatever the reason, someone or some group deliberately prevented Rae from meeting with Poundmaker; quite likely it was some of Riel's own men. They knew from the Sweetgrass council why the Indians had come to Battleford, and it was in their interests—if they were going to expand the agitation and involve the Battleford Indians—to see that the mission failed. Riel also had an agent active in the area for several months. In the fall of 1884, Joseph Jobin (sometimes Joubert), of Duck Lake, began teaching at nearby Bresaylor. Jobin's younger brother,

Local HBC manager William McKay left the safety of the fort to meet with the Cree. When he told a group of Indians to leave his store, they did so—without a word of protest. *Glenbow Archives NA-1193-5*

Ambroise, was a member of Riel's Exovedate, and the teacher's extracurricular activities consisted largely of trying to organize the local mixed-blood population for Riel. He was also known to be in regular contact with Batoche and often knew the latest developments before the local mounted police; he may have been involved in distributing ammunition to the local Indians. At the time of the Duck Lake hostilities, Jobin was living at a Métis encampment near Turtleford and brought a small force south to Battleford on the heels of Poundmaker.[34]

Rae's failure to meet with Poundmaker—something that hounded him for the rest of his Indian department career[35]—capped a long, disappointing afternoon for the Indians. They had travelled miles to affirm their treaty pledges only to be greeted by fear and suspicion. It was as if they carried some awful plague and had to be kept at a distance. No one inside the fort, not even their faint-hearted agent, was willing to believe their reason for coming to Battleford; it all seemed like an elaborate ruse. Thus, by the time Ballendine and McKay returned to the fort in the early evening, the Cree's patience finally gave way to frustration. They were tired, hungry, and more than a little confused—certainly ill-prepared for the chilling news that arrived from the south.

Following their cool reception at the Sweetgrass council, Riel's two messengers, Wawpass (Charles) Trottier and Mettaywaysis, headed southeast to the Eagle Hills, arriving at the Red Pheasant reserve the next day, 29 March. This was another pivotal reserve in the Battleford area, for the chief was an original signatory of Treaty Six and an elder statesman. And Wawpass did his best to impress Red Pheasant and his headmen. Recounting a string of seemingly miraculous events, he told them that the Métis leader was a god on a special mission and that he was being directed from heaven. He also said that Riel's forces, which included Americans, would soon be joining them, and that they could best prepare for their arrival by seizing the local stores. He then demanded an immediate declaration of intent—whether they were for Riel or the Queen—warning that those Indians who refused to support the Métis would be compelled to do so anyway. Like Little Pine, however, the gravely ill Red Pheasant was not swayed by the tales of Riel's greatness and declined the tobacco the two emissaries had offered as a gift. He also refused their request for a guide to the nearby Assiniboine reserves.[36]

This flat rebuff, the second in as many days, did not bode well for the Métis cause among the Battleford Indians. But William Lightfoot and three other Red Pheasant Indians apparently wanted to hear more about Riel and secretly agreed to take the messengers to the nearby Assiniboine reserves (Mosquito, Lean Man, and Grizzly Bear's Head) shortly after dusk.[37] At this meeting, with Heymozah of Grizzly Bear's Head band serving as interpreter, Wawpass repeated his stories about Riel's prowess. He also cautioned them that "he [Riel] had lots of soldiers and if we did not join them he would send them after us, that the Americans were going to help him."[38] These threats probably did not impress Chief Mosquito; not only had he distanced himself from the Cree political movement, but when Indian Agent Rae visited the reserve the previous day, he had promised not to become involved in the troubles.[39] Regrettably, one of his own band members used the visit of Riel's emissaries, and, more important, what Wawpass had said about the struggle to come, as a pretext to settle a personal dispute with the resident farm instructor.

James Payne, like many other government appointees, was not well liked by the Stoney Indians he supposedly served. Brusque and inflexible, he was perfectly suited to the task of enforcing the government's new rations policy. But his tenacity had exacted a devastating human toll. By the eve of the rebellion, the Mosquito band population had dropped by almost two-thirds.[40] The farm instructor's rigidity eventually led to even further tragedy. Payne's wife, the daughter of Grizzly Bear's Head, was treating her niece for tuberculosis. Whenever the girl visited, she simply walked into the house, as was customary among her people. This practice greatly annoyed Payne, and he warned her to knock before entering. One day, the girl forgot. An enraged Payne grabbed her and roughly threw her out the door. The fall caused a haemorrhage, and within a few days, claimed her life. Itka,[41] the girl's father, blamed Payne for her death and kept his festering resentment bottled up inside until he could strike. With the appearance of Riel's messengers, that moment had finally arrived. Taking his gun, Itka went to the farm instructor's house the next morning, calmly knocked on the door—as Payne would have wanted—and then shot him dead.[42] Ironically, just two days earlier, Payne had told Rae during his visit to the reserve that the Stoneys would come to the aid of the settlement if trouble erupted.[43]

Itka's actions had nothing to do with the Métis agitation; it was simply a case of a father's revenge. In fact, Judge Rouleau and his

Poundmaker and an ailing Little Pine (seated) waited in vain at the Battleford Indian office for Indian Agent Rae. *James Smith*

small party, fleeing from Battleford, had slept at Payne's house the night before—the same night that Riel's emissaries visited the reserve. Itka waited until Rouleau had left the next morning before settling his grudge with the farm instructor; had he wanted, he could have killed them all. Payne's murder, nonetheless, threw the Stoneys into turmoil. Some of the younger men, animated by Itka's bold act, decided that they would fight rather than see one of their own surrender to Canadian authorities. For years, they had heard stories of the now defunct Assiniboine warrior societies; here was their chance to recapture some of the tribe's former glory. Others knew from their relatives about the harsh treatment that the United States government meted out against Indian misconduct and feared that Canadian retribution would be equally brutal, especially given Payne's position. All seemed to agree that they had to leave—the two reserves were no longer safe. And in the confusion and anxiety following Payne's death, some headed towards Battleford, where they knew the Cree chiefs had gone with some of their band members.[44] The rest sought refuge in the nearby hills or headed south. That they literally ran away was underscored by the 101 bags of flour and 600 pounds of bacon left behind in the agency storehouse.[45]

The Stoneys' arrival and the news they brought with them had a disquieting effect on the Cree leaders gathered at the Battleford Indian school. Once word of Payne's murder spread to the people huddling inside the barracks, the Indians' purpose for visiting the agent would be squandered. They also faced losing control of their followers to more intemperate individuals. That seemed to be the case when several women started to help themselves to the contents of the abandoned buildings. All afternoon, they had resisted the temptation. But as evening fell and it became painfully apparent that they would probably end up with nothing after their long trip, they began to move hurriedly from home to home, taking whatever food and supplies they chanced upon. Soon others joined in—despite the chiefs' protestations—and a general melee ensued. Windows were broken, furniture destroyed, and personal possessions strewn about. By sunrise, the Indians had fled, leaving behind "print and cotton and calicos, and all sorts of dry goods, heaps of it lying in different places on the road."[46]

Much has been written about the looting of Battleford that night; it is generally regarded as a defining event in the town's collective memory. What is often overlooked, however, is that it was not a premeditated act. Nor did it last long. Robert Jefferson, the Poundmaker farm instructor, later recalled that the raiders had no sooner started their destructive work when they were overcome by guilt and took off into the dark—"[I]t was a regular stampede."[47] Above all, damage to the town was limited. According to the post journal, the looters did not burn any of the buildings that night. Principal Thomas Clarke also recorded in his diary for 31 March that small relief parties crossed the Battle River during the day to survey the overnight damage and retrieve food, clothing, and supplies from the stores and industrial school. It was four days later—after the Cree had left—that the first buildings were torched.[48] To the people hiding behind the stockade, none of that mattered. The pillaging of Battleford confirmed their initial suspicions about the Cree pilgrimage, and as more shocking rumours filtered in over the next few days, the incident took on more ominous overtones.

On the night the Cree deserted Battleford, Chief Red Pheasant had been trying to prevent further trouble among the Eagle Hills bands. Earlier that day, 30 March, the chief had received an invitation to join the Cree delegation at Battleford in their attempt to extract some concessions from Indian Agent Rae.[49] Although he had turned away Riel's emissaries the night before, Red Pheasant was reluctant to leave his reserve and become involved in the Battleford proceedings, probably because of his failing health and an old feud with Poundmaker.[50] But when word of the Payne murder on the neighbouring Mosquito reserve reached him, the chief evidently relented and agreed to go to Battleford the next day in an attempt to calm matters. In the meantime, during the middle of the night, Red Pheasant and his brother hurried to the home of their own farm instructor, George Applegarth, and frantically urged him to run away with his family and the reserve schoolteacher, Charles Cunningham; they told them to head south because the Métis were watching the trail to Battleford. At dawn, a raiding party arrived, ransacked Applegarth's house, and then pursued the fleeing whites for a few miles before giving up.[51]

Barney Tremont, a local rancher, was not so lucky. That same morning, a group of five Stoneys on their way to Battleford came upon Tremont, who was busy getting his wagon ready to go to town. Tremont was a notorious Indian hater—he had apparently once turned away from his door a half-frozen boy who had become lost in a blizzard.[52] When Waywahnitch asked for food and ammunition, the rancher flatly turned down the request. One of the other Stoneys then uttered a challenge, "Why don't you shoot him?" A warrior could not back down, and picking up Tremont's own gun, Waywahnitch shot him twice; another put an arrow in his heart.[53] The Indians then continued on to Gopsill (near present-day Prongua), and finding the tiny hamlet abandoned, set the buildings on fire. They caught up with the fleeing settlers a few miles later and confiscated most of their horses, wagons, and belongings before allowing them to proceed to the Battleford barracks—unharmed.[54] Clearly, Tremont's cold-blooded murder, like that of Payne the day before, had more to do with a personal grudge than a general Indian uprising. They were not indiscriminate killings. In both cases, the victims had offended Indian sensibilities, and when the opportunity arose, the men were struck down.

The Battleford residents knew only that several white people were dead; in fact, initial reports suggested that the Indians had also slain Applegarth, his wife and sister, and Cunningham.[55] Inspector William Morris, the senior mounted police officer at the fort in Crozier's absence, tried to put up a brave front in a telegram to his Ottawa superiors: "Am well fortified—have 200 determined men." But his bleak conclusion—"Indians extremely wild"—betrayed his true feelings.[56] Indian Agent Rae was much more frantic. After his aborted meeting with the Cree delegation, he had wired Commissioner

Chief Red Pheasant and his brother tried to prevent further bloodshed in the Eagle Hills district by warning local Indian officials to flee south to safety.
Glenbow Archives P1390-41

Dewdney: "Indians 300 strong in possession of Indian school and mean war."[57] The numbing news from the south simply confirmed this prediction: "The Stoneys are up in arms—on way in—it looks serious now."[58] This dramatic turn of events seemed to stun Dewdney, and he immediately began to speculate about a possible union of the Battleford and Fort Pitt Indians and the sizeable fighting force that would create. The occupants of the barracks had more immediate concerns. Although the Cree had withdrawn to the Poundmaker reserve, the townspeople believed that they were gathering there for an assault on Battleford, which had supposedly always been their intended target. In the minds of the settlers, the Indians' strategy was brutally simple: what they could not achieve through trickery would now be accomplished by sheer force. This fear of an imminent attack—"expected hourly"[59] as Principal Clarke put it—effectively kept the residents of the stockade under siege. And nothing would shake them of this notion until a relief force arrived.

The situation among the Indians, however, was anything but settled. Following the brief looting spree, the Cree made their way back to their reserves, fearing that the police would soon be after them for their petty thievery.[60] At one of the temporary camps along the way, near Cut Knife Creek, Chief Little Pine died. He had been weak for some time, and the dismal outcome of the Battleford pilgrimage and its probable impact on the Indian diplomatic movement undoubtedly hastened his demise. All that he had worked tirelessly for over the past year was destroyed in a matter of hours. Little Pine's death cast a pall over the Indians. It was bad enough that they were likely perceived as rebels after their humiliating departure from Battleford, but to lose a respected voice of wisdom and moderation at this time of crisis was doubly devastating—all the more so when news reached them that Chief Red Pheasant, seriously ill for weeks[61] and distressed over recent events, had also died.

The deaths of the two leading chiefs in the Battleford district pushed Poundmaker into the spotlight, as members of the local bands, alarmed by all that had befallen them, moved to his reserve. It is debatable, though, how much influence Poundmaker actually exercised at this time. Although he spoke on behalf of the chiefs at Battleford, farm instructors Joseph McKay and John Craig later testified at his trial that Poundmaker had little control over the Indians at the Sweetgrass council; the chiefs had the right to act independently.[62] And when the Cree hastily withdrew from

P.G. Laurie, editor of the *Saskatchewan Herald*, never forgave the local Indians for the looting and burning of Battleford and demanded the harshest punishment possible. *Saskatchewan Archives Board S-B75*

Battleford, it would have been the responsibility of the warrior or soldier society, formally called the Rattlers Society,[63] to protect the camp from a possible attack.

It is also noteworthy that the Cree made no attempt over the next few days to lay siege to the police barracks—something that could have been easily accomplished. Although the townspeople had madly piled up earth along the inside base of the stockade, there were gaping holes between the spindly posts of the palisade; one of the refugees joked that he could have shaken hands through the fort wall.[64] It would have been a simple matter to cut the telegraph wire, the residents' lifeline to the outside world; despatchers on horseback, meanwhile, could have been intercepted and detained. Most vulnerable, though, was the stockade's water supply. More than five hundred residents were entirely dependent on the nearby Battle River for their daily water needs. If the Cree had wanted, they could have blockaded the fort and waited for the occupants to surrender. But they chose not to exploit this or any other weakness. Instead, they

were more concerned with securing food—the very reason for going
to Battleford in the first place—and busied themselves rounding up
cattle from the abandoned farms in the area for their steadily growing
camp population.

The stockade residents, in the meantime, continued to send small
parties across the river in the first few days of April to retrieve supplies
from the hurriedly evacuated stores and homes. They faced stiff
competition, however, from a group of Métis determined to exploit
the situation to Riel's benefit. On the morning after the looting, Peter
Ballendine and several other men attempted to cross over to old town
but had to return to the stockade when someone fired on them.
Ballendine described this shooting incident at Poundmaker's trial
and insisted that the perpetrators were mixed-bloods, not Indians.[65]
Evidently, Riel's supporters were continuing their efforts to drive a
wedge between the local Indians and the Battleford residents. The
day before, they had prevented Agent Rae from meeting with
Poundmaker. Now, they were bent on continuing the ransacking of
the townsite that the Cree had started—only on a more systematic
basis.

On 1 April, occupants of the fort spotted four men robbing a store
and fired at them with the fort's cannon; a detail of the home guard
then rushed across the river and claimed the wagon and its booty for
the fort.[66] Two days later, Joseph Nolin, Sr., the brother of Charles, a
prominent Métis leader, and Joseph Vandal of Duck Lake were
caught plundering the Hudson's Bay store. The police then raided
the Métis camp at the junction of the Battle and Saskatchewan Rivers
and arrested local freighters Duncan Nolin and Basil Lafonde, among
others, for looting. This preemptive strike only intensified the campaign against Battleford. The next day, 4 April, a fifty-cart brigade
pulled into town in the early evening, started to empty the buildings
of their remaining supplies, and then set the Mahaffey and Clinkskill's
store and the Indian school stables on fire. For the first time in days,
small groups of Indians were also seen in the townsite and on the
surrounding hills. These men were Stoney warriors who had come
north to Battleford and evidently joined the local Métis camp. On 8
April, a group of them plundered the abandoned homes on the south
side of the river and then fought a brief skirmish with the home guard;
at least one was killed by a shell from the fort's seven-pounder.[67]

This harassment—perhaps more than any single event to that
point—convinced the residents of the stockade that all the surround-

ing reserves had joined the Métis agitation. Battleford had been expecting an attack in the wake of the Duck Lake skirmish, and the looting and burning of the town in the early days of April suggested that the final push against the fort was about to begin in earnest. That this campaign of terror was actually the work of Métis and a few Stoney and that the Cree were just as upset about how things had turned out at Battleford were inconsequential to the hundreds of people shut up in the stockade. The events of late March seemed to speak for themselves. A sizeable Cree party had come to Battleford with questionable motives a mere four days after an Indian-Métis force had soundly trounced Superintendent Crozier's men. And when the chiefs failed to lure Agent Rae out of the fort, the Indians revealed their true purpose by going on a mad, destructive rampage in town and killing several people in the outlying area. From the vantage point afforded by the inside of the stockade, there was only one possible explanation for the events of the past week—the local Indians had joined the rebel cause.[68] The one remaining question was whether their involvement might erupt into a full-scale uprising. It certainly appeared that way when a police courier from Fort Pitt arrived with the horrifying news of a massacre at Frog Lake.

chapter six

Spring of Blood

I N THE FIRST DAYS of the North-West Rebellion, there was one Indian leader who worried Canadian authorities more than any other—Big Bear. Once described as "the head and soul of all our Canadian Plains Indians,"[1] the Cree chief had been a thorn in the government's side for almost a decade. He had not only refused initially to take treaty but had spent the past few years trying to secure a broad alliance of the western bands in order to force Ottawa to provide better assistance. This activity made Big Bear, in the eyes of Indian Affairs officials, an enemy of the Canadian state. Naturally, it also attracted Louis Riel's attention, for he realized it would be easier to win over the Cree to the Métis cause if he had Big Bear as an ally. Above all, the chief's resolute leadership, in the face of government intransigence, had made his band the logical home for all those who were angry, disillusioned, or confused with the changes sweeping across the West. And when the blood of nine men[2] was spilled at Frog Lake in early April 1885, in an apparent coordinated effort with the Métis, the blame fell squarely on the shoulders of Big Bear.

The Canadian government had forced Big Bear to move to the Fort Pitt area, almost one hundred miles northwest of Battleford, in a deliberate attempt to isolate the powerful Cree leader and his five hundred followers. Indian Affairs officials did not want a further

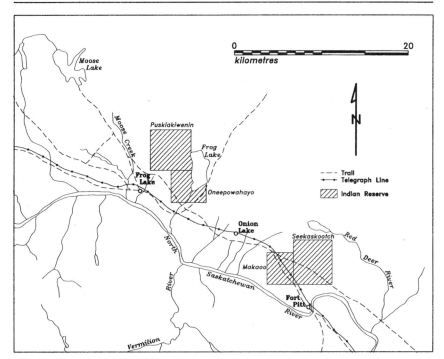

The Pitt district.

concentration of Indians in the Battleford district and therefore rejected his request in 1883 and again in 1884 for a reserve near Little Pine and Poundmaker. Nor did they want to facilitate his organizing work among the Plains Cree bands; it would be harder for him to achieve his purpose if he had to travel greater distances. Louis Riel's return to Canada in the early summer of 1884 did not alter this strategy. Although Big Bear had consistently refused to accept the government-selected reserve near Frog Lake and was busily pursuing his diplomatic offensive, officials like Assistant Indian Commissioner Hayter Reed continued to reason, "If we can keep Big Bear at Pitt no uneasiness need to be felt on the score of any general Indian difficulties." In the same letter, Reed suggested to Edgar Dewdney that "little need be feared" from Big Bear as long as the Métis behaved.[3]

But all was not well at Frog Lake. Although the tiny hamlet with its Indian agency, Hudson's Bay Company storehouse, Roman Catholic mission (Notre Dame de Bon Conseil), and new grist mill seemed destined for a promising future—there was even talk of a railway connection—tensions churned beneath the surface. Part of the problem were the two government officials that the Indians had to deal with on a daily basis. Thomas Quinn, the local Indian agent, was a tough-minded autocrat, who in the words of NWMP Superintendent Crozier was "very much disliked."[4] He had escaped death during the 1862 Sioux uprising in Minnesota—unlike his father—and seemed to fear nothing. Prior to assuming his duties at Frog Lake in May 1883, the slight though pugnacious Quinn had worked out of the Battleford Indian agency and assisted in moving bands in the Cypress Hills area, including Big Bear's, to the North Saskatchewan country.[5] In his new position, he adhered steadfastly to the Indian department's work-for-rations policy as if it were carved in stone. Nothing could deviate him from his course—not even his Sioux heritage or his Assiniboine wife. And he quickly earned a reputation as a mean-spirited, petty little man completely lacking in compassion. "I heard of you away over the other side of the Missouri River," the mercurial Little Poplar had once harangued him at Fort Pitt. "I started to come this way and the farther I came the more I heard. *You're* the man the government sent up here to say '*No!*' to everything the Indians asked you!"[6]

The other official, farm instructor John Delaney, was equally despised. It appears he was physically threatened at least twice—the second time in November 1884—when he refused to distribute food to starving Indians.[7] The more serious grievance against Delaney, however, was that he interpreted "Indian affairs" quite literally. During the winter of 1880-81, he regularly slept with a married woman, the wife of Sand Fly. When the offended husband drew a knife against the couple and was charged, Delaney attempted to cover up his indiscretion by paying the man twenty dollars and encouraging the pair to leave the Makaoo reserve. An investigation of the matter by Hayter Reed concluded that "the ill effects have in great measure been forgotten" and that it would be difficult to find a suitable replacement.[8]

There were also problems among the different Cree bands in the area. Although the government had sought the approval of Chief Oneepowahayo (Standing Man) before sending Big Bear's band to the Frog Lake area, the Woods Cree were uneasy about the presence of their Plains cousins, especially the more warlike members.[9] These same individuals also threatened to undermine Big Bear's diplomatic initiative. Men such as Wandering Spirit, formerly of the Young Chipewyan band, had been drawn to the Cree leader because of his unflinching resistance to government policies. But the old chief's tactics—of calmly outwaiting Ottawa in an effort to force officials to deal with his complaints—came at a cost. As long as Big Bear refused to select a reserve in the area, Indian Affairs would not distribute rations to his followers; it was a simple case of submit or starve. Band members eked out a miserable existence at Frog Lake by felling trees and cutting logs in exchange for rations. The unusually severe winter of 1884-85, however, often curtailed this work, and the Plains Cree were reduced to begging rations from an uncooperative Quinn. The situation eventually became so desperate that one of Big Bear's own sons, Imasees, and several of Wandering Spirit's warriors forced the old man to agree to select a reserve in the spring; otherwise, they threatened to desert him. By this point, according to Big Bear's biographer, he was a chief in name only.[10]

The activities of Riel's agents further complicated matters. Although Big Bear had repeatedly spurned his advances during the

Big Bear (extreme right) and band members at Fort Pitt in 1884. (Left to right) Four Sky Thunder, Sky Bird, Natoose, Napasis. *Saskatchewan Archives Board S-B134*

summer of 1884, the Métis leader had not given up. If and when the Métis decided on more radical action, Riel wanted to be in a position to influence the Cree chief. He therefore called on Father Alexis André, an Oblate from the Batoche area, to write Commissioner Dewdney and request—albeit unsuccessfully—that Michel Dumas be named farm instructor for the Fort Pitt reserves. This was the same man who would bring the One Arrow band to Batoche against its will after the declaration of Riel's provisional government.[11] There was also a small Métis wood-cutting party at Moose Creek, just west of Frog Lake, during the winter.[12] That two of the men had interesting family backgrounds was probably no coincidence. One of them was Adolphus Nolin, son of Charles Nolin, one of Riel's advisors and first defectors; Adolphus would later be involved in events in the Battleford area. The other was André Nault, Jr. The son of Riel's cousin and a major player in the 1869–70 Red River Resistance, the younger André had grown up with the knowledge that Riel had stopped the government surveyors at Red River on his father's land. What Nolin and Nault did in the area when not cutting wood is not known, but local officials suspected they were spies for Riel.[13]

Despite these various internal dynamics, there were no outward signs of impending trouble at Frog Lake, as the Métis and Canadian government slid towards a confrontation. In mid-February 1885, Peter Ballendine, Dewdney's confidential agent, happily announced that Big Bear had finally agreed on a reserve site for his band. "I must say that I never left any band of Indians more satisfied than those around Frog Lake," he advised Reed in an apparent attempt to trumpet his negotiating skills. "I only hope that they continue to be so."[14] Local officials evidently felt much the same way. "I had not heard a word of any trouble among our Indians," James K. Simpson, the post manager at Frog Lake and friend of Big Bear, testified at the Rebellion Claims Commission hearings a year later. "They were all quiet when I left."[15] And, later, when the militia recovered the diaries and record books of some of the dead men, Dewdney reported to the prime minister there was no evidence—even after Riel had tipped his hand—to indicate "that our Indians were even dissatisfied much less that they contemplated violence."[16] What was most encouraging about the Frog Lake situation was that Big Bear had been away hunting since 10 March, evidently oblivious to the events unfolding at Batoche.[17]

News of the Duck Lake hostilities reached Frog Lake in the late

Local Pitt officials in 1884. (Left to right) Thomas Quinn, Francis Dickens, James Simpson, Stanley Simpson, and Angus McKay. Quinn would lose his life the following spring when he refused to follow an order from Wandering Spirit. *Provincial Archives of Alberta B1680*

evening of Monday 30 March. Inspector Francis Dickens, the officer in charge of the NWMP detachment at nearby Fort Pitt and son of the famous British novelist, recommended that the white population temporarily abandon the settlement. But the residents, in complete contrast to their counterparts at Battleford, viewed Dickens's proposal as rather alarmist, and only the small police force withdrew to Pitt early the next morning, thereby removing a possible source of provocation but leaving the settlement undefended.[18] It is not clear how much the local Cree bands knew at this point. On 17 March, two days before the formal establishment of Riel's provisional government, two emissaries arrived from Batoche with a message for Big Bear.[19] Theresa Gowanlock, the young bride of one of the men building a new grist mill, later identified these "strangers" as Gregory Donaire and Peter Blondin and said that they claimed to have fled the Duck Lake area to avoid trouble and were looking for work. "They were constantly going to and fro among the Indians," Gowanlock recounted several months later, "and I cannot but believe that they were cognizant of everything that was going on, if not responsible in a great degree for the murders which were afterward committed."[20]

Around the same time, André Nault left the wood-cutting camp for Battleford to pick up supplies;[21] it is quite possible that he used the trip to consult with local Métis about ongoing developments. The Frog Lake police certainly believed that he was a conduit for Riel, for he was arrested on 26 March—the same day as the Duck Lake fight—and taken to Fort Pitt; he was released the next day for lack of evidence.[22]

The other likely source of information was Little Poplar, a relative of both Lucky Man and Imasees, who had his own following within Big Bear's band. A notorious lady's man and fanciful dresser, Little Poplar was widely admired for his fiercely independent ways and seemed destined for a future leadership role. He also had a reputation for being a hothead, and his spirited rantings about the government and its failings quickly gained him a following among the warrior element; he dared to voice what others only thought.[23] This kind of influence also attracted the attention of Indian Affairs officials, and by January 1885, a concerned Hayter Reed personally recommended to the prime minister that Little Poplar be silenced. Macdonald agreed, on the condition that there be sufficient evidence to support the arrest.[24] In late March, Little Poplar was camped in the Battleford area and slipped away when news of Crozier's defeat reached him. Although Indian Agent Rae reported he had gone to Fort Pitt to join Big Bear, his whereabouts for the next week are a mystery.[25] What is known, though, thanks to Dickens's post diary, is that Imasees and Kahweechatwaymat, Lucky Man's son who had sparked the Craig incident almost a year earlier, returned to Frog Lake on 28 March.[26] That the pair might have been with Little Poplar the past few days was just as important as the news of the Duck Lake clash they brought with them to Big Bear's camp.

On the morning of 31 March, after conferring secretly with the other white residents through the night, Thomas Quinn summoned Big Bear's band to a meeting at the Frog Lake agency. According to the oral story of Kamistatin (Baptiste Horse), a Woods Cree who worked in the Hudson's Bay Company store and personally witnessed the events, the Indians had no idea why Quinn sent for them.[27] While Quinn sat in a rocking chair, holding his young daughter in his lap, Big Bear's headmen sat at his feet in a circle—waiting. After some time, Quinn finally broke the silence and asked where Big Bear was. When he heard that he was away hunting and trapping at Little Bear Creek, the agent said that he wanted to see him because he had some news for him. Quinn then pulled out the letter that he had received the night before and announced, in a matter-of-fact manner, that there had been a fight at Duck Lake and that twelve policemen[28] had been killed. The meeting then broke up with the promise that messengers would go and retrieve Big Bear.[29]

The next morning, 1 April, or "Big Lie" day as it was known to the Indians, Big Bear's men gathered at Quinn's house again—this time with the old chief in attendance. Big Bear had first learned about the deteriorating situation at Batoche on 19 March when he came across Henry Halpin, the Hudson's Bay Company clerk at Cold Lake; he apparently was not overly concerned, for he continued to hunt.[30] By the time he returned to Frog Lake, however, he found his band in an agitated state thanks to Quinn's news.[31] The meeting at the agent's house was much the same as the day before. Quinn once again sat passively in his rocking chair with his daughter, while the Cree leaders were made to sit at his feet and wait what seemed like an eternity. Eventually, an exasperated Big Bear waved his hand in the direction of the younger men and said, "Were you trying to tell me a lie? You told me the Indian Agent wants you to come." Quinn then turned to Big Bear and asked him whether he had heard the news. The chief said yes, but that it would be best to hear it from the agent. Quinn took out the letter, recited its brief contents, then calmly put it away again.[32]

After several more minutes of tense silence, Wandering Spirit spoke up and told Quinn that he was worried that something might happen. "I used to enjoy killing a person. I used to enjoy it as if it tasted sweet, like eating something sweet," he recounted. "But since we now have laws, I left it behind . . . But our younger people are restless, they do not listen to us." The war chief then recommended that the best way to avoid trouble was for Quinn and the others to go to Fort Pitt and put someone else in charge of distributing rations until the Métis agitation was resolved. When the Indian agent responded that he had no intention of leaving, Wandering Spirit expressed disappointment that his advice was not taken. The meeting fell quiet again until Imasees suggested a possible compromise. "My father is very poor," he told Quinn. "He is going to have a feast and feed the people. And he's very poor. He has not been able to kill any game. Can you give some provisions or rations to him to feed the people?" The Indian agent, as usual, was unmoved and bluntly told Imasees that if he were to give rations to Big Bear it would be the same

Adolphus Nolin, September 1925. Forty years earlier, the Métis agent was active in the Pitt and Battleford districts. *Glenbow Archives NA-1193*

as if he gave the feast. When Imasees asked a second time, Quinn lost his temper and shouted that no food would be given out—nothing! This emphatic refusal touched off a minor furore among the young men gathered in the adjoining room, and they angrily called on their leaders to stop speaking to "that dog." The meeting concluded with some talk among Imasees and others about possibly going to Fort Pitt for rations, but the damage had been done.[33] As elder Fred Horse observed one hundred years later, "It was hunger which brought about anger to the Plainsmen . . . Their children were crying for food. They were hungry and the Indian Agent refused to give food."[34]

That evening, at the HBC store, Kamistatin told his wife to expect the worst. And it was not long in coming. Just before daybreak, the couple awoke to hear Kamistatin's brother pounding on their door; he had come to warn them that the agency store had been raided and that men had been sent to retrieve the white people who lived near the mill.[35] These acts were part of a larger plan that had been hatched the night before by Wandering Spirit, Imasees, and several of the younger warriors. Frustrated by their demeaning treatment at Quinn's hands and having lost faith in Big Bear's nonaggressive tactics, they decided to take the white people prisoners and help themselves to much-needed food and supplies. When Chief Oneepowahayo encountered one of Wandering Spirit's men riding the farm instructor's horse the following morning, he was told that the settlers were to be taken hostage—nothing else. No one was to be harmed.[36]

The Métis may also have had a hand in encouraging Wandering Spirit and Imasees to take action. According to Louis Goulet's reminiscences, one of the Métis woodcutters at nearby Moose Creek, Adolphus Nolin, was at the Indian camp the same night that Wandering Spirit and his soldiers decided to move against the local white population; when Nolin returned the next morning, he warned Goulet there would be trouble.[37] Considering their activities elsewhere, Riel and his sympathizers certainly had no qualms in taking advantage of Indian unrest or misfortune. And by working behind

On the morning of 2 April 1885, the war chief Wandering Spirit and several younger warriors decided to seize hostages at Frog Lake and help themselves to food and supplies. *Saskatchewan Archives Board R-A27292*

the scenes at Frog Lake, essentially as cheerleaders, they could have forced Big Bear's band into the rebellion—on their side.

Big Bear, for his part, was powerless to stop Wandering Spirit's plan—even though it clearly threatened to undermine all his efforts over the past decade. By erecting a soldiers' lodge and putting the camp on a war footing, Wandering Spirit had effectively become band leader, as was the custom in Indian society. All Big Bear could do was counsel restraint.[38] When the old chief discovered what was taking place early that morning, he hurried to the settlement and chastised the men who were now pillaging the HBC store. Later, he also tried to maintain peace at the church while the two priests performed their Holy Thursday service. And when the situation grew completely out of control, he sent a girl to get help from the Woods Cree at the nearby Kehiwin reserve.[39] In the end, though, Big Bear was helpless to prevent the rounding up of government officials and settlers, especially once the warriors found cases of alcohol-based liquid pain killer and several casks of communion wine during their looting.[40]

These stimulants altered the course of events that fateful day. What started out as a hostage-taking turned into a fatal confrontation. And, ironically, the man who set off the carnage was Agent Quinn or The Dragon Fly[41] as he was dubbed by the Plains Cree. Following the church service, Wandering Spirit ordered the prisoners, now being held at farm instructor Delaney's house, to move to a new camp on the shores of Frog Lake. Quinn stubbornly refused to budge—despite the obvious gravity of the situation—and told the hostages to go to his home instead. He then went to the HBC store to inform the people there of his decision. As he was returning to Delaney's house, he met Wandering Spirit on the trail.[42] John Horse or Duom, Kamistatin's son, was eleven years old at the time and had been following about ten yards behind the war chief. He witnessed the ensuing dispute. "Wandering Spirit called to him and said, 'We want you to go with the other white people to camp. They are just now leaving,'" he recalled. But Quinn, who kept walking, replied, "No, I am not going over. I will be staying at my house as before. I refuse to take orders from anybody here." Wandering Spirit then warned him a second and last time. "My brother I beg you to leave with the rest. It will save trouble for you and everybody here." When Quinn repeated that he was not going to any camp, the war chief uttered coldly, "Die then," as he loaded his rifle and forever silenced the agent who always said no.[43] "[H]ow stubborn this little man was," Imasees's daughter re-

Big Bear tried in vain to stop the murderous rampage at Frog Lake. *James Smith*

marked over seventy years later, "all he . . . had to do was consent to move away to the Main Camp and let my people help themselves."[44]

Quinn's shooting touched off a murderous rampage, as the warriors who were escorting the hostages to the Indian camp now became their executioners. It was as if they were trying to lash out against years of deprivation, abuse, and wounded pride. And their drunken state only made their revenge all the more gruesome—the bodies of several victims were mutilated or burned. By the time the shooting stopped, nine men lay dead, including farm instructor Delaney and two priests, Fathers Marchand and Fafard. Theresa Delaney and Theresa Gowanlock were spared—but early reports suggested that Mrs. Gowanlock had died with her husband.[45] The HBC clerk, W.B. Cameron, sometimes known as Glass Eyes because of his spectacles,[46] also managed to elude certain death, when a quick-thinking Kamistatin had him smuggled through the bush to the Indian camp disguised as a woman. Kamistatin's grandson, Fred Horse, later recalled how Cameron shook with fright for the next few days and was always holding onto his saviour. "My grandmother slept alone for a long time," he recounted jokingly. "Cameron took my grandfather away from my grandmother."[47]

When the shooting erupted, Big Bear was having breakfast with the HBC manager's wife and immediately rushed outside, yelling, "Stop! Stop!," in a vain attempt to rein in Wandering Spirit's warriors.[48] The Frog Lake massacre, as it became popularly known, had two major consequences for the old chief. His diplomatic crusade now lay in ruins, and as news of the ghastly event flashed across the country, Big Bear became a heinous beast in the hands of newspaper editors. It did not matter that he no longer exercised any authority over his followers or that he had done his best under the circumstances to restrain Wandering Spirit's soldiers. To the outside world, it was "Big Bear's band" that had committed unspeakable crimes that early spring day at Frog Lake, and as their leader, he was held personally responsible. Big Bear's image had also suffered when Indian Affairs authorities were misinformed several months earlier that the chief had advocated at the 1884 Duck Lake council that agents and officials be killed. Ironically, the same report noted that Big Bear "was not entirely his own maker in his conduct as his young men had a great deal to do with what he did."[49]

The nine deaths also implicated all the local Indians in the rebellion—even though many of the Woods Cree were away trapping at the time.[50] The violence exacerbated the already tense relations between the Woods Cree and their Plains cousins. When Chief Oneepowahayo heard several shots coming from the direction of the Indian agency, he hurried to the settlement and evicted a group of looters from the HBC manager's home. "I am surprised that you would allow your men to carry on like this," he admonished Big Bear after surveying the bodies of the victims. "If I had known of this I would have given twenty-five head of cattle to kill instead of massacring the white people the way you have done."[51] When Oneepowahayo arrived home, he found that some women from Big Bear's band had forcibly moved his wife, along with their lodge, to a new campsite under Plains Cree control. Other Woodland Cree, upon hearing the news, returned from their trapping grounds and were also made to join the growing camp. Although not technically prisoners, the Woods Cree were intimidated by the brutal killings and knew better than to provoke Wandering Spirit by trying to leave; a few even initially feared for their lives.[52]

Over the next few days, the two groups gradually arrived at an uneasy understanding. There had been tense moments, such as when a defiant, one-armed Chief Seekaskootch of the Onion Lake area strode into a council meeting the day after the murders and nearly came to blows with Wandering Spirit when he questioned his manhood. "I used to be at the front when we fought the Blackfoot Indians. You were behind then," he taunted the war chief. "It is a shame to see how you have butchered those innocent white people down there, but you cannot scare me."[53] Both groups realized, however, that fighting would only aggravate the situation, and Wandering Spirit's leadership went unchallenged for the time being. The Woods Cree, at the same time, took deliberate steps to prevent further trouble. While those in the Frog Lake camp sheltered the hostages from the brooding warriors during their first few days of captivity, Seekaskootch warned the farm instructor and the Anglican minister at Onion Lake to head for Pitt with their families. To ensure their safety, Seekaskootch had his son follow George Mann, while he personally escorted the Reverend Charles Quinney and his family to the fort.[54] Big Bear also shared these concerns and dispatched Lone Man, his son-in-law, to Cold Lake on 3 April, armed with a note from Cameron. Lone Man was to retrieve Henry Halpin, the HBC clerk, as well as John Fitzpatrick, the local farm instructor. When they arrived at Frog Lake two days later, Big Bear, "looking so miserable and tired," assured them that they were quite safe, but that they should not trust the young men.[55]

Almost two weeks after the Frog Lake massacre, Wandering Spirit decided on his next move—the capture of Fort Pitt. The decision made strategic sense; the fort, with its mounted police detachment, represented a potential threat. It would also provide much-needed provisions, as well as guns and ammunition. That Wandering Spirit and his soldiers waited several days before moving against the police would confirm, however, that what happened at Frog Lake in early April was unpremeditated. Had the Plains Cree been truly hostile and intent on waging war, they would have taken advantage of the element of surprise—in keeping with plains warfare—and attacked the police the next day, if not sooner, instead of allowing them time to fortify their position.

The timing of the advance against Pitt is also interesting. It occurred almost a week after Riel had sent out a special letter, in the aftermath of the Duck Lake victory, calling on potential supporters to "[D]o what you can" and "take the stores, the provisions, and the munitions."[56] Henry Halpin, in his reminiscences, reported that the Frog Lake camp received a number of messages from Métis head-

Following the Frog Lake murders, the occupants of Fort Pitt, above, prepared for an imminent Indian attack. *Hudson's Bay Company Archives, Provincial Archives of Manitoba/1987/363 F90/1, neg 67–73*

quarters and that messengers arrived from Duck Lake, asking for assistance, before the Indians started for Fort Pitt.[57] Abraham Montour, a Métis trader from Cold Lake, had also joined the Cree camp in early April and made no effort to disguise his unabashed support for Riel and his cause. A year earlier, Montour hosted the secret South Branch meeting at which the Métis decided to retrieve Riel from Montana.[58] The most damning evidence that the Indians were being manipulated, however, was provided by the Cree themselves. At a special council to try to negotiate the surrender of Fort Pitt, Seekaskootch, who had joined the Frog Lake camp after saving the officials at Onion Lake, said it was too late to withdraw "as we are pledged to Louis Riel to carry on what he got us to commence." One of the other warriors, meanwhile, warned "there were twenty ox-trains loaded with rifles and ammunition with ten thousand Americans to join them, and they also had all the half-breeds to fight with them." Wandering Spirit said much the same thing, adding that Qu'Appelle, Calgary, and Edmonton had already been taken, the railway torn up, and the telegraph cut down.[59] These were the same kind of lies that the Métis in the Battleford area had been spreading among the Indians there.

The occupants of Fort Pitt had learned about the Frog Lake murders the same day and had been anxiously awaiting an attack ever since. When the Indians failed to appear, an overwrought Inspector Dickens, nicknamed the "chicken stalker" by his father, sent out a three-man search party on 14 April to determine their whereabouts. The scouts had been gone for only a few hours when a large party of Cree, fresh from the burning of the Indian department buildings at Onion Lake, rode over the hill overlooking the fort in the late afternoon.[60] Although Big Bear's influence was still in abeyance, he had accompanied the warriors in a determined effort to prevent further bloodshed. The next morning, before the young men did something rash, especially since the cocky Little Poplar had joined their ranks, he called on the police to surrender the post on the understanding that they would be allowed to slip away.[61] It was good advice. Not only was the term "fort" a complete misnomer for Pitt—it consisted of no more than six stout buildings in a square—but like Battleford, the only source of water lay beyond the rickety stockade. The Indians also held the upper hand, in that they occupied the ridge

Big Bear used his limited influence to prevent further bloodshed at Fort Pitt in mid-April 1885. *James Smith*

above the buildings and could monitor any movements around the fort or along the North Saskatchewan River, some three hundred yards wide at this point. In a word, the situation was hopeless.[62]

While the police contemplated their predicament, W.J. McLean, the local HBC factor, went to meet with the Indian leaders. Since his arrival at Pitt the previous fall, the experienced McLean was struck by the acute sense of bitterness and betrayal that consumed the Plains Cree.[63] And despite his earnest, at times paternalistic, efforts that day to defuse the situation, he quickly realized that nothing would dissuade the Indians from taking the fort—one way or another. They had lost any remaining confidence in Ottawa's benevolence and regarded the fort as a symbol of past injustices at the hands of wooden officials. When McLean questioned their motives, one of the chiefs sharply informed him that, "It is not the Queen that we want to fight, but the government."[64] But before the parley's conclusion, the three scouts, who had been sent to find the Cree, galloped through the Indian camp in a mad dash to the fort. Their sudden appearance caught the warriors completely by surprise, and fearing an attack, they instinctively fired on the men, killing one, NWMP Corporal David Cowan, and wounding another.[65]

The death of Cowan served notice that the Cree were not to be provoked. McLean wisely agreed to an arrangement whereby the police would be allowed to leave unharmed if the rest of the fort's occupants—mostly HBC employees and their families—became prisoners. Inspector Dickens, who had approved McLean's mission,[66] was reluctant to abandon Pitt to the Indians, but really had no choice, especially when the trader made it clear in a note that the warriors could not be restrained much longer and that he and his family planned to give themselves up voluntarily.[67] Although it was the only way to get out of the situation, both Dickens and McLean were subsequently condemned for their actions that day; the commander of the North-West Field Force even suggested that the HBC trader should be executed for his treasonous behaviour.[68] Apparently, it was more honourable to die at the hands of Indians than exercise some common sense.

Another aspect of the situation that is often overlooked is that the Cree offered the occupants of the fort a peaceful resolution to the crisis. These were the same so-called villainous Indians who had committed the atrocities at Frog Lake and now had a virtual stranglehold on defenceless Pitt. Yet instead of attacking, they allowed the

W.J. McLean, the local HBC factor, realized that Pitt was indefensible and agreed to surrender voluntarily to Wandering Spirit. *Provincial Archives of Manitoba N13962*

police a chance to escape. Far from being on a bloodthirsty rampage, the Indians showed incredible restraint and only engaged the scouts because they appeared to threaten their safety. The Cree demonstrated their true temper when two of McLean's daughters, Kitty and Amelia, drove out in a wagon to check on the well-being of their father, just after the shooting incident, and returned unmolested.[69]

That evening, 15 April, while Dickens and his men boarded a scow and retreated down the ice-filled North Saskatchewan River to Battleford, the remaining occupants of the fort, including those who had fled there from Onion Lake, walked through the gate and into captivity. The majority of the new hostages were children; the McLeans, for example, had five girls and four boys. Several of the women, such as Mrs. McLean and Mrs. Quinney, were also pregnant. Although it was dark by the time the families had been settled into the makeshift camp, many of the Indians could not wait until morning to claim their prize and scurried the eight hundred yards down the hill and into the abandoned fort.[70] Nothing was spared in their frenzied search for spoils; they even ripped apart an organ in an innocent attempt to get at the source of the noise. Some of the McLeans' silverware would later be recovered in Montana.[71] At Big Bear's trial, prisoner Henry Halpin, who had accompanied the party from Frog Lake, testified that the old chief did not take part in the looting of Pitt.[72] It did not matter. As far as Canadian authorities were concerned, Big Bear was still leading his band at that time, and they added the sacking of the fort to his growing list of rebellion crimes. After all, it was he who had dictated the letter telling the police to give up the post or face the wrath of Wandering Spirit's warriors.

The mounted police left Fort Pitt unharmed and set off down the ice-choked North Saskatchewan River to Battleford. *Hudson's Bay Company Archives, Provincial Archives of Manitoba/1987/363 R34/30, neg N13504*

The capture of Fort Pitt marked the end of a dramatic two weeks for the Plains Cree. In late March, it had appeared that Big Bear's diplomatic efforts to bring about a broad Indian coalition were about to succeed, while his band members looked forward to taking up their own reserve and finally receiving rations on a regular basis. Now, with the death of ten people behind them and Fort Pitt in ruins, the old chief and his followers had been transformed into some of the vilest criminals the young dominion had ever known. The Cree of the area seemed to be so far along the road to open rebellion that several of the Métis who had accompanied the Indian party to Fort Pitt, including Adolphus Nolin, decided to leave directly for Battleford and Duck Lake.[73] But much of what had taken place during those cold, first two weeks of April had been spontaneous, if not provoked.

The murderous few minutes at Frog Lake were the unfortunate consequence of a mixture of hunger, stubbornness, and drink. The taking of Pitt, on the other hand, was evidently done at the urging of Riel and his supporters. None of this activity, starting with the initial plan to take hostages, had Big Bear's support. He had been pushed aside by the more volatile members of his band, such as Wandering Spirit and Imasees. These new leaders, in keeping with the pattern up to then, had no clear idea of what to do next—except to return to their families and wait. After packing up their booty from the fort and dispatching scouts to other parts of the country, the Cree started on the thirty-mile trek back to Frog Lake. It was a miserable march, for it had snowed heavily the night before, and the spring wind still had a bite in it. The Cree and their captives also carried the extra burden of wondering what lay ahead. Both knew that the Canadian government would respond—but how soon?

chapter seven

Making History

O NE OF THE MOST compelling images during the North-West Rebellion was that of
the five hundred men, women, and chil-
dren, penned like panic-stricken animals, within the crowded con-
fines of Fort Battleford. They were seen as the unfortunate hostages
of that madman Riel and his Indian henchmen, who were reportedly
regrouping for one final, deadly assault on the fort. Unless they were
rescued soon, the bloody tragedy of Frog Lake was sure to be
repeated—but on a mind-numbing scale. Popular myth aside, the sad
truth at the time was that the Cree were just as frightened and
bewildered as the townspeople cowering within the fort. Far from
joining the rebel cause, as events in late March had implied, the local
bands had anxiously gathered on the Poundmaker reserve, near Cut
Knife Creek, seeking emotional support and spiritual guidance. Not
only was their peace mission to Battleford in tatters, but they genuinely feared an attack from the very people whom they supposedly
held under siege. They decided that the best thing to do in the
confusion was wait out the brewing storm, in the vain hope that it
might pass them by. But in early May, a battle-hungry Canadian
officer disobeyed orders and launched an ill-advised, surprise attack
on the Cut Knife camp, shattering the uneasy calm. If not for the
restraint of the Indians, Canada would have experienced its own

Little Big Horn.[1] Though the Indians had been provoked, the engagement was seen as further evidence of their hostile intentions and raised the unsettling prospect of a full-scale Indian war.

When Louis Riel chose open rebellion over negotiation with the federal government, Major General Frederick Middleton, the sixty-year-old commander of the Canadian militia, assumed the task of organizing and leading the punitive force. Old Fred, as he was mockingly called by his men, decided from the outset to concentrate his amateur army's energies on the Métis stronghold at Batoche, believing that a quick knock-out blow there would effectively end all resistance. He was convinced that the threat to western communities, including Battleford, in the early days of the rebellion had been greatly exaggerated and that the dispersement of his men would only prolong the campaign, giving Riel more time to secure Indian assistance.[2]

Middleton's proposed plan of attack did not sit well with many communities across the West, which not only felt helplessly vulnerable but feared the worst from the approximately twenty-five thousand Indians living within the region. Moose Jaw, for example, had a CPR engine ready to evacuate women and children should the small population of neighbouring Sioux raid the town.[3] The situation at Broadview, just south of the Crooked Lake reserves, was equally tense. Even though the four local bands had affirmed their neutrality, an armed volunteer militia patrolled the village, while area farmers made plans to form barricades with their implements.[4] Then, there was Battleford. Since the end of March, the beleaguered residents of the stockade had been pleading with Canadian authorities to send someone to save them. Otherwise, they faced annihilation. This sense of impending doom coloured the fort's every message. A note sent to Prince Albert on 7 April, one day after Middleton's army had started from Fort Qu'Appelle for its showdown with Riel, was typical. "[T]ribes have risen and surround us on every side," the officer in charge of the Battleford barracks reported despairingly to NWMP Commissioner Irvine. "I believe it is their intention to exterminate the Whites in this Section . . . I have about 400 women and children in barracks, and their situation is anything but pleasant."[5]

General Middleton was well aware of the panic and dread gripping Battleford and other communities when he devised his strategy for dealing with Riel. But he refused to divide his force and fight a protracted war on several fronts; since the Métis prophet was the spiritual force behind the agitation, his wings had to be clipped as quickly as possible. Middleton also discounted the fighting prowess of the Métis and Indians and concluded that the threat to western settlements existed largely in people's minds. Stories about the blockade of Prince Albert, for example, were proven unfounded when his chief transport officer made a hurried visit to the community. The situation at Battleford was assumed to be much the same.[6] Middleton acted as if any and all resistance across the North-West would melt away like the spring snow once his force arrived. It was simply a matter of getting there. "On march," he hastily wired the minister of the Militia from the Touchwood station the morning of 10 April. "Telegraphic communications with Battleford and through it with Prince Albert—neither in immediate danger but want us... Cannot wait."[7]

Favourable reports coming in from the local reserves also influenced Middleton's assessment of the situation. During the first few days of April, while the general drilled his raw recruits at Fort Qu'Appelle, there was every indication that there was little, if anything, to fear from the

Major General Fred Middleton wanted to concentrate his amateur army's energies on the Métis stronghold at Batoche, but the terrible news from Frog Lake forced him to send secondary columns to Battleford and Pitt. *Saskatchewan Archives Board R–A5070*

Indians located along or near the CPR main line. On 3 April, Allan McDonald, the Indian agent for the Treaty Four district, visited the File Hills reserves (Little Black Bear, Star Blanket, Okanese, and Peepeekisis), just northeast of Fort Qu'Appelle. There, Okanese, the senior chief, told him that the bands "intended remaining on their reserves and working."[8] This was the third cluster of reserves in the area—after Touchwood and Crooked Lakes—to affirm its allegiance during those first anxious days following the Duck Lake battle.

Reports from Lawrence Herchmer of the neighbouring Treaty Two district were equally encouraging. On 30 March, he had quickly dashed off a note to Commissioner Dewdney indicating that "all the Indians in my Agency are quiet . . . and appear to take no interest whatever in the affairs of the Rebellion's Half Breeds, their sympathies being entirely with the Government."[9] When Herchmer visited the Oak River reserve a few days later and explained the troubles to the resident Sioux, the band immediately offered the services of twenty scouts.[10] He also learned during his travels that an Indian from Beardy's reserve who had taken part in the fight had already been through the Moose Mountain reserves (Pheasant Rump and White Bear) and been told that "they would have nothing to do with the rebels" as long as their treaty promises were fulfilled.[11]

These reports seemed to justify Middleton's strategy of concentrating on Riel and suggested that any rearguard action against Canadian forces was highly improbable. He could go forward with confidence over the open prairie, knowing that his supply lines were secure and that his troops were unlikely to be tested until they reached rebel territory, if at all. The terrible news of the Frog Lake massacre implied, however, that the rebellion virus had spread northwest and infected the Cree of the North Saskatchewan country. Middleton had little choice, given the growing government concern, but to amend his plan. And on 11 April, after less than a week in the field, he instructed Lieutenant Colonel W.D. Otter and his five hundred men to proceed directly from Swift Current to Battleford, instead of descending the South Saskatchewan River to Batoche as originally arranged. Another assault force would march north from Calgary to Edmonton and then eastward along the North Saskatchewan River. Middleton largely regarded these two secondary columns as a security measure; his sights remained fixed firmly on Batoche.[12] The general was one of the few senior officials to discount the idea of a coordinated Indian-Métis uprising. As late as 14 April, the day before the siege of Fort Pitt, he privately questioned the reliability of police reports coming in from Prince Albert and Battleford—but added, "I fear the chance of their being right."[13]

The rerouting of Otter's force to Battleford did not come soon enough for the hundreds of townspeople who had taken refuge within the stockade. They had been expecting Poundmaker to attack since late March, and were even more concerned after the Frog Lake murders.[14] As they waited to be liberated, each passing day only added to their sense of paranoia—and their anger with the Canadian government for not taking their plight seriously. Ironically, by the time Middleton finally agreed to send a relief column to Battleford, there was "not an Ind[ian] to be seen near town."[15] On the same day that Otter received his new orders, Inspector Morris, the NWMP officer in charge of the fort, sent out the first of two police scouts to uncover the whereabouts and size of the Poundmaker camp. That the first man returned from nearby Bresaylor to report that the Cree chief had evidently returned to his reserve did nothing to allay the fears of the Battleford refugees—he could be waiting for reinforcements from Big Bear's band. Nor did it occur to the townspeople that the local Indians might be as upset as they were about the Frog Lake tragedy—instead, the residents believed they were next. As Morris cautiously noted in the post journal for 12 April, "Everything *apparently* quiet."[16]

This calm was soon shattered. On 6 April, the same day that Middleton launched his campaign, Riel's council unanimously passed a motion "that two men be sent to Fort Battle[ford], and, if it is possible to do so, destroy Fort Battle[ford], seize the stores and munitions, and bring the forces and animals here."[17] This resolution formed the basis of a new letter,[18] once again extolling the virtues of the Métis cause and its divine support, that was carried to the Battleford area by Chicicum and Norbert Delorme. Theirs was a crucial mission: assume control of the Cut Knife camp and bring the Indians to Batoche.

Riel could not have chosen a better pair for his handiwork. Chicicum, a member of Beardy's band, was probably the same messenger who had visited some of the Treaty Two reserves in search of fresh recruits; William Tompkins, one of Riel's prisoners at Batoche, later testified that Chicicum had told him in early April that he had been away for a few days and was leaving again.[19] Chicicum had also developed a special spiritual bond with the Métis leader

Chicicum, a member of Beardy's band, was one of two emissaries that Riel sent to the Cut Knife camp to bring the Indians to Batoche. *Saskatoon Public Library Local History Room 1859*

stemming from their days together in Montana in the early 1880s. In his Batoche journal, a rambling collection of thoughts about his mission and God's directives, Riel scribbled on the day of the Duck Lake battle a series of divine messages that he had received. Among them was the command: *"You will give to Tchekikam (Chicicum) what he will demand of you."*[20] The forty-eight-year-old Delorme, on the other hand, was a hand-picked member of the Exovedate and one of Gabriel Dumont's closest strategists—Delorme's St. Laurent home served as military headquarters for the Métis campaign.[21] Riel probably chose him for the Battleford mission, though, because of his close affinity with the Plains Cree. Not only did Delorme have an Indian name, Mankachee, but some seven years earlier, he was one of fourteen Métis petitioners who had asked that a special reserve be set aside for their exclusive use in the Cypress Hills area.[22] Now, in 1885, he was also arguably the most militant member of Riel's flock. On a list of prominent individuals prepared for the subsequent rebellion trials, someone has written, "one of the worst," beside his name.[23]

By the time Chicicum and Delorme reached the Battleford area the second week of April,[24] most of the Indians were camped on the Poundmaker reserve along a creek not far from the base of Cut Knife Hill, a large prominent rise of land named for an earlier Cree victory. They had instinctively gathered there in a common search for security; not unlike the behaviour of the people hiding within the barrack walls. Like the Battleford residents, they too were afraid of being attacked—not only for the looting incident, but also for the Frog Lake murders—and believed that the hill and its commanding view of the surrounding countryside offered the best defence. Many were also distressed, if not in shock, over the recent deaths of Little Pine and Red Pheasant and the apparent spread of the Métis rebellion westward and were unwilling to remain on their home reserves. Their world was collapsing around them, and they were desperately looking for leadership—and answers. This did not mean, however, that Chief Poundmaker was in any sense the undisputed leader of the Cut Knife camp. Although the young chief was noted for his powers and had even prophesied an attack, the Assiniboine warriors who returned from Battleford with the Cree had erected a soldiers' tent in the camp. As a civil chief, Poundmaker's authority was limited, all the more so since his followers were outnumbered by the other bands.

The two Métis emissaries lost little time in taking advantage of the situation. At a hastily called meeting in the warriors' tent, Delorme read Riel's letter aloud, first in French and then in Cree. "Rise; face the enemy, and if you can do so, take Battleford—destroy it—save all the goods and provisions, and come to us," it implored. "With your numbers, you can perhaps send us a detachment of 40 or 50 men. All you do, do it for the love of God . . . and be certain that faith does wonders."[25] Delorme then spoke at considerable length about Riel's sacred mission, how his work had the active support of the Americans, and how those who refused to fight on his behalf would suffer the consequences.[26] This closing threat, according to Robert Jefferson, the local farm instructor, did not sit well with Poundmaker, who distrusted the messengers and their purpose. The chief was also alarmed by Riel's call for assistance; the Indians had earlier been told that the Métis would score an easy victory over government forces.[27] But Poundmaker could do little more than voice his opinion, since Chicicum and Delorme had allied themselves with the more aggressive members of the camp, in particular the Assiniboine. Nor were the two emissaries alone in their endeavour. Joseph Jobin, Riel's agent in the Battleford area, and André Nault were already there, and they were soon joined by Adolphus Nolin, fresh from the siege of Fort Pitt.[28]

The Métis presence at the Cut Knife camp had an immediate impact on nearby Battleford. After several peaceful days, Inspector Morris reported on 14 April—within hours of the arrival of Chicicum and Delorme—that a group of Assiniboine scouts had warned a small party from the fort that Poundmaker had crossed the Battle River with six bands and planned to take the barracks the next day.[29] This news prompted a flurry of trench-digging around the walls of the stockade, but the Indians never came and the general alert was called off a few days later. Warriors from the Cut Knife camp, in the meantime, were busy in the surrounding countryside. In an apparent effort to amass a larger fighting force, Delorme instructed his Cut Knife allies to round up any Cree bands who were still on their reserves. This was accomplished in two ways. At Moosomin and Thunderchild, the cattle were driven off in the expectation that the bands would be forced to follow—or face possible starvation.[30] Others were intimidated into joining. Peaychew, a hardliner from Red Pheasant's band, together with a large Stoney force on horseback, confronted some of Little Pine's men who had gathered at the reserve storehouse. "You are cowards if you do not fight," Peaychew shouted while rifles were discharged into the air. "Anyone of you who refuses to fight can don and wear his wife's dress."[31]

In keeping with Métis strategy elsewhere, Delorme also took a large armed force to the neutral Métis settlement at Bresaylor to bring back hostages. About two weeks earlier, following his return from Battleford, Poundmaker had personally promised to do what he could to guarantee the safety of the settlers; he now tried to keep that pledge and sent two men ahead to warn them that the raiding party was on its way and that he had no control over it. Upon learning of the raiding party heading their way, the Bresaylor residents initially balked at the idea of going to Cut

Joseph Jobin, Bresaylor school teacher and Riel's agent in the Battleford area, was identified as president of the Cut Knife Hill camp during the rebellion trials. *Loretta Jobin*

Knife, but quickly realized that resistance was futile, especially when they learned that Delorme was heading the group—they apparently knew of his reputation from his Red River days. Some fifteen families, as well as the priest Louis Cochin, were taken captive. More important, however, was the seizure of three hundred head of cattle needed to feed the growing Cut Knife camp.[32]

Over the next week, Riel's agents attempted to consolidate their control over the Cut Knife camp, which now numbered over one thousand people. Much of this work was done in small councils, as witnessed by Robert Jefferson, the resident farm instructor. Speaking to a group from Red Pheasant's band one day, Chicicum recounted in glowing terms the lopsided victory at Duck Lake and how Riel was confidently preparing to meet the so-called forces of evil at Batoche. He also outlined how the railway was to be destroyed, the police corralled like animals, and all signs of the government wiped out across the West. He even promised that the land would be returned to its original inhabitants.[33] This kind of talk undoubtedly encouraged some of the warriors and may even have won over some new converts. It also made life somewhat precarious for the prisoners. Poundmaker and his supporters had to intervene on several occasions to prevent them from being harmed.[34] But besides dancing at the soldiers' tent and patrolling the countryside, the young men made no move towards Batoche, let alone Battleford—Riel's very purpose in sending Chicicum and Delorme to the area.

The reason that the Cree remained at Cut Knife throughout April was because their intentions were peaceful. They lived in constant fear that the government would punish them for what happened at Battleford and Frog Lake and essentially came together at Cut Knife—and stayed there—for defensive reasons. If anything, the failure of the Indians to attack Battleford confirms that they were not an integral part of the Métis rebellion and that they had their own strategies for dealing with the Canadian government—and taking up arms was not one of them. They also made no attempt to hide their whereabouts throughout the so-called siege, and the occupants of the fort knew that the main Indian camp was some forty miles away.

While the Cut Knife camp watched and waited, Otter's relief column marched steadily northward from Swift Current. By 21 April, the five-hundred-man force had reached the Bear Hills, some fifty miles south of the Assiniboine reserves where farm instructor Payne had been murdered. The following day, it skirmished briefly with a

small Assiniboine party, but met no other resistance as it pushed towards its goal.[35] Otter's approach effectively killed Riel's plan for the taking of Battleford. In one of their last defiant acts, however, the scouts who had been watching the fort—most likely Stoney warriors and Métis agitators—set fire to the Hudson's Bay Company store on 22 April. The next night, they burned the home of Judge Rouleau, the man who had fled in terror in late March and would later be called upon to preside over the local rebellion trials. The torching of Rouleau's house was particularly galling, for Otter's men were camped only a few miles distant and could see the glow from the fire in the early evening sky. It appeared as if the Indians were spoiling for a fight and that an attack was imminent.[36] But by the time the column marched triumphantly into old town the next morning and set up headquarters at the Indian industrial school, renamed Fort Otter, the Indians who had supposedly held the residents of the barracks in mortal fear for three long weeks had vanished.

In relieving Battleford, Otter had achieved his purpose. Both he and his men were disappointed, however, that they did not see any action. Nor were they thrilled with the prospect of sitting out the next few weeks of the war at Battleford, while Middleton grabbed all the glory. Two days after his arrival, then, Otter concocted a plan to march against the Cut Knife camp in the simple belief that the Indians would surrender. One writer has suggested that had the Assiniboines not killed Payne and Tremont and then joined the Cree at Cut Knife, Otter would probably have left the camp alone; after all, the only crime the Cree had committed was some hurried looting.[37] This argument does not take into account, though, the ugly mood in Battleford after the so-called siege had been lifted. People who had been forced to endure several weeks of cramped confinement wanted revenge, especially after surveying the damage inflicted on the town and their homes.[38] They felt violated and called on the troops to punish the perpetrators. "The petted Indians are the bad ones," P.G. Laurie announced in a *Saskatchewan Herald* editorial prepared while inside the barracks.

> The Assiniboine have been treated as being of a superior race, and are the first to shed the blood of their benefactors. Poundmaker has been petted and feted and stands in the front rank as a raider. Little Pine, bribed to come north and kept in comfort, hastens to the carnage. Big Bear, who has for years enjoyed the privilege of eating of the bread of idleness, shows his gratitude by killing his priests and his best friends in cold blood . . . The petted Indians have proved the bad ones, and this gives weight to the old adage that the only good Indians are the dead ones.[39]

Otter's men, on the other hand, could not help but be stirred by the emotional outpouring that greeted their arrival on the scene; the poor people had been terrorized for weeks, and they were their saviours. They also learned first-hand from Inspector Dickens and his police detachment, who had reached Battleford only a few days earlier, about the ignoble surrender of Fort Pitt and their forced flight down the ice-filled North Saskatchewan River. When these latest developments were added to what had occurred in the Battleford region since late March—not to mention the taunting fires set the night before the column's arrival—there appeared to be ample reason for striking back at the Indians. Someone had to hand these rebels their first defeat. That someone, Otter believed, was himself. Although the Canadian-born career soldier had been given command of his own military column in the North-West campaign, Otter craved advancement and saw a quick defeat of the Cut Knife forces as the surest way to promotion. On 26 April, he wired General Middleton and Indian Commissioner Edgar Dewdney, who doubled as lieutenant governor for the North-West Territories, about his planned move against the Indians. "I would propose taking part of my force at once to punish Poundmaker," he reported. "Great depredations commit-

Colonel Otter decided to march against the Cut Knife camp in defiance of Middleton's orders. *Ontario Archives S604*

ted. Immediate decisive action necessary. Do you approve?"[40] Middleton answered the same day, as did Dewdney—but their telegrams suggested different courses of action. Whereas the general counselled caution, telling Otter to remain at Battleford until he learned more about the size and location of the Cut Knife camp, Dewdney decided that Poundmaker's allegiance was now dispensable and gave his blessing to the use of force: "Think you cannot act too energetically or Indians will collect in large numbers."[41]

Otter apparently saw nothing contradictory in the two responses and dispatched scouts to locate the Indian camp and determine the best route for a surprise attack. He then made another attempt on 30 April to secure Middleton's approval for the expedition: "Am I to attack? Please give me definite instructions."[42] The general, still licking his wounds from a Métis ambush at Fish Creek a few days earlier, had not changed his mind. "Fighting these men entails heavy responsibility," he lectured from afar. "Had better for the present content yourself with holding Battleford and patrolling about the country."[43] This was not the answer Otter wanted, and he decided to go anyway on the pretext that he was conducting a reconnaissance of the area. It was a decision that Middleton deeply regretted. "Otter has . . . gone off contrary to the spirit of my orders to attack Poundmaker and I am rather uneasy," he wrote Dewdney several days later. "He and all his forces are untried in actual fighting."[44]

The news of Otter's arrival at Battleford, in the meantime, had had a disquieting effect on the Cut Knife camp. Up to then, the Cree had steadfastly refused to become involved in the rebellion and tried to keep their distance from the trouble. Now they might be forced to fight, especially if Otter decided to march against them. This imminent threat of attack caused the Rattlers Society, led by Fine Day of the Strike-Him-on-the-Back band, to assume responsibility for the camp's protection and join the Assiniboine soldiers' lodge in the centre of the encampment.[45] These warrior societies were to have disbanded with the signing of the treaties, but they still enjoyed considerable influence, especially during times of crisis. Such a war footing now existed for the Cree. The soldiers threatened to punish anyone who questioned their authority or tried to leave, including Poundmaker, the peace chief.

Otter's presence at Battleford also worked to the advantage of Riel's disciples, who had been warning for the past few weeks that the Canadian government preferred to crush the Indians rather than honour its treaty promises; it seemed they were speaking the truth after all. The Métis agents, as a result, began to enjoy greater influence in the camp, especially with the warriors.[46] One of their first acts in the days following Otter's arrival at Battleford was to ask farm instructor Robert Jefferson to prepare a letter to Riel on 29 April, under the names of Poundmaker and four other Cree, asking for reinforcements from Batoche.[47] "I want to hear news of the progress of God's work. If any event has occurred since your messengers came away let me know of it," it opened.

> We wait still for you, as we are unable to take the fort without help . . . It would give us—encourage us much to see you, and make us work more heartily. Up to the present everything has gone well with us, but we are constantly expecting the soldiers to visit us here.[48]

Although it is not clear who dictated the letter, Chicicum was probably one of the authors; he was present in Poundmaker's tent when it was composed and took it directly to Joseph Jobin, who reviewed and altered it and then added his own postscript: "When this reaches you send us news immediately, as we are anxious to hear the news . . . send as many men as possible."[49]

At Poundmaker's trial, the prosecution pointed to the Cut Knife

Poundmaker was forced to sign a letter to Riel calling for his support in the taking of Battleford. *James Smith*

letter as indisputable proof that the chief not only conspired with Riel, but actively sought his support in the taking of Battleford. Curiously, though, the letter was riddled with errors of fact. It claimed, for example, that Big Bear was on his way eastward and that the Blackfoot had destroyed a force of sixty policemen at the Elbow of the South Saskatchewan River. These mistakes may have been partly attributable to Robert Jefferson's imperfect understanding of Cree—something that became apparent when he was cross-examined about the preparation of the letter. It was also revealed during the trial that Poundmaker's name had been placed on the letter against his wishes. Jefferson, who was asked to record what was said at the meeting, testified that Oopinowaywin or Sheds the Hair, one of Poundmaker's own headmen, ordered him to sign the chief's name to the document.[50] The names of the other Indians at the bottom of the letter are also significant. Peaychew and Mussinass, headmen of the Red Pheasant and Strike-Him-on-the-Back bands, respectively, were noted warriors, while Mettaywaysis had been one of Riel's messengers to the Battleford district in late March. Finally, the thrust of the letter not only bears the unmistakable imprint of Riel's sympathizers, but in calling for assistance, also seems deliberately designed to force Poundmaker's hand. Jobin was certainly optimistic and left the next day for Batoche with the letter, as well as a short note from Chicicum, in which he made no secret of his purpose in trying to involve the local Cree in the rebellion. "I am very well pleased with my work as I see it in this camp," he reported to Riel. "Hope you will pray for me."[51]

This call for help fell several hours short. On 1 May, the same day that Jobin rode into Batoche to secure help in moving the Poundmaker camp, Colonel Otter left Battleford in the late afternoon with a flying force of about 325 men, including seventy-five mounted policemen and several members of the local militia. Because of the distance to the Indian camp and since it was to be a lightning raid—one diary account suggested they were "on the war path"[52]—the infantry travelled by wagon; Otter also took along two light cannons and a Gatling gun that the manufacturer had loaned to the field force as a demonstration weapon. The troops sped westward along the Battle River, and after stopping for a late evening rest, resumed their march through the night. Otter planned to swoop down on the unsuspecting camp and force its surrender. But as the scouts neared Cut Knife at dawn, they were shocked to find that the Indians, who had been spotted a few days earlier on the east side of the creek, had moved their camp several hundred yards to the west. Otter had no choice but to push on across the creek and through the bordering marshland.

Surprisingly, the Cut Knife camp did not have any scouts watching for Otter's approach. An old man, Kohsakahtigant or Jacob with Long Tangled Hair, however, heard the rumble of the wagons and immediately spread the alarm. Jacob was the possessor of "manitouassini" or Old Man Stone. In return for yearly offerings of tobacco, sweetgrass, and cloth, the sacred stone would warn its owner of visitors and storms or assist in curing illnesses. That night, Old Man Stone woke Jacob and would not let him sleep; his protector was trying to alert him to the coming of the troops.[53] Jacob's warning sent Delorme and a handful of Assiniboine riding out to check Otter's advance,[54] while the rest of the warriors scrambled to take up positions in the shallow wooded ravines that ran down to the creek from the new camp. All those not engaged in the fighting, including Poundmaker, fled south and watched the encounter from the relative safety of Cut Knife Hill.[55] It is commonly assumed that the battle took place on the hill; yet, as one of Otter's own men remarked forty-five years later when the Historic Sites and Monuments Board of Canada proposed to erect a commemorative cairn there, "the large hill . . . to the southwest of our position about two miles . . . was really outside the area of the engagement."[56]

The rousing of the Indians foiled Otter's plan to surprise the camp. He still believed, though, that his superior weaponry, if quickly deployed, could force the Indians to surrender, and he directed that the two cannons and Gatling be fired on the Indian village. The whiz of the bullets ripping through tents and splintering poles, interspersed by the boom of incoming cannon balls, sent the women and children screaming for cover in the bush. But the guns were virtually useless against the concealed warriors, who dashed up and down the length of the ravines, stopping to fire on the exposed troops or just waving a blanket on a stick. These peekaboo tactics proved so confusing that Otter thought he was dealing with a much larger force instead of the fifty or more men who actually took part in the battle; they also frustrated his troops, who did not know where to shoot.[57] Little did they realize that they could have easily overrun the camp.

When the fighting erupted, the warriors' primary concern was to keep the troops from advancing farther and harming the women, children, and elders. But as the poorly armed Indians gained confidence, they began to work their way down towards the creek in a kind of pincer movement. There were a num-

War chief Fine Day of the Strike-Him-on-the-Back band directed the Cree counterattack at the Cut Knife battle. *National Archives of Canada PA28837*

ber of acts of personal bravery and sacrifice that morning. A grieving father, who had recently lost a daughter to malnutrition, stood up and ran yelling towards the troops before being shot down. A refugee Nez Perce warrior from the United States, who had fled north following the defeat of Chief Joseph in 1877, gallantly tried to disrupt the firing of the big field guns on the camp and was cut down. And an Assiniboine boy, barely a teenager, was killed while armed with only his bow and a few arrows. More of Otter's men would likely have been injured, if not for the lack of ammunition. As it was, the warriors were constantly coming back for more bullets and even stones, which were being treated with medicine so that they would inflict more damage.[58]

By noon, Otter realized that his position was hopeless; his troops were quickly tiring from their lack of sleep and were vulnerable to a counterattack. In going to Cut Knife and engaging the Indians on their own terrain, he had stirred up a hornets' nest and was being stung from nearly all quarters; if he stayed much longer, he might be swarmed. He consequently ordered his men to withdraw, and while some held off the Indians until the wagons were loaded with the dead and wounded, others dropped back and guarded the force's escape route across the creek. It was a difficult retreat through the marshy, hummocky creek bottom, even more so once the shock of what had befallen them finally began to sink in. But to their relief—and ultimate survival—the Indians did not follow. Although several warriors had mounted horses and were ready to pursue, Poundmaker stopped them. "They have come here to fight us and we have fought them; now let them go."[59]

One author has suggested it would not have been possible for the Cree chief to prevent the warriors from harassing Otter's retreating column, for he was not a member of the soldiers' society and had no authority under the circumstances.[60] But prisoners in the Cut Knife camp and descendants of Indians who were present at the battle all agree that Poundmaker intervened.[61] He was able to do so because Masatimwas, or Sailing Horse, a headman of Little Pine's band and respected veteran of the Blackfoot wars, had given Poundmaker his sacred pipe-stem, the Oskichi. Masatimwas had sustained a severe abdominal wound during the early part of the battle. As he neared death, he summoned Poundmaker and handed him the Oskichi, the symbol of his authority, to be used in times of acute crisis to invoke the power of the Creator. When the Cree chief later told the warriors to leave the retreating soldiers alone, he held the Oskichi high over his head and they obeyed.[62] Masatimwas, for his part, survived his horrible wound after spending a fitful night under a buffalo robe with the Oskichi at his side.[63]

Otter's party limped into Battleford some ten hours later. On the return ride, one dazed, young mounted policeman confidently told the war correspondent for the Montreal *Star*, "We're making history, eh."[64] He was right. What reporter Howard Kennedy would later describe as the "most disastrous fight of the campaign" had been costly: fourteen men had been wounded and eight killed, including one poor soul who had been left behind. The Indian dead numbered around five—although it is difficult to ascertain the exact figure because of the general reluctance of those involved to speak about their activities that day.[65]

Otter filed his official account of the engagement on 5 May. He claimed that when his column arrived in the Battleford area, Poundmaker "was hesitating between peace and war" and that he took "a reconnaissance in force" to Cut Knife "in order to make

Poundmaker stopped the Cut Knife warriors from pursuing the retreating soldiers. *James Smith*

Poundmaker declare himself." He also maintained that the raid had been a success, in that the Cree chief's intentions were now clear and that his troops had performed admirably, especially when "Big Bear, or at least his men, had effected a junction before my arrival, as the number of enemy was fully five hundred fighting men, including some fifty halfbreeds."[66] This blatant distortion of the facts was perhaps understandable at the time, because Otter had clearly disobeyed orders and was desperate to salvage something from his defeat at the hands of the Indians. He even went so far as to suggest that Poundmaker had lost over one hundred men.[67] In fact, for the rest of his life, Otter promoted the falsehood that his raid had had a decisive bearing on the suppression of the rebellion, to the point where he modified the draft wording on the commemorative Historic Sites plaque in 1923 to suggest that his men had prevented a union of Poundmaker and Big Bear[68]—something that clearly contradicted one of his own stated reasons for retreating almost forty years earlier.

However Otter tried to obscure the truth, there was no denying that his march against Cut Knife had made a muck of things. The Indian camp, despite the presence of several of Riel's most devoted Métis followers who argued for the destruction of Battleford, had not only kept its distance from the unfolding troubles, but had assumed a defensive posture. It is possible that the Indians would have avoided a confrontation with Otter's force and moved away had they not been taken by surprise that early spring morning. By attacking Cut Knife, Otter had made a peaceful resolution of the situation extremely doubtful, if not impossible, and did more in a few short hours to push the Indians into the arms of the Métis than Riel and his followers had been able to accomplish over several months. And Canadian officials knew it. "This engagement ends hope of an amicable settlement of the difficulties that have arisen," Hayter Reed pessimistically advised Dewdney from Battleford on 5 May. "It is probable that an Indian war is on our hands."[69] If it did break out, Otter would be lucky to take part in it. As Robert Jefferson observed over fifty years after the Cut Knife Hill battle, "But for the grace of God and the complaisance of Otter's Indian opponent, it would have been left to strangers to name it, for there would have been no survivors."[70]

It was up to Riel and the Métis to decide what would happen next in the area. Otter was still smarting from his near defeat, and the Indians were recovering from the trauma of the attack. The situation at Battleford, meanwhile, had unexpectedly been reversed. Whereas

Battleford Indians (including three former warriors) at a special ceremony commemorating the fiftieth anniversary of the battle. *Saskatoon Public Library Local History Room LH9424*

the occupants of the fort had once feared for their lives, it was the Cut Knife camp that had nearly been overrun if not for the bravery of the warriors. And while Battleford now enjoyed the protection of Otter's well-armed force, the Indians remained extremely vulnerable—not only to attack, but to the insidious activities of Riel's agents. There was little that Poundmaker could do. Commissioner Dewdney secretly advised the prime minister less than a week after Otter's actions, "I have heard a few days ago . . . that Poundmaker wanted to come to terms, but . . . the young men who ruled in the war Council would not hear of it and carried the day."[71] This was exactly the kind of situation the Métis were prepared to exploit. The Cut Knife camp was wanted at Batoche. Riel had ordered it, and his disciples would see to it, by force if necessary.

chapter eight

A Rope
about Their Necks

O NE OF THE DARKEST FEARS of the commander of the Canadian forces during the
North-West Rebellion was that the Métis
would conduct a guerilla campaign. Drawing on their familiarity with
the countryside, small parties of mobile fighters could have raided
settlements or harassed the advancing military column, then slipped
away as quickly as they had struck. It was the kind of war that would
have demoralized General Middleton's inexperienced forces and
effectively blunted, if not undermined, his strategy for dealing with
the rebels.[1] But apart from allowing an ambush at Fish Creek in late
April 1885, Louis Riel chose to make his stand at Batoche, confident
that God would not fail him in the end. This decision—to wait
faithfully at Batoche for divine intervention—ultimately sealed the
Métis's fate, for they gave up any chance of prolonging the conflict
and forcing the Canadian government to negotiate. It also meant that
the Indians were deliberately dragged into the conflict. In order to
bolster Riel's small army, the Métis brought a Dakota (Sioux) band
north to Batoche and, together with some captive Cree already there,
forced them to fight on the rebel side. This participation in the two
major engagements in the area was damning proof of an Indian-Métis

alliance and called into doubt earlier expressions of Indian loyalty. That Poundmaker's camp was moving eastward at the time of the fall of Batoche, apparently to join Riel, only made things look worse. Canadian officials concluded that the Indians were more deeply involved in the rebellion than had first been believed.

It is debatable whether Louis Riel expected to fight a war in 1885. Some fifteen years earlier, he and his Métis followers had seized control of the Red River Settlement and forced the Canadian government to bring the region into confederation as the province of Manitoba, complete with land guarantees for the mixed-blood population. He now seemed intent on following the same strategy. In the first few days of his provisional government, he took hostages and tried to bring about the surrender of Fort Carlton in order to bargain from a position of strength. The circumstances in 1885, however, were completely different from those of his earlier resistance—the most significant being the arrival of the Canadian military in the region in a matter of weeks. The Métis leader consequently had little choice in late March but to embark on his threatened "war of extermination."[2]

How this war was fought is extremely revealing. At Duck Lake, the Métis allowed Superintendent Crozier and his beaten men to retreat from the battlefield; they could have followed and cut them down. Similarly, they simply watched as the mounted police abandoned Fort Carlton and fled north to Prince Albert. By the time that General Middleton's force left Fort Qu'Appelle at the end of the first week of April, the Métis had made no attempt to take advantage of their position and go on the offensive; instead, they prepared to meet the Canadian response by entrenching at Batoche.[3] All of these decisions were made at the urging of Riel. He was the one who held back the Métis at Duck Lake and later Fort Carlton in order to avoid further bloodshed. He had also encouraged his followers to do nothing to interfere with the advance of Middleton's men, but rather lie in wait for them on Métis home ground. And he did so for religious, not military, reasons. As a prophet with a divine mission, Riel believed that God was on his side—he spoke daily of revelations—and counted on this spiritual backing to smite his enemies and confirm his sacred destiny. There was nothing to fear, then, from the approaching army; his followers merely had to have faith in his ability to bring about a "miraculous deliverance."[4]

Riel's decision to meet Middleton at Batoche in effect handcuffed his adjutant general, Gabriel Dumont. Although in the past the Métis had traditionally followed defensive tactics whenever threatened, Dumont wanted to attack the untried militiamen in the early weeks of the campaign at a place and time of his choosing; the skills and discipline that had characterized the buffalo hunt would now be applied against a two-legged quarry in a hit-and-run raid.[5] Riel, however, refused to endorse this plan, and Dumont, being a good disciple, grudgingly went along with his master. This did not mean that the veteran plains hunter abandoned his gun for his rosary. Although Dumont deferred to Riel's prophetic powers, he took concrete steps in early April to fortify Métis headquarters by creating an elaborate system of trenches on both sides of the river and along the trails leading to Batoche.[6] He also realized that if his army was to have any hope of repulsing the Canadian force, he would have to find more recruits for the cause. Too many of the local Métis had refused to take part in Riel's brave new world; only an estimated 250 out of a total regional Métis population of some 1500 were prepared to defend Batoche.[7] This is why, then, with the official endorsement of the Exovedate, messengers were dispatched to Indian reserves in the first days of the campaign with an invitation to join the Métis and strike back against their oppressors.[8] The Cree and other First Nations were to be involved—willingly or unwillingly.

By the end of March, Dumont's search for allies had gone badly. Except for some men from Beardy's reserve and a handful of mixed-blood supporters from Petequakey, the only other Indians in Riel's camp were those from One Arrow—and Dumont, with Michel Dumas's assistance, had to bring them there by force. All other bands preferred to uphold their treaty pledges and avoid the struggle; as one Indian agent neatly summed up the situation to Edgar Dewdney, "Everything is quiet and no apprehension is felt."[9] This failure to win over the Indians called for more aggressive tactics, and in early April, about twenty Métis horsemen surrounded the Dakota reserve at Moose Woods, just south of the hamlet of Saskatoon, and escorted the elderly Chief Whitecap (Wapahaska) and his band, along with all of their livestock, north to Batoche.[10] This was the second time in as many weeks that the Métis had come to the reserve. In the days immediately following the declaration of Riel's provisional government, Chief Whitecap had turned away two messengers from Batoche, refusing to join the rebels—a pledge he repeated after the Duck Lake fight to Gerald Willoughby, a Saskatoon trader and one of the few local men who could speak Dakota.[11] Now, Whitecap and

In the days immediately following the declaration of Riel's provisional government, Chief Whitecap affirmed his loyalty to the Queen. *Saskatoon Public Library
Local History Room PH91-369*

his band were literally being abducted at gunpoint. And there was
nothing that could be done about it.

Whitecap's predicament was painfully apparent when the party
passed through Saskatoon on its way to Métis headquarters. While
camped a few miles south of the village, the chief had tried unsuccessfully to meet with Willoughby to explain his situation. The chief then
sent his brother to Saskatoon early the next morning with a plea for
help; he wanted the local citizens to rescue them. The Métis escort,
however, was twice as large as the armed force that Willoughby was
able to muster, and when the Indians and their captors neared the
village, all the Saskatoon group could do was question whether the
Indians really wanted to go to the front. One of the Métis riders
retorted gruffly, "Whitecap can speak for himself." When Willoughby
questioned the visibly upset chief about his intentions, he shrugged
his shoulders and simply said he did not know. The Métis then shoved
themselves between the two men, effectively preventing any further
discussion, and hurried on with their reluctant recruits, sweeping
eastward around the village and through the present-day university

grounds. A frustrated Willoughby followed at a distance and finally caught up with Whitecap when he stopped to warm himself with a cup of tea at a house on the other side of Saskatoon. During their private conversation, the chief explained that he was afraid of being harmed if he turned back. He also assured the Saskatoon trader that he did not support the rebellion. When Willoughby responded that the government would regard him as a rebel and likely throw him off his reserve if he went to Batoche, Whitecap became indignant and repeated several times that he would not fight.[12]

Whitecap and his band were abducted for several reasons. First, any Indians in the Carlton area who were likely to join the Métis had already done so by now. And if Dumont tried to commandeer other bands to the north, he risked a confrontation with the mounted police who had taken refuge at Prince Albert. Whitecap's band, on the other hand, was relatively isolated and could be moved with little interference, especially since they were nontreaty Indians and perhaps more vulnerable to this kind of pressure. The Dakota also had a reputation as warriors, having fled to British territory some two

An armed Métis escort prevented Chief Whitecap from being rescued by his friends in Saskatoon. *James Smith*

Charles Trottier was named a member of Riel's governing council for his efforts in bringing Whitecap and his band to Batoche. *Glenbow Archives NA-1036-8*

decades earlier following their part in the 1862 Minnesota uprising;[13] if they fought once against white settlers, it was likely assumed that they might be willing to do so again. The most obvious explanation for their abduction, however, was the reserve's proximity to the Métis settlement at Prairie-Ronde (near present-day Dundurn). The leader or chief of this community was the Red-River-born Charles "Wawpass" Trottier, a winterer in the area since the mid-1850s and close friend and relative of Dumont. Trottier had hunted and traded with the Dakota for almost a generation, as well as developed kinship ties with them through his large, extended family.[14] He saw them as possible Métis allies, and upon completing a similar mission to the Indians in the Battleford area in late March, decided to bring the Dakota north—over Whitecap's objections—to help Riel's cause.

Trottier was immediately named a member of the Exovedate upon his arrival at Batoche on 6 April—most likely in recognition of his standing among the South Branch population and his recent work among the Indians. Whitecap joined him on the governing council four days later.[15] It was a curious appointment, since the Dakota chief was the only First Nations member of the Exovedate; there was not a single Cree representative, despite the supposed support of the nearby reserves. And, as Whitecap was unable to understand what took place during the meetings since he spoke neither French, English, nor Cree, he chose not to attend. By the second week of April, however, the Métis were anxious to strengthen their forces at Batoche. They had just dispatched two special agents, Chicicum and Delorme, to retrieve the Indians from the Battleford area. And by creating the impression that Whitecap not only supported Riel's government, but also took an active role in it—even though he was really there under duress—they might be able to win over other neutral bands.

Canadian officials, on the other hand, should have been under no illusion about the circumstances behind Whitecap's presence at Métis headquarters. On 5 April, Lawrence Herchmer, the Treaty Two Indian agent stationed at Birtle, Manitoba, advised Indian Commissioner Edgar Dewdney that "Whitecap and his Sioux are with the Rebels . . . on compulsion." He went on to explain how a local woman had just returned from visiting her brother in the area and been told that "after repeated refusals to join the rebels, a large party surrounded his camp [Whitecap] and drove them into the rebel camp by force . . . the Old Chief intends to desert the first chance he gets with his men."[16] What was not known at the time and has only become clear in recent interviews with reserve elders is that Whitecap probably saved Saskatoon from certain destruction. The Métis were apparently ready to plunder the tiny hamlet if they encountered any resistance, but Whitecap agreed to go to Batoche on the understanding that his white friends were left alone.[17]

The Sioux's arrival did not substantially increase the fighting force at Dumont's disposal; prisoner John Astley later reported only about twenty men accompanied Whitecap.[18] Their knowledge of the land between Prince Albert and Fort Qu'Appelle, however, made them a valued addition to Riel's camp, and they were quickly dispatched in small parties to watch for the Canadian army's approach. The scouts did not have to go far, for by 17 April, Middleton had followed the telegraph line from Fort Qu'Appelle as far as Clarke's Crossing on the South Saskatchewan River, a mere thirty miles from Batoche. For the next few days, while the general rested his troops in preparation for the final assault on Métis headquarters, the Dakota carefully noted the strength and deployment of the camp. Unknown to them, they were also being watched, and three of them, including Whitecap's adopted son, Blackbird, were captured by a group of French's Scouts led by Lord Melgund, Middleton's chief of staff and a future governor general.

The Dakota, instead of keeping quiet, not only professed their innocence—they had been forced to join Riel—but divulged the small size of the Métis army;[19] in fact, their capture may not have been accidental. As for the other scouts, they returned safely to Batoche with their information and were formally thanked at the afternoon sitting of the council on 22 April. One individual, Wechawecopewin, was singled out and presented with a horse "in recognition of the courageous, honorable and Christian conduct he showed in the reconnaissance of Clarke's Crossing."[20] Such blandishments may have been designed to keep the Indians on side.

On Thursday 23 April, General Middleton resumed his march northward, after ferrying one-half of his men to the other (western) side of the South Saskatchewan River. This division of his force went against textbook tactics, but the general believed that it was the only way to surround Batoche since the village occupied both sides of the river; he was also confident that either four-hundred-man column could easily handle the smaller Métis army—if it did not scatter.[21]

Three Dakota scouts told their captors that they had been forced to join Riel.
Provincial Archives of Manitoba/N14579

The proximity of the Canadian forces reopened the question of where the Métis should meet them. The day before, probably in response to concerns raised by the scouting reports, Riel submitted a note to the Exovedate, in which he admitted that "it would be of great benefit to us to go and attack and harass," but that such action would leave Batoche open to a possible attack from Prince Albert. He also claimed that his guiding spirit had told him that his men should not stray because they would be needed "to defend every inch of

As the Canadian punitive force marched north from the Qu'Appelle Valley to Batoche, General Middleton was confident that his force would crush any opposition. Little did he realize that an ambush was waiting for him at Fish Creek. *National Archives of Canada C1876*

ground."[22] Dumont, on the other hand, was alarmed that Middleton was only two days' march away, and when he learned that the troops were on the move again, he successfully convinced the council to launch a surprise attack.[23] The division of Middleton's force may also have contributed to this decision.

Dumont, Riel, and about two hundred men, including Dakota and Cree, left Batoche in the late afternoon of 23 April and stopped to eat later that evening near Tourond's Coulee, about ten miles distant. While they rested—half were on foot—a messenger arrived with news that the police had left Prince Albert; although this report later proved false, Riel hurriedly returned to Batoche with about fifty men. Dumont and the others continued south, planning to surprise the Middleton camp early the next morning. But the two Dakota scouts, who had been sent ahead, could not find the column in the darkness, and by the time they did, the camp was already stirring. This forced a frustrated Dumont to change his plans. He decided to wait for the troops at Tourond's Coulee, where the Batoche trail swung inland from the river, down through a wide ravine, and then across Fish Creek, a tributary of the South Saskatchewan. It was an ideal setting for an ambush. Once Middleton's men began to descend to the creek bottom, they would be easy targets for snipers concealed behind the brush and trees that lined the coulee. Before the trap could be sprung, though, shooting erupted when Middleton's advance scouts, already alerted by signs of recent campfires in the area, spotted Dumont and some of his men hiding behind a poplar bluff ahead of the coulee.[24] This skirmish ended any hope of surprising the troops. It actually reversed the situation, as the Métis horsemen now galloped for the safety of the coulee under a hail of fire.

The battle of Fish Creek was its most intense—and deadly—during the first few minutes. As the troops hurried forward to confront their unseen foe, they quickly discovered that their position on the open prairie left them dangerously exposed. Each time they charged forward to the edge of the ravine in a bold attempt to flush out Dumont's men, they were repelled by a barrage of bullets. One war correspondent said it was like attacking a "human hornet's nest."[25] After an hour, the fight had degenerated into a stalemate—a situation made more pronounced by the drizzle that began to fall in the early afternoon. Although Middleton enjoyed a decided advantage in firepower, the bullets and shells that his men steadily directed towards the coulee sailed harmlessly over the heads of the concealed fighters. The Métis and Indians, on the other hand, found themselves pinned down and unable to do much more than watch for any new assaults, especially from the flanks. They had not expected to be the ones under attack. Nor were they prepared to fight a long, protracted battle. A large number bowed to the hopelessness of their position after the artillery had started its bombardment and slipped away when they could, so that by mid-afternoon, there were no more than fifty fighters stranded in the upper part of the ravine. Middleton, meanwhile, had been joined by men and guns from the other side of the river and carefully weighed the consequences of rushing the coulee. In the end, he decided that his troops had suffered enough that day and ordered a withdrawal in the early evening. The remaining Métis, somewhat surprised but no less relieved by this action, did the same.[26]

Although Dumont's plan to ambush Middleton had backfired, Fish Creek was still a victory for the Métis—from both a numerical and psychological perspective. Whereas Middleton's four-hundred-man force suffered over fifty casualties, including ten dead, the Métis escaped with only six fatalities; their loss of fifty horses, killed while tethered on the far side of the ravine, was far more serious.[27] The

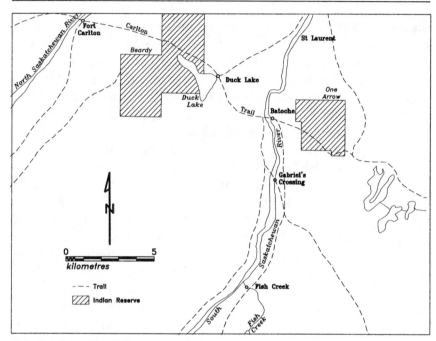

Fish Creek and Batoche area.

battle also affected the thinking of the two leaders. While Dumont could boast that his army had held off a superior force and was ready to do the same at Batoche, Middleton was shaken by the fierce resistance of the Métis and the comparatively poor showing of his inexperienced troops. The once-confident Middleton was left wary and cautious. He decided to postpone his date with Riel until his demoralized men were rested and reinforced and he had a battle plan in place. There would be no more surprises.

The Fish Creek encounter had also convinced a sceptical Middleton that there was some substance to the notion of an Indian-Métis union, something he had personally doubted at the outset of the campaign. Not only had three Dakota scouts been captured spying on behalf of the Métis a week before the battle, but during the actual engagement, Indians were seen fighting on the rebel side. In fact, two of the Fish Creek dead were Dakota. One, the son of Little Crow, had been shot at the beginning of the battle, when he went forward from the coulee two or three times and taunted the soldiers with his cries; while lying mortally wounded, he sang his death song until his last breath. The other Dakota victim, whose name is unknown, died instantly when he was struck by a shell from one of the guns.[28] For

Canadian officials, this involvement betrayed the true sympathies of the Indians. It did not seem to matter that the scouts had told Middleton whatever he wanted to know or that several of Whitecap's men had fled the area after the battle and sought refuge on Dakota reserves in the Fort Qu'Appelle and Prince Albert regions.[29] That they were there—apparently supporting the Métis cause—was viewed as proof of an alliance. And it was not restricted to Fish Creek. The same thing had happened at Duck Lake several weeks earlier and seemed to be underway at Battleford and further west at Frog Lake and Fort Pitt. Obviously, the Indians had accepted Riel's leadership and were prepared to do his bidding. How else could one explain their behaviour?

Middleton's solution was to confine the Indians to their reserves. On 6 May, one day after he received Colonel Otter's report on the Cut Knife battle, he wired Indian Commissioner Edgar Dewdney "to issue proclamation warning breeds and Indians to return to their Reserves and that all found away will be treated as rebels."[30] The reasoning behind this request was simple. Still smarting from the beating his troops had suffered at Fish Creek, the general wanted to limit the size of the rebel force he was likely to face at Batoche, as well

Following the battle of Fish Creek (the aftermath of which is shown here), General Middleton asked Edgar Dewdney to issue a proclamation ordering all Indians to remain on their reserves. *National Archives of Canada C3461*

as avoid, if possible, a costly Indian war the country could not afford. His fight was with Riel, and he wanted the Indians on the sidelines. Dewdney welcomed the idea, and within hours of receiving Middleton's telegram, issued a notice that

> all good and loyal Indians should remain quietly on their Reserves where they will be perfectly safe and receive the protection of the soldiers; and that any Indian being off his Reserve without special permission in writing from some authorized person, is liable to be arrested on suspicion of being a rebel, and punished as such.[31]

When Dewdney sent a copy of the notice to Prime Minister Macdonald the next day, he suggested it be proclaimed a government order; he also recommended that an act be passed empowering him, as lieutenant governor, to declare martial law should the need arise.[32]

Dewdney justified these restrictive features on the grounds that Middleton's troops might not be able to tell whether Indians found off their reserves were "hostile or friendly" and that it was for "their own safety" not to be mistaken as rebels.[33] On the surface, it seemed a sensible policy. Trigger-happy soldiers, stationed throughout the North-West, might be tempted to extract revenge for their fallen

Indian Commissioner Dewdney (seated centre with bowler) and Indian leaders in the Regina region. The heavy military presence was designed to ensure Indian neutrality. *National Archives of Canada PA118751*

comrades at Fish Creek and Cut Knife. And the Indians were less likely to be attacked if they stayed home and quietly went about their work in the fields and gardens. In reality, though, Dewdney had other, more devious reasons for introducing the notice—reasons that had nothing to do with Indian welfare or Middelton's campaign. For the past year or more, the Indian Affairs department had been trying to find a way to control the Indians under its supervision.[34] Middleton's request provided Dewdney with an excuse—and a good one at that—for implementing such a policy. The Indian commissioner was also desperate to regain control of a situation that had been badly handled since the start of the rebellion. Although several chiefs had publicly declared their allegiance to the Crown, these expressions of loyalty had not impressed Indian Affairs officials; they seemed to believe that the Indians were secretly waiting to see how Riel fared and would likely join the Métis if Middleton stumbled.[35] To prevent such an outcome, Dewdney used a mixture of kindness and intimidation. Whereas several bands had been on the brink of starvation over the past winter, food and supplies were now readily available in amounts that sometimes exceeded treaty provisions.[36] This open hand was counterbalanced by a clenched fist. Troops pouring into the West during the first weeks of the campaign were trained or stationed on or near reserves throughout the Qu'Appelle region in a concerted attempt to keep the Indians in check.[37]

These bullying tactics—not unlike those employed by the Métis—did not sit well with local officials. In early April, for example, in response to the arming of Broadview citizens, an alarmed Agent McDonald had bluntly warned Dewdney, "The Indians should not be intimidated."[38] The bands were also uneasy, if not confused, by the presence of so many troops in the area, especially since their leaders had promised not to join the rebellion. Many were afraid that the army might unexpectedly turn and attack them, as had been the case in the United States. "We have good thoughts in our hearts," Chiefs Pasquah and Muscowpetung of the Qu'Appelle Valley reserves telegraphed the prime minister three days before Fish Creek, "surprised to see soldiers coming here, don't know reason why . . . don't think anything disloyal of us, it hurts us . . . Governor Dewdney told us no matter if war is around our Reserves we should not fight, we would not be molested, we hold on to that . . . we want peace."[39] Piapot, whose reserve was closest to the territorial capital at Regina, sent a similar message at the end of the month. "It is eleven years since I gave

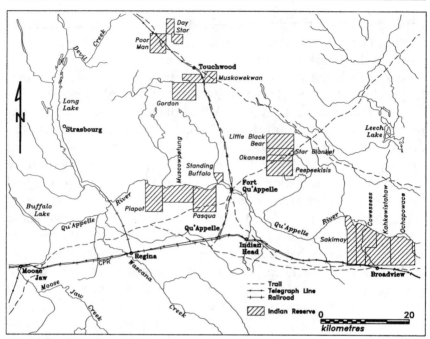

The Regina district.

up fighting," he told Macdonald. "When I took the Government Treaty I touched the pen not to interfere with the white man and the white man not to interfere with me."[40]

Instead of calming the Indians, then, the troops created a potentially explosive situation on the reserves. Such was the case when a detachment of infantry headed towards the File Hills reserves on 25 April. The young men, fearing they were to be rounded up and disarmed, prepared to do battle; only the last-minute intervention of Agent McDonald prevented bloodshed.[41] A similar situation developed in the Touchwood Hills in early May when local bands came together to defend themselves as a large number of troops passed through the reserves on their way north.[42] Many other Indians simply fled their reserves out of fear. Such incidents threatened to undermine Dewdney's strategy for keeping the Indians neutral during the rebellion. And when Middleton proposed that Indians be compelled to remain on the reserves, Dewdney promptly issued the notice, believing it would provide the extra leverage needed to keep the bands under his thumb. It did not occur to him to take the chiefs at their word and keep the troops as far away from the reserves as possible.

Dewdney's notice would be used during Poundmaker's trial to argue that the Cree chief was guilty of rebellious activity for having left his reserve.[43] But at the time it was introduced, the Indian commissioner had been led to believe by the reports from Battleford that Poundmaker had been "settled with."[44] This assessment was far from the truth. Dewdney and others would probably have been horrified to learn that the Cut Knife camp was headed towards Batoche—at the urging of the Métis. On 1 May, exactly a week after the Fish Creek victory, Joseph Jobin rode into Batoche, carrying the letter of support purportedly signed by Poundmaker and the other Indian leaders. It was a prophetic event, for only three days earlier, Riel's guiding spirit had been told that help was on the way; he consequently had Jobin write a short note in the margin of his diary, confirming that his prediction had been fulfilled.[45] The Exovedate, meanwhile, took more concrete action and unanimously decided at its afternoon sitting to send seven men[46] to Cut Knife, including Charles Trottier and two Indians, to bring the Poundmaker camp to Batoche. Jobin was also recognized for his supportive work in the Battleford area and joined his younger brother, Ambroise, as a member of the governing council.

The Batoche emissaries reached the Cut Knife camp on 4 May, a mere two days after the Otter attack. At a hurriedly convened council meeting, Jobin read aloud yet another letter from Riel—this time recounting in glowing terms the fight at Fish Creek and calling for two hundred men to "take General Middleton prisoner."[47] He then ordered some cattle killed for a feast. Poundmaker was deeply troubled by the delegation's arrival and the request for help. He knew the camp was still getting over the shock of the recent battle and was extremely vulnerable to Jobin's entreaties. He also sensed that Riel desperately needed Indian assistance to defeat Middleton. The Cree had steadfastly avoided such a commitment since Riel's return to Canada the previous summer. There was little that Poundmaker could do, however, to blunt the influence of the Métis emissaries, especially when Jobin was named president of the camp and the militants controlled everything.[48] In fact, when the chief tried to slip away with several of his followers to Manitou Lake and eventual refuge with his stepfather, Crowfoot, a combined Assiniboine-Métis force brought him back, and he became, in effect, a prisoner.[49] He was too valuable an asset to Riel's cause. And when the Métis finally convinced the warriors to head for Batoche, Poundmaker was forced to go along with them.

Middleton was also on the move again. On 7 May, more than two weeks after the Fish Creek fiasco, the general resumed his march northward with almost nine hundred men, heavy artillery, and a fortified river steamer, the *Northcote*. He still planned to surround Métis headquarters, but because of Otter's recent drubbing at Cut Knife, he decided to use only his own men in the assault: a small force on the stern wheeler would attack the village from the river, while the main party would move overland from the southeast. The Batoche army, in comparison, probably numbered no more than four hundred men, including fewer than sixty Indians from the Beardy, One Arrow, and Whitecap reserves. The Cree occupied entrenchments around the west village, while the Dakota were positioned on the opposite side of the river near the church and rectory.[50] It is debatable how much military support the Indians actually offered Riel; not only were many aged and even more poorly armed than the Métis, but there was no specific evidence at their subsequent trials that they had been actively involved in the fighting.[51] Middleton tried to further weaken their morale by sending Whitecap's captured son to Batoche on 3 May with copies of a proclamation indicating that those who returned to their reserves would be "protected and pardoned" and that the troops were only interested in fighting "Riel, his council and his chief accomplices."[52] The Exovedate dismissed this message as a hoax.[53]

The Canadian troops finally swooped down on Batoche on the morning of Saturday 9 May.[54] Middleton's plan collapsed, however, when the Métis lowered a ferry cable across the South Saskatchewan and pulled over the smokestacks of the *Northcote*, sending the steamer drifting helplessly down river. The land forces, in the meantime, only managed to get as close as the church and rectory, sometimes referred to today as mission ridge, before being forced to draw back under heavy fire from well-concealed pits that lined the fields down to the east village; they took refuge that night in a large fortified zareba that they constructed just to the south.

Over the next two days, while the two sides were engaged in general skirmishing, Middleton developed a new plan of attack, which he tried to implement the morning of 12 May. He sent a small diversionary force to the open prairie region to the east of the village in an effort to draw the Métis away from their defences along mission ridge and the river bank. But because of the strong winds that day, the main body did not hear the guns of the feinting action and failed

When Chief Beardy (seated left) travelled to Prince Albert to meet with General Middleton (standing left) and ask for rations, he was singled out for his reserve's apparent role in the rebellion and its collusion with the Métis. *Saskatchewan Archives Board R–B2064*

to advance. An enraged Middleton berated the officers in charge of the infantry before returning to camp for lunch. This stinging rebuke, coming after days of growing restlessness, sparked an impromptu advance on the village that quickly gained momentum and easily overran the defenders, who were anticipating an attack from the east. The battle for Batoche was over in minutes—largely because the remaining defenders had all but exhausted their ammunition and were unable to offer any resistance. Many paid with their lives. Whereas Middleton lost only eight men during the four-day battle, the Batoche dead may have numbered as high as two dozen.[55] Two Dakota were killed: one apparently was Whitecap's son, who, ironically, had carried Middleton's message that no harm would come to those who returned home, the other a twelve-year-old girl who was accidentally killed during the fighting.[56] Riel was much luckier. He had prayed for a miracle throughout the siege and had initially escaped, but decided to surrender three days later in a bid to take his cause to the courts.

The fall of Batoche was the first Canadian victory of the North-West campaign and did much to restore the swagger to Middleton's step. It also marked the end of the Métis provisional government, and with it, Riel's brief reign as prophet of the new world; his unshakeable belief in his divine mission had pushed his followers towards open rebellion, but failed to save them in the end. The other losers at Batoche that May were the Indians—many of whom were in the trenches against their will.

Although Chiefs Whitecap and One Arrow claimed to have had no part in the actual fighting, they, and several of their men, were immediately taken into custody at Carlton as rebels. Gabriel Dumont and Michel Dumas, two prominent players in the Métis agitation, on the other hand, managed to elude the troops and slip away to the United States, while many of their soldiers were simply disarmed and told to return to their homes. Even Indians who had refused to take part in the fighting, such as Chief Beardy, were suspect. Although a few of his men had sympathized with Riel—in most cases, those who had close connections with the local Métis communities—Beardy remained on his reserve throughout the spring and evidently watched the deciding battle from the safety of a hollow on the other side of the river.[57] But when the chief travelled to Prince Albert on 24 May to meet with Middleton and ask for rations for his hungry people, he was singled out for his reserve's apparent role in the start of the troubles and its collusion with the Métis. The accusations greatly offended the chief, and when Middleton called his leadership into question and tried to get him to admit his guilt, he took off his Treaty Six medal and handed it to the general. "If you believe me you will return it."[58] Middleton was unmoved by the solemnness of the gesture and took away the medal and those of Beardy's councillors. He then dismissed the chief, threatening to "destroy his settlement and his band" if there was a hint of any further trouble.[59]

Poundmaker fared little better at Middleton's hands. When Batoche fell on 12 May, the Cut Knife warriors, led by Riel's agents, were moving southeastward through the Eagle Hills, having swept around Battleford to avoid detection by Otter's men. Two days later, they surrounded a supply train heading north on the Swift Current trail and took most of the teamsters hostage. The news of the wagons' capture was the first indication that the Cut Knife camp was moving towards Batoche,[60] and more than anything else to that point, reinforced the image of Poundmaker as Riel's faithful lieutenant, hurrying east with much-needed reinforcements. But history has generally ignored the subsequent testimony of two captured teamsters who reported that the Métis ruled the camp and that Poundmaker was noticeably silent at any councils.[61] The other curious thing about the march to Batoche was its extremely slow progress. It should have taken the camp no more than a week to reach Riel's headquarters—just in time to help repulse Middleton. But ten days after the Métis delegates had arrived at Cut Knife with their urgent message for help, the Indians were still in the Battleford vicinity. Poundmaker's general lack of cooperation effectively prevented Riel's messengers from succeeding with their mission.

The Cut Knife party first learned of the fall of Batoche on 17 May at the east end of the Eagle Hills; news of Riel's surrender followed two days later.[62] Realizing that the resistance was in ruins, the Métis immediately left for home to ascertain the fate of family and friends. Several—including Delorme, Trottier, and Chicicum—would eventually flee to the United States and never stand trial for their rebellion activities. The Indians, on the other hand, found themselves stranded

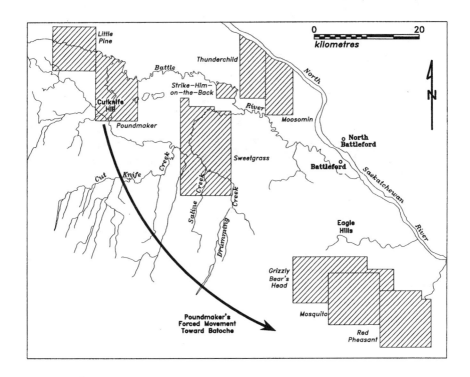

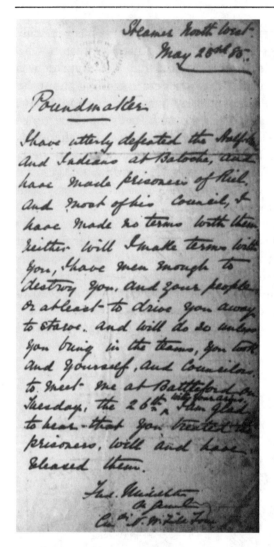

and turned to Poundma-
ker, the diplomat, to
reach a peace settlement
with Canadian authori-
ties. He responded by
asking farm instructor
Robert Jefferson, one of
the Métis's former pris-
oners, to prepare a letter
to Middleton, asking for
terms of surrender.[63]

The general, fresh
from his defeat of Riel,
was in no mood to be gen-
erous. "I have enough
men to destroy you and
your people or, at least,
to drive you away to
starve," he threatened,
"and will do so unless you
bring in . . . yourself and
Councillors, with your
arms, to meet me at
Battleford on Monday, the 26th."[64] It was not the kind of response
that made it easy for the Indians to head back. But Poundmaker knew
it was useless to flee or try to fight and encouraged his followers to
think of the young people and their future. "I would prefer to
surrender myself at the risk of being hanged rather than to shed
streams of blood by a resistance which has no more reason to be."[65]

On the morning of 26 May, exactly two months after the Duck
Lake skirmish, Poundmaker proudly led his people into Battleford
under a white flag of truce. After surrendering their weapons at
Middleton's insistence as proof of their unconditional submission,

the chief and warrior society leaders gathered in a large semicircle at the feet of the general, who looked down upon them imperiously from his chair. The meeting started badly for the Indians. When Poundmaker came forward to exchange greetings, the general waved him away, stating through his interpreter that he did not shake hands with rebels. Middleton then opened the discussions by accusing the Indians of "pilfering like rats." Poundmaker replied, "I felt that I had a rope about my neck and something drawing me all the time."[66] He then tried to explain that the young men wanted to fight and that he had little influence over them, especially with the Métis in their camp. He also insisted that he had not promised to help Riel and that the Indians were simply defending themselves when they were attacked at Cut Knife—"my people made war gently."[67] Middleton, however, dismissed his statements as lies, telling him at one point, "You have been on the warpath since the troubles began . . . committed murders and kept the country in alarm."[68] Tatwaseen (or Breaking-Through-the-Ice) then asked that his mother be allowed to speak on behalf of the women and children. When Middleton curtly replied that women did not address war councils, Poundmaker wondered

On the morning of 26 May 1885, Poundmaker (seated centre) proudly led his people into Battleford and surrendered to General Middleton. *National Archives of Canada C2769*

aloud why the Queen, the Great Mother, always presided at their supreme councils. This response brought an approving shout from the Indians and even sent a ripple of laughter through the officers and men when it was translated.[69] The meeting came to a close when one of Poundmaker's headmen asked how they were to make a living that summer. Standing for extra emphasis, Middleton told the Indians that the government would take care of them if they behaved themselves and returned to their reserves, but that all would suffer if there was any more trouble. He also announced that Poundmaker was to be taken into custody and that the men who had committed the murders in the Battleford vicinity would have to give themselves up. Itka and Waywahnitch came forward and surrendered to the general. As they were being led away with Poundmaker, an Assiniboine woman cried out, "The Almighty sees; our children and country have been taken."[70]

Father Louis Cochin, who had been held captive by the Métis in the Cut Knife camp for over a month, could not understand why Middleton had treated Poundmaker so contemptuously, especially when the Cree chief had done everything within his power to counsel

Poundmaker (centre) was taken into custody for his apparent role in the looting of Battleford and the Cut Knife battle. *National Archives of Canada C4593*

restraint and avoid any entanglement with Riel. "Poundmaker delivered himself up voluntarily," Cochin recalled in his reminiscences. "It was on the part of an Indian a generous act and heroic, more worthy of pardon and even of reward, than of prison and fetters."[71] The general, however, was simply a soldier who had been given the task of putting down the rebellion as quickly as possible. And in doing his job, he considered anyone appearing to assist Riel—whether it be Poundmaker, Whitecap, or One Arrow—to be the enemy. That the Indians took part in the battles at Fish Creek, Cut Knife, and Batoche seemed, to him, irrefutable proof of their duplicity.

Indian Affairs officials knew otherwise. In a letter to the prime minister on 7 May, two days before the siege of Batoche, Edgar Dewdney revealed that several bands had been compelled to join Riel under threat of death and that the warrior society, not Poundmaker, controlled the Cut Knife camp. But instead of communicating this information to Middleton, Dewdney decided the Indians should "have a good lesson before any olive branch is held out to them,"[72] and he did nothing to protect them from the wrath of Canadian troops, let alone refute the idea that the Indians and Métis were acting in concert. He preferred to let the North-West Field Force "thrash" any Indians implicated in the troubles, believing that it would "make them anxious to . . . get back to their Reserves." And with the defeat of Riel and surrender of Poundmaker, the recalcitrant Big Bear was next.

chapter nine

Too Many Scared People

I F THERE WAS A SINGLE ACT that best served to implicate the Indians in the Métis rebellion, it was the Frog Lake murders. Coming within days of the Duck Lake clash, the nine tragic deaths not only suggested that Big Bear looked to Louis Riel for leadership, but that the Cree were wild, ruthless savages who would do anything as their part of the alliance. What happened that spring in the North Saskatchewan country, however, was an isolated, spontaneous incident perpetrated by men spurred to action by hunger, frustration, and alcohol. Wandering Spirit and his warriors had no sooner taken Fort Pitt when they faced the vexing question of what to do next. They realized that Canadian authorities would likely send a punitive force to deal with them. They also knew that Louis Riel wanted them to help capture Battleford and then come to the defence of Batoche. But instead of preparing to meet the Canadian military response or moving east to join the Métis, the Indians simply waited in the Fort Pitt area—much like their counterparts at Cut Knife had done. They did not want to fight. Nor were they willing to surrender. They therefore tried to remain aloof while the rebellion ran its course. And when they were forced to engage the Canadian army in late May and early June, they did so in self-defence, then retreated. It was a curious way to fight a war. If anything, the Indians' behaviour during the spring of 1885 confirmed that they were not part of Riel's rebellion.

When Wandering Spirit's party returned to Frog Lake with the Fort Pitt prisoners on 19 April 1885, he and his soldiers seemed undisputed masters of the region. They had not only rid themselves of the bull-headed Indian agent who always said no, but forced the equally hated mounted police to flee for their lives. They had also gained access to food and provisions that had been deliberately withheld from them as part of the government's policy of subjugation. And they had gathered together a following that probably numbered around one thousand people.[1] It was all fondly reminiscent of the days before treaty. The only thing missing was the great buffalo herds.

The situation in the Frog Lake camp, though, was anything but settled. Wandering Spirit may have shoved Big Bear and his diplomatic initiative aside at the start of April, but the Frog Lake slayings shocked many band members, and they continued to follow the war chief out of a sense of crisis and not necessarily in support of his actions. Something terrible had happened—albeit accidentally—and they looked to the soldier society to protect them from further trouble. Tensions also continued between the Plains Cree and their woodland counterparts, many of whom had decided to move to the Frog Lake camp because they feared possible reprisals at the hands of Wandering Spirit's warriors.[2] Others, such as a group of Chipewyan families and the priest from St. Raphael's mission at Cold Lake, were forced to join in late April when they were reportedly told that a marauding band of mixed-bloods was "scouring the woods in order to ... massacre all who refused to turn out."[3] When the Chipewyans learned they had fallen into a trap, they were forcibly prevented from leaving the camp, even though they offered a team of oxen and several head of cattle to buy their freedom.

The behind-the-scene activities of Big Bear and the prisoners versus those of Riel's agents also divided the camp. Even though the old Cree chief was no longer in control of his band and never openly challenged Wandering Spirit, he was deeply worried about the consequences of the warriors' actions and worked quietly to prevent an escalation of the troubles.[4] Several of the captives, in particular the two Bay traders, William McLean and James Simpson, did much the same thing by privately counselling the Woods Cree to avoid any

Big Bear's son, Imasees, contradicted his father at every opportunity and eventually assumed leadership of the band. *National Archives of Canada PA27861*

involvement with the rebellion.[5] André Nault and Abraham Montour, on the other hand, actively promoted the idea that the Cree and the Métis faced a common foe and were constantly prodding the camp leaders to go to Riel's aid; they had a definite agenda and were determined to carry it out, even if it meant distorting the truth. A letter that Montour sent to the Lac la Biche area in mid-April, for example, was apparently riddled with false claims and exaggerations about the Métis cause and what had transpired since the start of the troubles.[6]

These various forces and strains within the Frog Lake camp made any concerted action difficult, such as moving east to unite with Riel's army. It is extremely doubtful, though, whether Wandering Spirit and his supporters had made any plans beyond the capture of Fort Pitt and the rounding up of nearby bands. What they had done so far was largely reactive—starting when Indian Agent Quinn had repeatedly refused to obey the war chief; it was not part of a coordinated plan with the Métis. Once the threat to their safety had been removed with the retreat of the mounted police down river, they decided to wait peacefully at Frog Lake to see how the rebellion would unfold. They spent the last two weeks of April feasting, dancing, gaming, and visiting in the camp.[7]

These activities did little to ease the underlying current of fear and apprehension. While many of the individuals and families who had been taken prisoner enjoyed a kind of loose custody once their reliability had been determined and even carried weapons to help hunt for food, they knew that any escape attempt threatened the lives of all the captives. The Woods Cree faced a similar situation. They could not resist the temptation of helping themselves to the plunder of the past two weeks, but also realized that any attempt to leave the camp would incur the wrath of the warriors. This sense of uneasiness was perhaps best exemplified when Paskayak, an old, sickly woman in a delirious state, threatened to turn into a flesh-eating cannibal—a wetiko—and had to be clubbed, beheaded, and burned in order to protect the camp.[8] It was a bad omen.

The situation to the west and north was little better. As news of the Frog Lake murders swept westward towards Edmonton, members of the Blue Quill and Little Hunter bands broke into the government storehouse at Saddle Lake on 3 April.[9] This impromptu raid was the only incident of its kind at the time, but because it came on the heels of the massacre, white residents saw it as the beginning of the rebellion in the district. Settlers along the North Saskatchewan,

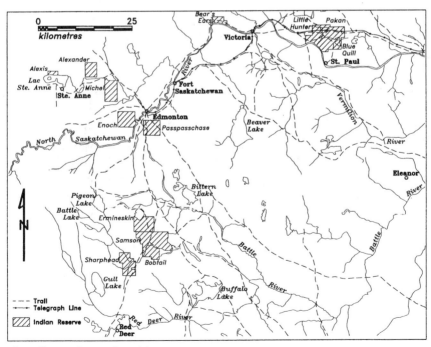

The Alberta district (north).

between Frog Lake and the foothills, sought refuge in the nearby forest or fled to Fort Edmonton. Even people who interacted with the local bands on a regular basis, such as HBC men Harrison Young of Lac la Biche and Peter Erasmus of Whitefish, abandoned their posts and headed for the safety of Edmonton.

This behaviour both confused and alarmed the Indians. They had done nothing wrong, yet people were deserting the area as if the Métis rebellion was rapidly gaining the upper hand. When Wandering Spirit's messengers subsequently visited the area and threatened the Beaver Lake band unless it joined the Frog Lake camp, the local Indians took advantage of the traders' absence and raided the two abandoned posts on 26 April.[10] Chief Pakan of the Whitefish Lake reserve, however, would not be bullied. Even though the chief had constantly complained about his reserve allotment size and had even visited Indian Commissioner Edgar Dewdney in Regina to complain about the matter in 1884, he ignored an initial warning from Big Bear to join the Frog Lake camp or flee the area and advised his followers to remain loyal. This determination to avoid any entanglement with the Plains Cree eventually led to bloodshed, when one of Wandering Spirit's emissaries was shot dead during a tense confrontation on Pakan's reserve. Fearing retribution from the Frog Lake camp, Pakan and his followers had little choice under the circumstances but to join those already hiding in the bush.[11]

There was also minor trouble to the northeast at Green Lake, a major Hudson's Bay Company trans-shipment depot. When J.N. Sinclair, the clerk in charge of the post, learned about the Duck Lake fight on 15 April, he immediately began to cache whatever arms and provisions he could along the lakeshore to hide them from the rebels. This was no small chore, since the warehouse contained all the supplies for the northern posts. Sinclair and his assistants were still busy moving goods when about thirty Indians from the Island Lake and Waterhen bands, apparently led by Kahpeeschoose (Cut Hand), arrived on the morning of 26 April. Sinclair tried to defuse the situation by offering food and ammunition, but the Cree, already excited by the news from Fort Pitt, rushed into the store when he unlocked the door. Throughout the incident, none of the Bay employees were harmed; they were allowed to depart safely that same day for Île à la Crosse, leaving the Indians to help themselves to the holdings of the abandoned depot before joining the Frog Lake camp. Nor were they alone in their looting. Solomon Vennes, a Métis from

Batoche and an independent trader in the region, was seen with the Cree party the day of the raid and was later found in possession of HBC goods. Whether he was working for Riel is not clear, but a Métis emissary was reportedly working among the local bands.[12] What was also significant is that the raiders were acting on their own—without the authority of their leaders. A number of the Island Lake Indians, moreover, had not entered the Fort Pitt treaty, and some who had, under different chiefs, had not collected their annuity payments for several years.[13]

Collectively, these events did not make for an Indian uprising. But their occurrence—largely in response to developments in the Fort Pitt area—suggested the rebellion had the potential to sweep across the North-West to the Rockies like a wind-whipped prairie fire.[14] This is what settlers throughout the district of Alberta had feared since the beginning of the troubles, especially given the size of the local Indian population. Two days after word of the Frog Lake murders and Saddle Lake raid reached Edmonton, the crown timber agent sent a despondent letter to his superiors about the sense of impending doom that gripped the town—made worse by a downed telegraph line. "We do not know the hour the Indians in our midst will rise," he wrote on 9 April, "and if they do, God only knows the consequences . . . without outside assistance, [we] will be at the Indians' mercy."[15] Little did he realize that the Indians on the surrounding reserves were equally distressed by the news. The overreaction of the white population only made things worse.

Such was the case on the Bears' Hills reserves (present-day Hobbema), where four Cree bands (Samson, Ermineskin, Bobtail, Muddy Bull) and one Assiniboine (Sharphead) were concentrated near the Battle River, some fifty miles south of Edmonton. Within days of the Frog Lake killings, a courier galloped "at steeplechase speed" through the area on his way to Calgary; he stopped long enough to announce that all the bands to the northeast had joined Riel and that Edmonton was about to be attacked. This alarming news, according to Father Constantine Scollen, who had spent more than thirty years in the North-West, greatly excited the Indians, "but the climax of all was to see the Whites running for their lives," including Samuel Lucas, the local Indian agent. "Just imagine the consternation of the Indians when witnessing all this commotion," he related to a fellow priest on 20 April. "The Indians were amazed and frightened. They thought the Whites had received letters bearing terrible news and were hiding the real state of affairs from them . . . that the days of the Whiteman were at last numbered in the N–W."[16] At a special council meeting, the chiefs and headmen called for peace, but several of the young men ignored them and raided the abandoned HBC store at Battle Crossing and some empty homes on 11 April. They were acting out of desperation. Thomas Taylor, the local HBC clerk, testified a year later at the Rebellion Claims Commission hearings that the looters believed that Fort Edmonton had fallen and that they would be without supplies unless they seized the local goods. He also reported that they left untouched the abandoned store of the rival American trader, because the United States was reportedly supporting Riel's movement.[17]

The Bears' Hills commotion lasted little more than a day. It ended at an emotionally charged council meeting the next night, when Bobtail broke up a war dance, and Ermineskin, who was married to Poundmaker's sister, convinced the young men to return their booty.[18] After that, everything was quiet in the region. In fact, Lucas's new problem was to convince the Muddy Bull and Sharphead bands, who had fled in fear to the Battle Lake area, to return to their reserves. When they had first heard of the troubles, they asked the local Methodist minister at Wolf Creek mission to prepare a letter to Indian Commissioner Dewdney on 10 April, in which they promised "to have nothing to do with the insurgents and . . . remain loyal till death."[19] Unfortunately, these kinds of pledges, like those made by Indian leaders elsewhere, were discounted by Edmonton residents, who desperately hoped their "worst fears may be averted by the arrival of troops."[20]

The situation in southern Alberta, meanwhile, bordered on mass hysteria. The news of the mounted police routing at Duck Lake sent shockwaves through the region—farms and ranches were abandoned overnight, and home guards sprang up in the larger communities. What the settlers dreaded were the five thousand Indians who made up the Blackfoot confederacy (the Blood, Blackfoot, Peigan, Sarcee, and Stoney) joining their Cree cousins to the north and fighting alongside Riel's forces. They were not alone in their thinking. "Fear you must expect outbreak," an agitated NWMP Superintendent John Cotton cabled Ottawa from Fort Macleod on 4 April. "I have lived too long among Indians not to know there is mischief brewing."[21] What he and others should have known, however, is that the Blackfoot and Cree were traditional enemies and that many Blackfoot, in particular

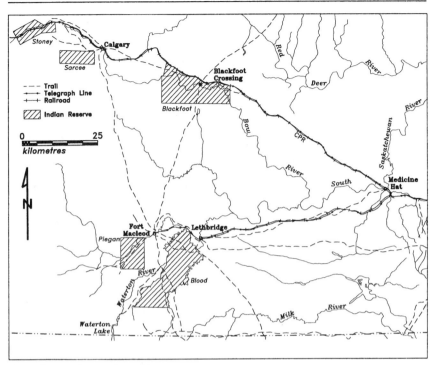

The Alberta district (south).

Red Crow, the Blood chief, would sooner serve the government side.[22] The Blackfoot, furthermore, had been decimated by the twin scourges of hunger and disease and could muster no more than six hundred men of all ages.[23] They would have been hard pressed to defend their own territory, let alone wipe out Calgary. The government had also sent the chiefs to Regina and Winnipeg the previous summer in order to impress upon them the strength and power of white civilization in the event of any future trouble; they realized that it was better to remain loyal to their treaty commitments and extract concessions from the Canadian government.[24]

Commissioner Dewdney, for his part, believed that the cooperation of the Treaty Seven Indians was essential if Ottawa hoped to confine the unrest to the Saskatchewan country. He therefore lost little time in approving the lavish distribution of previously scarce rations. He also placed Cecil Denny, a former mountie and Indian agent, in charge of government dealings with the southern Alberta tribes, on the understanding that he was to keep the Indians peaceful at any cost.[25] His most publicized move, though, was arranging through Father Albert Lacombe to meet with the Blackfoot tribe at Gleichen on 11 April. The council, in Chief Crowfoot's words, "was all good—not one bad word." In exchange for Dewdney's promise of protection and food, the Blackfoot chief affirmed his allegiance—a pledge he repeated in a special telegram to the prime minister. "Should any Indians come to us and ask us to join them in war," Crowfoot told Macdonald, "we will send them away. I have sent messengers to the Bloods and Peigans . . . to tell them . . . what we intend to do about the trouble . . . We will remain loyal to the Queen whatever happens."[26] This assurance should have relaxed tensions in the region, particularly since it enjoyed wide broadcast. But the white population continued to be haunted by the spectre of an Indian revolt. "There are too many scared people in the country," an exasperated Denny complained to Dewdney almost three weeks after the Gleichen meeting.[27] These scared people included the Indians, who could not understand the settlers' fears. If anyone should feel threatened, it was the Blackfoot. When Superintendent Cotton, special agent Denny, and a small police force visited the Blood reserve—unannounced—in early April, it so unnerved the Indians that it took several meetings and the issuing of extra rations before they calmed down.[28]

Clearly, Ottawa had nothing to fear from the Treaty Seven Indians or from the reserves around Edmonton. But during the first two weeks of the hostilities, when it seemed that Big Bear would side with Riel and was prepared to influence other bands to join him, General Middleton decided on 9 April to send a separate military column north from Calgary to subdue the Cree chief. The man named to head the Alberta Field Force was Thomas Bland Strange, a retired British army officer who had founded the Military Colonization Ranch east of Calgary in 1882. Three days after the Duck Lake disaster, the minister of the Militia had asked Major-General Strange, or "Gunner Jingo" as he liked to style himself, whether he could raise a corps for the defence of southern Alberta.[29] Now, the veteran had been given the job of "over-awing the Indians in the district"[30] by marching north from Calgary to Edmonton and then along the North Saskatchewan to Big Bear's lair. It was a curious appointment— Strange was an eccentric and had nothing but utter disdain for Indians. The last thing the Canadian government needed was someone to aggravate an already strained situation. Yet Strange was known to be "very bitter" towards his Indian neighbours.[31] "With all savages,"

The eccentric Thomas Bland Strange was given the job of putting down any Indian unrest in Alberta and subdividing Big Bear's band. *Glenbow Archives NA-1353-16*

he would later remark in his autobiography, "leniency has no meaning but cowardice."[32] His appointment as commander of the Alberta column proved a serious mistake, and it was not long before Denny was complaining about the general's rash behaviour. He had ordered the men guarding his ranch, for example, to shoot any Indian *on sight!*[33]

On 20 April, Strange started for Edmonton, heading a force that eventually numbered around one thousand men, including a small party of mounted police scouts under Inspector Sam Steele. They expected the worst. The first reports from Frog Lake suggested that Mrs. Gowanlock had been murdered trying to protect her husband, while Mrs. Delaney had been defiled by her captors. There were also unsubstantiated rumours that Fort Pitt had fallen and that the Indians along the North Saskatchewan were terrorizing the Edmonton region.[34] As a result, the men acted as if they were entering enemy territory as they worked their way north. And each mile that they put behind them only hardened their resolve. Nothing—least of all the mud-riddled trail—would prevent them from setting things right. "Our revenge must be a terrible one," a captain in the Winnipeg Light Infantry wrote a friend in Minnesota. "Pray for our being able to get the brutes within reach of our sniders. We ask no more."[35]

By the time Strange reached the Bears' Hills reserves on 29 April, the Indians were "comparatively quiet & very sorry for having been led astray."[36] They had returned the cattle stolen from the government farm, started to repair the damage from the looting, and even sown a few acres of wheat. The real test of their allegiance, however, occurred in mid-April when all but a restless few flatly rejected an invitation from four Cut Knife messengers to join the Métis insurgents. As Agent Lucas summed up the situation: "They are not guiltless but I think some credit is due them."[37] But General Strange was not in a forgiving mood and refused to shake hands with the chiefs, let alone acknowledge their remorse for what Father Scollen described as "a small trifle, a little stealing."[38] Instead, he sternly cautioned the Indians that any future unrest would be severely punished. He also banned the distribution of ammunition and stationed a small garrison at the local Hudson's Bay store and the agency farm. He also put on a display of force by marching his red-coated infantry, with fixed bayonets, through the reserves to the music of the column band.[39] Strange was endeavouring to assert the power of the Canadian government. But all he did was stir up an already unsettled situation. No sooner had the general pushed on to Edmonton than an anxious Lucas was complaining that the Indians were now "sullen and discontented," that several had gone into hiding because of the presence of the troops, and that those who remained behind had no desire to work. Not even the promise of extra rations eased their concerns.[40]

General Strange reached Edmonton on 1 May, a week after the Fish Creek skirmish and a day before the Cut Knife battle. Although the general's advance scouts had encountered not a hint of trouble in the area, he was greeted in Edmonton like a liberating hero—much like Otter had been treated at Battleford. The occupants of the fort had lived in terror for most of the past three weeks and believed that the timely arrival of the troops had saved the town from certain destruction at Indian hands. It did not seem to matter that their makeshift stockade was never tested or that the volunteers did not fire a single shot in defence. All they knew—or imagined in their panic— was that the surrounding countryside was awash with disloyal bands, and that the threat to Edmonton would not end until Strange had turned back the rebel tide.[41] This perception of what lay beyond Edmonton undoubtedly rubbed off on the general and made his mission to Frog Lake—to punish Big Bear and save the hostages— seem all the more critical. But by the time the column began its descent of the North Saskatchewan on 14 May, six weeks after the Frog Lake killings, any initial unrest among the local Indians had long since passed.[42] The only irritants were the almost constant rain and the leaky scows carrying half the force.[43]

Strange's approach from the west was the second crisis that the Frog Lake camp had faced in as many weeks. In late April, a letter had arrived from Norbert Delorme, Riel's firebrand in the Cut Knife camp, addressed to his brother-in-law John Pritchard, the local mixed-blood interpreter for the Indian department and one of Wandering Spirit's prisoners.[44] Claiming to speak on behalf of Chief Poundmaker and knowing that Métis agents were operating there to provide extra leverage, Delorme invited Big Bear to bring his men east, whereupon the two camps would take Fort Battleford and then move on to Batoche. To facilitate the union, Delorme promised cattle, horses, and carts.

The message precipitated the first serious division in the camp since the murders. Whereas Wandering Spirit, at the urging of Nault and Montour, was evidently prepared to accept the in-

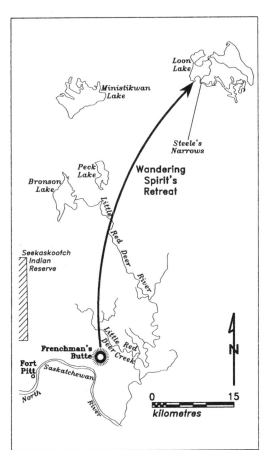

Frenchman's Butte and Loon Lake.

vitation, the Woods Cree were not only opposed to joining Poundmaker but wondered why the chief had not sent his own message.[45] The council remained deadlocked for two days until it was unanimously agreed to send couriers to Cut Knife to report on the situation there.[46]

These men returned from the Battleford district on the evening of 4 May. The news they brought was not good. The two Woods Cree couriers had arrived in the area just in time to witness Colonel Otter's attack on the Cut Knife camp. Although they did not stay to watch the outcome, they saw that both soldiers and mounted police were involved in the battle and that they were armed with powerful weapons. This information momentarily stunned the camp, and for the first time since being removed as chief, Big Bear publicly chided the warriors. "You have heard the report brought to you by the couriers . . . what are you going to do about it?" he asked the following morning. "You were in a hurry to commence trouble, and now you have it. The soldiers of the Queen have come to fight you and very shortly you will have to show how you can fight them."[47] Instead of taking any decisive action, however, the camp leaders remained stalemated and could agree only to head towards Fort Pitt and wait to hear from Poundmaker. Because of the sheer numbers involved, this move took several days, and it was not until 15 May, the day after Strange started from Edmonton, that the camp was reestablished about two miles from the fort on the east bank of Pipestone Creek. From here, the Indians scavenged Pitt for whatever had been missed a month earlier and, in one of their few acts of defiance, set fire to the buildings that had housed the police.[48]

The camp's next move—or lack of one—affirmed the Indians' passive intentions. For the past six weeks, the perpetrators of one of the most bloody acts during the rebellion had remained peacefully in the area, uncertain what to do or where to go. It had not been an easy wait. Throughout the period, Riel's agents had continually urged the Plains warriors to make for Batoche and help the Métis cause. They now faced a second, equally demanding challenge, when messengers from Saddle Lake reported that redcoats had arrived in the Edmonton area. True supporters of the rebellion would have either answered Riel's call or made battle preparations—or even run away, as many of the Métis fighters would do following the collapse of Riel's regime. But all they did was send out another pair of couriers—one from each camp faction—to ascertain Poundmaker's fate. When these men returned with news that the Cut Knife camp had been deserted,

Little Poplar and about thirty Plains warriors, weary of waiting, tried to coerce their woodland brothers into going directly to Riel's aid. Their posturing and taunting almost led to a fight and ultimately left the camp no closer to Batoche.[49]

Half Blackfoot Chief, a member of Big Bear's band, tried to heal this growing rift between the Plains and Woods Cree by vowing to hold a thirst dance at the base of a nearby kame, known locally as Frenchman's Butte. Undertaken for renewal and thanksgiving, the ceremony was a major commitment for both the sponsor and the camp, and as such, underlined the Indians' search for direction and guidance in a time of great crisis; it did not mean, as some commentators have suggested, that the Indians were making warriors.[50] But the sacred lodge, with its ritually felled rafters and centre pole, had no sooner been erected, when scouts interrupted the celebrants to announce that they had spotted soldiers at Fort Pitt.[51] The troops' arrival—coming on 26 May, the same day Poundmaker was surrendering at Battleford—threw the camp into turmoil. Not only were the Indians unprepared for a fight, but the curtailment of the thirst dance signified pending misfortune.[52] Above all, the moment of decision had finally arrived. After some bickering over what to do with the hostages—whether to abandon them or bring them along—Wandering Spirit ordered the camp to head north to a more defensible position along the valley of Red Deer Creek.[53]

That evening, Maymenook, a Saddle Lake Indian, and about a dozen warriors went on a horse-stealing raid to Fort Pitt. Steele's Scouts intercepted them, and in the ensuing exchange, Maymenook was shot dead and his body grossly mutilated, apparently in retribution for the horrifying remains the troops had found at Frog Lake.[54] The skirmishing continued the next day, as small parties of warriors attempted to check the advance of Strange and his men as they headed north from Fort Pitt. The rest of the camp, meanwhile, readied for an attack and spent the day digging two lines of pits on the north side of the creek valley: the first row along the crest of the ridge for the fighters, and the second in a shallow depression behind the hogback for the protection of all noncombatants.[55] These rearguard trenches were quite large, often able to hold several families, and still dominate the landscape today. It is obvious from an examination of the Indian position that they were determined to safeguard their women and children, as well as the prisoners.

The Battle of Frenchman's Butte, as it was incorrectly named at the time,[56] started on the morning of Thursday 28 May, when Strange shelled the north side of the valley with a few rounds from his cannon and then ordered his men forward. As the troops poured down the southern face of the ravine, they came under heavy fire from the concealed pits on the other side, and discovered to their chagrin that muskeg lined the creek bottom. Wandering Spirit had chosen his position well. Strange abandoned a frontal assault and countered by sending Steele's men to probe the eastern flank, but once again they faced a yawning swamp-filled stretch between them and the Indians. The general was reduced to using his nine-pounder in an attempt to inflict whatever damage he could.[57] Once the gunners found the correct range, they pounded two pits in quick succession, mortally wounding Kahweechatwaymat, who had taken part in the Frog Lake murders;[58] he suffered a slow, agonizing death. By this point, some three hours after the battle began, both sides expected the other to attack and decided to withdraw to safer ground. Strange believed the Cree occupied "an impregnable position"[59] and was not prepared, in his words, "to commit Custer."[60] He would later be criticized for letting Big Bear slip through his fingers.[61] The Indians fought bravely

The Battle of Frenchman's Butte was a draw—in large part because of the defensive position that the Indians occupied along the north side of the Red Deer Creek valley. *Glenbow Archives P1390-4*

under the inspired leadership of Wandering Spirit and Little Poplar, but their ancient firearms were no match for the destructive power of the "gun that speaks twice,"[62] and they withdrew in the face of the punishing bombardment.[63]

General Strange declared his first engagement with the Indians a draw—an assessment widely repeated ever since. But in digging entrenchments along the north side of Red Deer Creek, the Cree were simply trying to defend themselves and avoid capture. It was not their intention to fight, let alone rout Strange's force. They were merely trying to keep the troops at bay. In a sense, then, Frenchman's Butte was a victory for the Cree, but a hollow one. Although the Indian defenders held their ground for most of the morning, they were thoroughly shaken by the intensity of the assault and decided to pull away, rather than face the troops again. It had been a harrowing experience—one they did not want to repeat.[64]

The engagement also prompted the camp to break into its constituent bands. The Chipewyans from Cold Lake and some of the Woods Cree slipped away in the early morning fog before Strange launched his offensive. They were followed by small groups of prisoners, including many of the Frog Lake survivors, who took advantage of the commotion caused by the shelling to escape.[65] The battle also further tarnished Big Bear's reputation—even though the former chief was some two miles behind the trenches, with women and children, during the actual fighting. Several of the hostages later testified that Big Bear had no voice in matters—his harangue was an isolated act—and that his son, Imasees, deliberately contradicted him at every turn.[66] This shift in leadership was not known, or understood, by government and military officials. All they knew was that Big Bear's band was at the heart of the troubles in the Pitt area and that the old man bore ultimate responsibility for any rebellion crimes. As one of the most influential Indian leaders of the past few years, he must surely have had a direct hand in the events that spring.

The remaining Indians fled north that same day, trying to put as much distance as possible between themselves and the troops. It was an arduous trek. To discourage pursuit, Wandering Spirit deliberately avoided trails and waterways.[67] And, in their scramble to get away, they had abandoned most of their horses and carts, provisions, and tents at the battle site. Perhaps most disheartening, though, was that they had become fugitives in their own land—unable to go home and unsure of what the future held. The Cree found temporary

Sam Steele of the mounted police and a small force surprised the retreating Indians at Loon Lake. *Provincial Archives of Alberta B1968*

refuge near the Horse Lakes, where they rested for two days while warriors slipped back to the trenches to retrieve some belongings. The discovery that Strange had also withdrawn provided some comfort, but the mood among the refugees remained bleak; there were also fewer of them, as small groups of hostages, Indians, and mixed-bloods, including Riel's agents, continued to wander off into the dense forest. A false alarm had the camp on the move again. For the next few days, they tramped through a steady, at times heavy, rain until they reached the southwest corner of the western basin of Loon or Makwa Lake—cold and soaked—on 2 June. Any hope of safe haven was dashed the next morning when an advance party under Inspector Steele attacked the Indians and the remaining prisoners.

The skirmish at Steele's Narrows, or Rat Foot Hill as it was known locally, marked the last battle of the rebellion. It was comparable to the Cut Knife battle almost a month earlier. On 1 June, Steele and a force of about sixty policemen and soldiers had returned to the Red Deer Valley to reconnoitre the area and try to pick up Big Bear's trail. Convinced that the Indians were on the run, they set off late that night through the woods at a gruelling pace and covered the fifty miles to Loon Lake by mid-morning on 3 June. Here, they found the Cree camped on both sides of the narrows and swooped down on them—guns blazing—much like Colonel Otter had done at Cut Knife. The Indians repelled the attack as best they could, but those stranded on the same side of the narrows as Steele bore the brunt of the firefight.[68]

When the shooting stopped, after about half an hour, five warriors lay dead, including Chief Seekaskootch, one of the Woods Cree leaders who had acted as a counterbalance to the more aggressive Plains Cree. The toll could have been much higher, for several Indians and hostages, including the children of HBC factor William McLean, were fording the narrows when Steele's party arrived and narrowly missed being hit during the engagement. Big Bear, for his part, had expected the worst and placed his powerful bear-claw necklace around his neck for protection.[69]

Following the battle, Steele withdrew a short distance and waited for reinforcements. The Cree used the opportunity to flee up the western shore of the lake to the north end (or "island" that separates the two lake basins), where they sombrely buried their dead.[70] The Indians were tired, starving, and despondent. But like hunted animals, they had to keep moving to avoid the reach of the soldiers, who

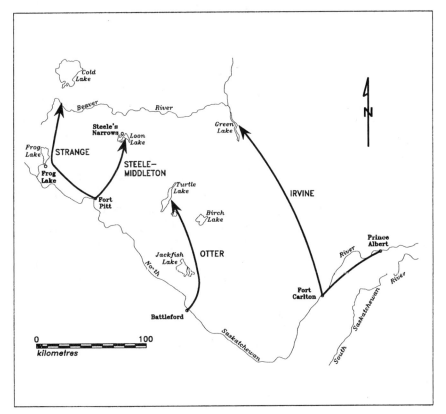

The pursuit of Big Bear.

Two Cree women who surrendered at Battleford in early July 1885. *Ontario Archives ACC16462-62 and ACC16462-61*

they believed would soon be after them. They pushed on across the swift-flowing channel that separated the two lake basins and then plunged into a muskeg that was still frozen in places, yet deep enough to mire several of their oxen. The wading of the "big swamp," as Kitty McLean called it,[71] was an act of desperation—a fact driven home by the suicide of Sitting in the Doorway, an old crippled woman who had lost the will to go on and hung herself under a big tree along the north shore of the lake.[72] It also accelerated the breakup of the camp, and within a few days the two groups finally separated after two months together as unhappy bedfellows; the Plains Cree headed east and then south in the direction of Battleford, while the Woods Cree continued north towards the Beaver River. There was also a change of leadership. Wandering Spirit apparently decided it was safer to travel with the woodland people and the remaining hostages.[73] His defection meant that Imasees assumed leadership of his father's band.

The flight of the Indians kept the Canadian troops busy for most of June. With the capture of Riel and surrender of Poundmaker, General Middleton was determined to apprehend Big Bear and bring the campaign to a successful conclusion, even if it meant tying up his troops for several weeks in a seemingly futile chase. He decided to move upriver from Battleford at the end of May with about four hundred cavalry and infantry and had been at Fort Pitt for only a day when a courier arrived with news of the Loon Lake skirmish—the first reports suggested that Steele's men had killed fifteen Indians.[74] Confident that the Cree could be overtaken, the general hurriedly joined the pursuit with a large mounted force and two gatling guns. He also ordered three other columns north in an effort to snare the wily old chief if he tried to escape south: Commissioner Irvine of the NWMP would march from Prince Albert to Green Lake; Colonel Otter from Battleford to Turtle Lake; and General Strange from Frog Lake to Cold Lake. But the largest manhunt in Canadian history came up empty-handed. As one of the Otter brigade members sarcastically confided to his diary on 12 June: "tramped up hill and down hill but no BB [Big Bear]."[75]

Middleton reached Loon Lake five days after the engagement, but after inspecting the wide expanse of muskeg that lay ahead of him, he elected to return to Pitt. Several of his men saw this decision as nothing less than an ignominious retreat, especially after they had expended so much energy just to get there.[76] Indian Affairs officials were equally critical of the Canadian army's failure to run down the Cree and complained privately to Edgar Dewdney that Middleton's plodding pace had allowed Big Bear to slip from his grasp. "I think more could have been done if time had been the essence of movement," Hayter Reed summed up the last few disappointing weeks of the campaign,

One of the fugitive Indians (possibly Four Sky Thunder) who surrendered at Battleford instead of fleeing to the United States. *Ontario Archives ACC16462-66*

When Big Bear surrendered at Carlton on 4 July 1885, he had been reduced to a shell of his former self, and his strategy for dealing with the Canadian government lay in total ruin. *Saskatchewan Archives Board R–A8812*

"but it was not, so the Indians escaped."[77] Middleton, who had earlier vowed to follow Big Bear "as long as I am able to,"[78] justified his return to Fort Pitt by reasoning "he must come back sooner or later or starve."[79] When he did, his men would be ready for him. He also took some solace in the reports from the escaped prisoners that none of the women had suffered any indignities. "It is a great relief to have this good news," he confided to the minister of the Militia, "and only shows what infamous lies are concocted in this North-West."[80]

Two weeks after the Loon Lake skirmish, the fugitive Indians could hold out no longer. On 18 June, Chief Keehewin dispatched William McLean, his family, and the last few prisoners with a peace offering to General Middleton. The Woods Cree sought assurances that they would not face arrest as rebels if they surrendered, and asked to deal directly with the general and not a government official.

"It was the people the Government sent to deal with us," Keehewin had told McLean, "that has been the cause of you and us being in such great trouble now."[81] The Plains Cree also decided that they could not wander in the northern wilderness for much longer, and at a council meeting on 25 June, Imasees announced his intention to seek asylum in the United States; several of the warriors joined him, including Little Poplar.[82] The rest of the band decided to give themselves up and either wandered into the nearest settlement or turned themselves over to one of the military columns looking for them. These defections meant that Big Bear—by then, the most wanted man in the North-West—was effectively abandoned. By the time he gave himself up to authorities near Fort Carlton on 4 July, he had been reduced to a shell of his former self, and his strategy for dealing with the Canadian government lay in total ruin.

Big Bear's surrender is often cited as the end of the North-West Rebellion, and with it, the collapse of the Indian-Métis alliance. This interpretation is entirely at odds with events in the Fort Pitt area. Not only had Big Bear been pushed aside by more aggressive members of his band, but when he did speak out, his was a voice of restraint. The Frog Lake camp had remained peacefully in the area for several weeks, not wanting to get involved in the troubles; the leaders looked upon Riel's overtures with caution, if not suspicion, and fought the Canadian troops only in self-defence. The Indian Affairs department had maliciously chosen to see the Cree as rebels, as Riel's rough-and-ready accomplices, perpetrators of one of the most brutal acts of the rebellion. Once it became clear that General Middleton held the upper hand in the campaign and began mopping up the remaining trouble spots, Hayter Reed joined him at Battleford as his private advisor. In fact, the assistant Indian commissioner was in the Loon Lake area when the last of the Frog Lake prisoners were released. Reed would play a crucial role in deciding the Indians' fate in the months ahead. Writing to Dewdney from Fort Pitt on 23 June, he described the Plains Cree as the "leading demons" during the rebellion and recommended that the government "not . . . feed them an ounce until next spring."[83] Even harsher measures would follow. "One of the great faults of our [military] leaders," Reed counselled Dewdney in the same letter, "is that they do not understand the Indian character, and do not know when he is defeated, and when to follow up an advantage." Reed thought he did. And he had the power to do something about it.

chapter ten

Stabbing the Queen in the Behind

W HEN LOUIS RIEL chose open rebellion over negotiation, he derailed the diplomatic offensive that had consumed the lives of Big Bear, Little Pine, and other Cree leaders since being evicted from the Cypress Hills. Not only did the grand council, scheduled for the summer of 1885 at Duck Lake, not take place, but several prominent chiefs were accused of being willing allies of the Métis. In fact, the First Nations had never been more vulnerable in their relations with Ottawa as they were in the months following the fighting. Canadian authorities keenly appreciated that Riel's activities had handed them a club, and they were determined to use it to beat into the ground—once and forever—all remaining vestiges of Indian autonomy. These actions, culminating in the mass execution of eight warriors in late November 1885, went beyond punishing Indians for their crimes and restoring the peaceful image of the western Canadian settlement frontier. Indian officials had been desperately searching for a way to destroy the treaty rights movement, which had gained unprecedented momentum during the summer and fall of 1884, and used the Indians' apparent involvement in the rebellion to pursue a public and private campaign against the First Nations. Over fifty

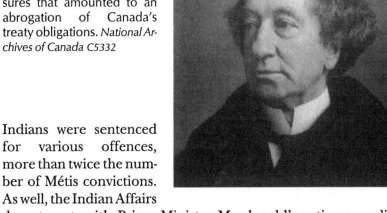

Prime Minister Macdonald, the most senior Indian official in the country, privately endorsed a number of measures that amounted to an abrogation of Canada's treaty obligations. *National Archives of Canada C5332*

Indians were sentenced for various offences, more than twice the number of Métis convictions. As well, the Indian Affairs department, with Prime Minister Macdonald's active compliance, privately contemplated a number of restrictive measures that amounted to an abrogation of Canada's treaty obligations. It was as if the Indians, and not Riel and his followers, were the culprits. And Ottawa was determined to see that they were never led astray again.

The six weeks following the fall of Batoche and the surrender of Riel were largely anticlimactic. Although the Canadian military expended considerable energy trying to track down Big Bear in the muskeg-riddled forest north of Fort Pitt, the other Indian leaders who had evidently been embroiled in the rebellion turned themselves over to Canadian authorities as instructed. Beardy, One Arrow, and Whitecap all reported to General Middleton after the capture of Métis headquarters, while Poundmaker led his camp into Battleford, once his Métis captors had abandoned him southeast of the Eagle Hills. In the early summer, even Big Bear and Wandering Spirit eventually surrendered—once they were no longer being pursued in earnest. Middleton would take credit for the chiefs' submissive behaviour, convinced that the Indians knew better than to tangle with his force, especially after its drubbing of the Métis army. He travelled triumphantly up and down the North Saskatchewan by steamer in late May and June, overseeing the surrender of various bands like some liberating hero who would make the country safe again.

The Indians' cooperation, however, had less to do with Middleton's victory at Batoche than their belief that they were the true victims of Riel's intrigues and that they had done little, if

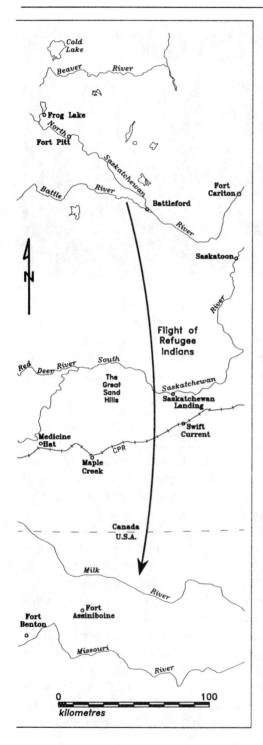

Flight of Refugee Indians

anything, wrong that spring. Most had tried to avoid the conflict or worked actively to prevent an escalation of the unrest. Others had been forced to participate under compulsion or fought in self-defence. Once the hostilities had ended, then, the bands who had been displaced for one reason or another wandered into the nearest community, hungry and exhausted, but relieved that the troubles had passed. They were anxious to return to some semblance of normalcy, and many gladly returned to their reserves and immediately started to work their fields and gardens.[1] Despite Commissioner Edgar Dewdney's initial concerns following Poundmaker's surrender,[2] very few Indians fled to the United States on the heels of Riel's agents. The exceptions were Imasees, Little Poplar, and Lucky Man, and their extended families, who slipped around Battleford and then headed due south to Montana, following a route almost parallel to Saskatchewan's present-day number four highway. Their flight went undetected, apart from the momentary alarm raised by the accidental shooting of a man who refused to give up his boat so that the refugees could cross the South Saskatchewan River.[3]

Dewdney was well aware that the majority of Indians had remained aloof from the Métis during the rebellion, while only a few bands were driven to the rebel side by a mixture of force and lies. In a long, reflective letter to Prime Minister Macdonald in early June 1885, with Big Bear still on the run, Canada's most senior official in the West laid the blame for much of the death and destruction over the past few weeks on the pernicious activities of Riel and his emissaries. He also severely criticized the behaviour of those settlers who had abandoned their homes in panic and confusion, and in doing so, created the false impression that the insurgents were carrying the day. "That they [the Cree] ever thought, intended or wished that the uprising should have reached the proportion it has," he emphatically told Sir John, "I do not believe."[4]

But Dewdney's understanding of the Indian situation had its limits. In the same letter, he advised the prime minister that the "break[ing] loose" of a few bands had turned "a Half-breed revolt of small magnitude into an uprising of large dimensions." According to the commissioner, the country had come perilously close to "an Indian war from one end of the Territories to the other." Dewdney realized that this assessment of the gravity of the situation was totally unrealistic and dangerously misleading. Nor was he sympathetic to the bands that had been tampered with and were innocent of any misconduct. Why should he be? Watching the conflict unfold from the territorial capital, Dewdney saw in the rebellion an unprecedented opportunity to rid himself and the Canadian government of troublesome Indian leaders and their nagging call for revision of the treaties. Though privately he knew better, it was to his advantage to portray the Indians as reckless allies of Riel who would cause trouble in the future unless reined in.[5]

Dewdney's campaign against the Indians began to take shape in mid-June. He sent three letters to the prime minister in the space of seven days. In them, he reported that Agent Ansdell Macrae had found several incriminating notes that Riel had sent the Cree in the Battleford district, including the one calling on them to destroy the fort.[6] He also urged Lawrence Vankoughnet, the deputy superintendent general of Indian Affairs, to withhold annuity payments from the Indians until he could determine who had "participated in anyway whatever in the late rebellion"[7]—the money could be used to replace livestock, farm equipment, and any other government property that had been lost or destroyed. He even went so far as to suggest the breaking up of several reserves. "Some bands have violated the terms of the treaty made with them," Dewdney concluded, "and . . . it will be for the govt to say what will be done with them and their reserves."

This tough talk found a receptive audience in Ottawa, and on 3 July, the day before the surrender of Big Bear, Dewdney was instructed to "quietly collect evidence" against all Indians suspected of any wrongdoing, no matter how trivial.[8] Local agents and farm instructors had already been doing this, for they looked upon the troubles as a chance to strengthen their own hand over their charges, as well as extract a measure of revenge against recalcitrant chiefs and individuals. In the Battleford district, for example, Macrae had been visiting the outlying reserves since late May, collecting evidence and lining up witnesses for the expected trials of those who had been at Cut Knife.[9] To the south, meanwhile, in the Qu'Appelle district, Treaty Four Agent Allan McDonald was demanding that the File Hills chiefs and headmen be deposed for allowing the slaughter of twenty head of cattle on the four reserves. His earlier concern for the bands' welfare, especially when the Canadian troops had first arrived in the region, had given way to intense anger and suspicion, and he wanted General Middleton to deal with them as he had with the disloyal Indians in the Saskatchewan country. There was no room in his heart for leniency; the guilty parties had to be harshly punished. "Action of this kind will settle all difficulties in the future," McDonald implored, "an example . . . must be made."[10] Dewdney agreed, and at a Regina hearing in early July, two of the File Hills chiefs, Peepeekisis and Star Blanket, were reprimanded for being off their reserve.[11] It was just the beginning.

Hayter Reed, Dewdney's ambitious assistant, was given the job of determining the loyalty of the bands. Reed had been in the field since late March, spending almost two months hunkered down in Prince Albert with Mounted Police Commissioner Irvine before proceeding westward to Battleford and then on to Pitt with Middleton's entourage; he was there when HBC trader William McLean and his family, the last of Wandering Spirit's hostages, ambled out of the bush north of Loon Lake in mid-June. This experience hardened Reed's resolve— if that was possible—and he returned to Regina convinced that only a program of repression against the First Nations would set things right.[12] He was personally offended by the Indians' conduct. How dare they cast off the government hand that fed them. He also believed that they enjoyed far too much freedom and that drastic measures were necessary in order to squeeze every last savage ounce out of them. As a result, Reed tackled the job of determining who had been unfaithful with a vicious enthusiasm; all agents were called upon to submit a summary report for each band, emphasizing any transgressions.[13] He also started work on a list of recommendations for future management of the Indians that would ultimately shape and inform his career as Dewdney's successor. The Canadian military had had their crack at subduing the Cree, now it was Reed's turn.

While this private campaign against the Indians took shape, preparations were also underway for a series of trials in Regina. The first and most famous trial—both then and now—was that of Louis Riel, who appeared in a Regina courtroom on 20 July charged with committing high treason. Guided by the hand of God, Riel had surrendered to Middleton three days after the fall of Batoche in the naive hope that he could use his trial as a platform for his cause. Although his lawyers claimed that their client was insane, the Métis leader's eloquent closing address to the jury was not that of a madman. He was found guilty and sentenced to death.[14]

The mass exodus of lawyers, journalists, and other interested parties from Regina following Riel's prosecution did not mean that

The trial of Louis Riel. Following his conviction for high treason in late July 1885, there was a mass exodus of lawyers and journalists from Regina. The first of several Indian trials started two weeks later. *National Archives of Canada C1877*

the court docket was empty. Another 129 people were being held on rebellion-related charges: eighty-one Indians, forty-six Métis, and two whites. These arrests and detentions were part of the Macdonald administration's strategy to divert attention from its mishandling of western affairs; primitive Native peoples, not government mismanagement, had spawned the recent unrest.[15] This interpretation dovetailed nicely with the needs of the Indian Affairs department. If a large number of Indians were convicted as rebels, Dewdney and Reed would enjoy a relatively free hand in the future. That the majority of those charged were innocent was immaterial.

Much has been written about the fairness of Riel's trial and whether justice was served. The Indian trials, in comparison, were a travesty. The First Nations defendants were unfamiliar with the court system and its procedures, and as a consequence, failed to challenge testimony, free themselves from self-incrimination, or appeal verdicts. They also understood little, if any, English and often did not know what was being said or argued, especially since the court translator was used sparingly.[16] Above all, the Indians stood before the court alone. Only a handful of the accused had legal counsel. Nor did they have the benefit of political pressure as exerted by francophone members of Parliament and the Roman Catholic clergy on the Métis's behalf. It did not help that the juries were composed of white, Protestant settlers, the same people who had lived in fear of an Indian attack during the rebellion. The Canadian courts imposed a system of determining guilt and assigning punishment that was unfamiliar to the Indians. It began with the difficulty of translating the charge of treason-felony: "feloniously and wickedly did conspire, consult, confederate, assemble, and meet together with divers other evil-disposed persons . . . to raise, make and levy insurrection and rebellion against our said Lady the Queen within this realm."[17]

The first indication that the Indian defendants were to be treated differently occurred at Battleford in mid-May. Inspector Francis Dickens, as senior NWMP officer, presided over a series of preliminary hearings to decide whether those Métis being held in detention at the fort should proceed to trial. No such hearings were held for the Indian prisoners.[18] Apparently, the Conservative government was also ready to proceed without providing any legal representation for the Indians until Sandford Fleming, the former CPR engineer-in-chief, raised the matter with Vankoughnet in mid-June. Prime Minister Macdonald, in turn, sought the advice of his attorney general, who

A triumphant Middleton poses in a buckskin outfit in an Ottawa photo studio. *National Archives of Canada PA27155*

believed that it would be "eminently fair" to provide Poundmaker and the other wards of the Crown with a lawyer from western Canada.[19] This defence counsel was not expected to make any difference to the outcome of the trials. On 5 July, deputy minister of Justice George Burbidge, who had travelled to Regina to handle personally the case against Riel, wired Ottawa that Manitoba's Stony Mountain Penitentiary should be enlarged to accommodate all the new prisoners.[20] The prime minister also interfered in the judicial process when he instructed Burbidge in early August to indict those Indians who had been involved in the Frog Lake killings with murder, instead of treason-felony, even though there were clear parallels with the Métis defendants.[21] Treason-felony, a noncapital offence, was punishable by life imprisonment or a lesser term, whereas the murder charge meant an automatic death penalty. Macdonald was determined to make an example of the Indians and thereby guarantee the safety of western settlement, one of his cherished national policies. He regarded his Indian charges as an irrelevant, primitive people—to be eliminated as a separate race and remade into good Euro-Canadians. It was his administration's ultimate goal to "assimilate the Indian people in all respects with the inhabitants of the Dominion, as speedily as they are fit for change."[22]

The first major Indian trial was that of One Arrow, the Willow Cree chief who had been forced to go to Batoche after the declaration of Riel's provisional government. Beverly Robertson, an experienced Winnipeg lawyer who had been hired by the Crown counsel in mid-July, handled his defence. Robertson had to juggle his new duties with a busy private practice and did not arrive in Regina until a few days before One Arrow's 13 August trial. Things started badly. The elderly chief found the proceedings thoroughly confusing, even more so when the treason-felony indictment was translated as "knocking off the Queen's bonnet and stabbing her in the behind with the sword." There was no Cree equivalent for words such as conspiracy, traitor, or rebellion. "Are you drunk?" a perplexed One Arrow reportedly asked the court interpreter.[23]

The case against One Arrow rested on the contention that he had openly associated with the Métis at Batoche and thereby breached his treaty "allegiance to the Government, the country, and the Queen."[24] Not one prosecution witness was able to say, however, that the Willow Cree leader had actually fired a shot or was even directing his band at Duck Lake and Batoche. And when the government's star witness, surveyor John Astley, testified that he had seen One Arrow and Riel talking together, the defence pointed out that Astley did not understand a word of Cree. It did not matter though. One Arrow's mere presence in the rebel camp made him guilty. Besides, as Astley casually remarked, the chief had the reputation for being a "worthless hound" who was "more fond of loafing around than working."[25]

At the conclusion of the Crown's evidence, Robertson tried to have the charge withdrawn, maintaining "not a tittle of evidence"[26] had been produced to link One Arrow directly to the uprising. Failing that, he tried to counter the suggestion that the chief had been disloyal by appealing to the jury's prejudices. "An Indian has no notion of the nature of civilized society . . . no notion of the importance of maintaining law and order," he admonished the jury. "Let us show that we really are superior to the unhappy race to which he belongs."[27] But it was hopeless. "I cannot acquire his confidence," Robertson remarked candidly. "I don't know the Indians well enough, and I have not been able to get anyone to assist me." He continued, "The most that I can do is to sit here and watch the case made by the Crown, appeal to you to consider it leniently, and to bear in mind the difficulties of this poor man's position."[28]

The six-man jury required only a few minutes to return with a verdict of guilty, and One Arrow was remanded for sentencing late the next afternoon. At this point, the real story behind the band's presence at Batoche began to emerge. When asked by Judge Hugh Richardson whether he had anything to say, an overwrought One Arrow tried to explain through the court interpreter that he could not have taken up arms or painted his face because he had just lost a grandchild. He also claimed that his fighting days were long past and that he would never break his treaty pledge. "All that was said against me was thrown upon me falsely," he asserted. "I was taken to the place, Batoche's, to join Riel by Gabriel [Dumont]. I did not take myself to the place. They took me there . . . I know that I have done nothing wrong, I can't see where I have done anything wrong against anybody so I beg of you to let me go, to let me go free."[29] Sadly, there was no one to corroborate One Arrow's account, and his plea sounded like a last-minute fabrication to save himself. Certainly, the judge was unmoved, and in keeping with the jury's recommendation that no mercy be shown, sentenced One Arrow to three years in the Manitoba penitentiary.

It was a harsh outcome, given the circumstances, but even more so when compared with the treatment of several of the Métis defendants. An hour before One Arrow learned his fate, Judge Richardson had passed sentence on twenty-six Métis soldiers who had been rounded up in the weeks after the rebellion. These men, mostly rank-and-file followers of Riel, had first come before the court as a group on 4 August. Although all had pleaded guilty to treason-felony

Once Riel's trial ended, the remaining Métis prisoners, shown here, were dealt with collectively by the Crown. *Saskatchewan Archives Board R-D121*

at the time, the prosecution requested that sentencing be delayed until the judge had had an opportunity to consider the particular circumstances of each individual case; the Crown argued that the prisoners had been "led away by evil counsels."[30]

When the court convened for sentencing on 14 August, no less than thirty affidavits had been secured by the defence—many sworn out by leading local citizens—attesting that the Métis defendants were a poor, ignorant lot who were not responsible for their actions. Father Alexis André, who had verbally wrangled with Riel, for example, declared that, except for a few hard-nosed disciples who had fled the country, "not one of the other half-breeds had the least idea or suspicion that there was any probability or danger of rebellion."[31] HBC clerk Lawrence Clarke also made a lengthy, emotional appeal on behalf of the group immediately prior to their sentencing, in which he argued that the prisoners did not even understand the nature of the charge against them. "We are not dealing with cultivated intellect," Clarke told the judge. "We are dealing with wild men of the territories . . . who were in the habit from early days . . . to follow a leader in the territories, to follow a leader in the buffalo hunt, to follow a leader wherever they went . . . and they looked up to that leader as their hope."[32] Judge Richardson then read his decision, sentencing eleven men to seven years, three to four years, and four to one year. He discharged the remaining eight on the understanding that the court might recall them at a later date. They joined another four men who had been released in early August. Adolphus Nolin, who had been at Frog Lake and Cut Knife, was one of these men. Apparently, the Métis could be excused for being, in Clarke's words, "the creatures of circumstances,"[33] whereas One Arrow could not.

Poundmaker's trial followed three days later. Ottawa was determined to proceed with the prosecution, even though Dewdney had known since mid-May, some two weeks before his surrender, that Poundmaker had no control over the Assiniboine warriors and that the Cut Knife camp was divided into war and peace factions.[34] The Indian commissioner was also aware that Crowfoot, the influential Blackfoot chief, felt great distress at his adopted son's arrest and was anxious about his fate. Nothing, not even the truth, however, would deter Ottawa from proceeding with its plan to decapitate the Cree political movement. Almost a year and a half earlier, in February 1884, Dewdney had complained to the prime minister that Poundmaker was "a leader in mischief" and how he sought "freedom from the wiles

Judge Hugh Richardson (right) shaking hands with Peter Hourie, the court interpreter for the Indian trials. *Saskatchewan Archives Board R–B1401*

of this cunning individual." He had added, "If any trouble arises, on his head will rest much of the guilt."[35] The Macdonald government now believed it had more than enough evidence to remove Poundmaker from the scene and thereby rob the Battleford bands of their leadership.

The Crown's case against Poundmaker was seductively simple—he was Riel's ally. In his opening statement to the jury, prosecutor David Scott maintained that Poundmaker had not only conspired with the Métis leader, but had actually levied war on three distinct occasions: the month-long siege of Fort Battleford, the engagement with Colonel Otter's force at Cut Knife, and the capture of the government supply train southeast of the Eagle Hills. The most damning piece of evidence, though, was Poundmaker's name on the letter of support that Joseph Jobin carried to Riel at Batoche.[36] So confident was the prosecution of its case that Scott claimed that the more serious charge of treason could have easily been proven.[37]

Testimony over the course of the two-day trial revealed there was a reasonable, alternative explanation for the behaviour of Poundmaker and his followers. When Scott tried to prove that the band had deserted its reserve in the wake of the Duck Lake battle and planned to sack Battleford, one of the prosecution's own witnesses had to admit under cross-examination that the Indians regularly performed begging dances for the townspeople and that none of these visits had resulted in vandalism, let alone violence.[38] And when Scott tried to evoke sympathy for the hundreds of frightened people who had taken refuge within the stockade walls, both Peter Ballendine and William McKay were forced to divulge under oath that they had heard from a messenger that the Indians were coming to Battleford to see Indian Agent Rae.[39] Robertson similarly dissected the Crown's version of the other two instances of Poundmaker's war activities, while at the same time eliciting names and descriptions of the otherwise shadowy Métis agents who had been specifically dispatched to the region to bring the local bands to Riel's side. The most controversial part of the trial came when farm instructor Robert Jefferson asserted that Poundmaker willingly agreed to have his name placed on the letter of support to Riel. Under intense questioning by Robertson about the matter, Jefferson first expressed confusion, then reported that he could not remember, and finally confessed that he could be mistaken. It was also pathetically clear during his testimony that he feared for his life in the Cut Knife camp and did what the Métis leaders told him to do without asking questions.[40]

In his address to the jury, Robertson continued to hammer away at the idea of an alternative version of events in the Battleford area, claiming that "Poundmaker's influence, such as it was, was always exercised in the interests of peace and humanity—always, but there was a stronger influence here, an influence that he could not countervail, the influence of those half-breeds with the Stonys [sic] at their back."[41] As in the One Arrow case, he also publicly questioned the fairness of trying an Indian in a white man's court. "I ask you to remember," Robertson pleaded with the jury, "that this poor man is an Indian, that although he is defended here, he is very imperfectly defended . . . if I had a white man to defend . . . it would be a very different thing."[42] The prosecution, in response, took direct aim at the suggestion that Poundmaker was "perfectly helpless"[43] and raised the question again and again—that if Poundmaker was so loyal, if he was truly a man of peace, why did he not surrender at either Battleford or Cut Knife? The jury agreed, and after a short deliberation, found him guilty.

Before being sentenced, Poundmaker was given the opportunity to address the court. "Everything that is bad that has been laid against me this summer," he replied through the interpreter,

there is nothing of it true . . . I did everything to stop bloodshed. If I had not done so there would have been plenty of blood spilled this summer . . . and now that I have done so . . . I will have to suffer for their sakes, that I have saved the lives of so many. So I shake hands, gentlemen, with the whole of you.[44]

Sadly, these efforts earned him a three-year prison term at Stony Mountain. It could have been much worse. Judge Richardson, himself a former resident of Battleford, suggested in his closing remarks that Poundmaker was fortunate because he could have been charged with treason and sentenced to death. The Cree chief did not see it that way. As he was hustled out of the courtroom, with the judge's sentence barely off his lips, Poundmaker shouted, "I would prefer to be hung than to be in that place."[45]

Poundmaker's conviction did little to appease Battleford. P.G. Laurie, of the *Saskatchewan Herald*, angrily denounced the trial as a "farce" and the sentence as "ridiculously short."[46] This same bitterness coloured an editorial some three weeks later, in which Laurie suggested that Poundmaker had received "what is the Indians' highest ambition to attain—plenty to eat and nothing to do . . . He said he preferred death to imprisonment, and it is a pity he was not accommodated."[47] The Toronto-based *The Week* saw the trial in an entirely different light. After reviewing a summary of the key testimony, "Lex" concluded that the Crown's case was "very weak and inconclusive."[48] In particular, the columnist noted that Poundmaker was actually on his reserve while camped at Cut Knife and that it was the Canadian military that attacked the Indians. "Considering the whole case," Lex observed, "it is very doubtful whether there has not been a great injustice done to a man who was our friend throughout . . . and yet this man is condemned as a felon to imprisonment for three years, and because he is an Indian not a voice is raised to say one word for him."[49] Defence lawyer Beverly Robertson could not have agreed more. But the sentiments expressed in the article were no substitute for reality, a reality that seemed to have no place for compassion and understanding of the Indian situation. And it did not take much reflection for Robertson to realize, especially after the demoralizing outcome of the One Arrow and Poundmaker trials, that his efforts were futile and that it was just a matter of going through the motions as quickly as possible. He consequently wrote the Crown counsel upon his return to Winnipeg and instructed them to "be ready to try a considerable number of Indians in rapid succession the next time I come up to Regina and let me know at least a few days beforehand

Defendants Big Bear (seated second from left) and Poundmaker (seated far right) photographed during their Regina trials. Beverly Robertson (right rear), a Winnipeg lawyer, was hired by the government to provide legal counsel for the Indians. *Saskatchewan Archives Board R-A2146*

what overt acts are charged against them respectively."[50]

The next series of Regina trials got underway in mid-September. Big Bear first appeared before Judge Richardson on 3 September, but because Robertson had still not returned from Winnipeg, the judge postponed the trial for eight days. The delay took its toll. Held in custody for over two months, the elderly chief seemed initially lost in court and had to be reminded at the start of proceedings that he was charged with treason-felony. According to surviving prosecution documents, the Crown considered the case against Big Bear to be weak.[51] In fact, in his opening remarks, Scott suggested that he might not be able to show that Big Bear was in charge of his band or that he had played a part in the Frog Lake killings. As in the trial of One Arrow, however, the prosecution was content to base its case on guilt through association. "You must understand," Scott lectured the jury, "that if he were acting with these parties at that time in open rebellion against the Government of the country . . . then . . . he was in open rebellion against the Government of the country and ought to be punished."[52] Ironically, the case against Big Bear might have been dismissed on a technicality, if Robertson had properly prepared for his defence. The formal indictment gave the wrong date for the siege of Fort Pitt—an error that was repeated several times by the Crown.[53]

The trial itself confirmed that Big Bear, like Poundmaker, had done everything within his power to promote peace. The image that emerged from the testimony was that the Cree chief was anything but a rebel: he tried to stop the slaughter at Frog Lake, he arranged for the emergency evacuation of Fort Pitt, he was several miles behind the lines at Frenchman's Butte, and he kept a protective eye on Wandering Spirit's prisoners. Unfortunately, such evidence, no matter how favourable, could not counteract his reputation as a troublesome leader whose band had committed one of the vilest acts in Canadian history. This was glaringly apparent during the hearing, when defence witness and former hostage Henry Halpin reported that Stanley Simpson, another prisoner, had confronted him in private, for agreeing to appear on Big Bear's behalf. "He thought it was strange, very strange, any white man should get on the defence of an Indian," Halpin told the court. "His idea was that Indians should have been hung."[54]

In his address to the jury, Robertson tried a different tack from the two earlier trials and argued that Big Bear was obliged to remain with his band even though he disagreed with the warriors' actions. He could not simply leave, especially during a time of crisis, when the war chief had assumed leadership. This explanation of Indian behaviour was barely understood, much less believed, by the jury. They preferred the prosecution interpretation that it was Big Bear's duty "not to be found in the rebel camp, but to be found where law and order prevailed."[55] And in keeping with past decisions, they found the elderly chief guilty after only a few minutes' deliberation—but this time recommended mercy. This verdict set the stage for Big Bear's last and perhaps finest speech as leader of the Plains Cree. Returning to court two weeks later to be formally sentenced, he used the occasion to protest his innocence and at the same time make a special plea on behalf of his people. "I think I should have something to say about the occurrences which brought me here in chains," he began.

I knew little of the killing at Frog Lake beyond hearing the shots fired. When any wrong was brewing I did my best to stop it in the beginning. The turbulent ones of the band got beyond my control and shed the blood of those I would have protected . . . When the white men were few in the country I gave them the hand of brotherhood. I am sorry so few are here who can witness for my friendly acts. Can anyone stand out and say that I ordered the death of a priest or an agent? You think I encouraged my people to take part in the trouble. I did not. I advised against it . . . I look around this room and see it crowded with faces far handsomer than my own. (Laughter) I have ruled my country for a long time. Now I am in chains and will be sent to prison . . . At present I am dead to my people. Many of my band are hiding in the woods, paralysed with terror. Cannot this court send them a pardon? My own children!—perhaps they are starving and outcast, too, afraid to appear in the light of day. If the government does not come to help them before the winter sets in, my band will surely perish. But I have too much confidence in the Great Grandmother to fear that starvation will be allowed to overtake my people . . . I am old and ugly, but I have tried to do good. Pity the children of my tribe! Pity the old and helpless of my people! I speak with a single tongue; and because Big Bear has always been the friend of the white man, send out and pardon and give them help! How! Aquisanee—I have spoken![56]

A profound silence followed his last word, only to be shattered by Judge Richardson and the pounding of his gavel—three years at Stony Mountain Penitentiary.

The next pair of trials was something of a farce. On 16 September, nine members of Big Bear's band, who had been arrested near Fort Carlton, were tried for treason-felony. This was not the first time that the court had dealt with more than one defendant, but because of the difficulty in pronouncing the Cree names, the men were each assigned a number. In the resulting chaos, the lawyers and witnesses were never sure if they were talking about the same person.[57] Robertson, meanwhile, did not bother to mount a defence; he called no witnesses and declined to make a closing statement. In the end, all nine were found guilty and sentenced to two years. An almost identical scene took place the next day—this time for five Indians, one from One Arrow and four from Whitecap. Once again, the defendants were given numbers, and even though there were fewer of them, the trial was equally confusing, since the two bands had arrived at Batoche at different times. Judge Richardson had no problem keeping things straight and sentenced four of the men to three years for being in the rebel camp; the fifth, The Hole, a member of Whitecap's band, received only six months. These sentences were consistent with the punishment of the three chiefs. But what was curious, if not revealing, is how André Nault and Abraham Montour, two of Riel's agents, had been treated in the same courtroom only days earlier. Charged with treason-felony for their part in events at Frog Lake and Frenchman's Butte, the pair had their hearing postponed because of the absence of witnesses; the case would later be silently dropped.[58]

The last Regina trial was that of Whitecap, the Dakota chief who had been conscripted by the Métis in early April. General Middleton had detained and interrogated Whitecap after the fall of Batoche, but released him upon hearing his story. Once the government's lawyers discovered that the chief had been a member of Riel's governing council, however, the mounted police took him into custody until his trial for treason-felony on 18 September.[59] Whitecap's situation was identical to that of One Arrow; he had been present at Métis headquarters and was, according to the Crown, little better than the rebels themselves—especially since he was the only Indian member of Riel's governing council. But unlike One Arrow's hearing, Robertson had a white witness, the Dakota-speaking Gerald Willoughby of Saskatoon, who verified that Whitecap and his band had been

An Indian begging dance during the Regina trials. *National Archives of Canada* C7524

kidnapped by a large Métis force and that the citizens of Saskatoon were helpless to stop it. And whereas One Arrow had been character-ized as a worthless hound, Willoughby described Whitecap as a loyal Indian who was always a welcome guest in homes throughout the district.[60]

This kind of testimony was hard to refute. In fact, according to the surviving department of Justice notes about the trial, prosecutor Scott had scribbled, "coercion of half breeds," on one of the pages.[61] Robertson, by this time, had become cynical of the process and began his address to the jury with a stinging attack on the objectivity of the court. "Since the conviction of Big Bear," he observed sarcastically, "I have felt that it is almost a hopeless task to obtain from a jury in Regina a fair consideration of the case of an Indian. It has seemed to me it is only necessary to say in this town to a jury, there is an Indian, and we will put him in the dock to convict him."[62] A frustrated Robertson also took issue with Judge Richardson's interpretation of the law and twice interrupted his instructions to the jury. He did not need to worry, though; the jury returned within fifteen minutes with a verdict of not guilty. Richardson, who normally lectured the ac-cused before passing sentence, seemed surprised by the acquittal and pronounced simply, "[Y]ou are now a free man again."[63]

The Macdonald government had planned to hold all the rebellion trials in Regina. But once it weighed the costs of transporting all the prisoners and witnesses to the territorial capital, it decided that it would be more expedient to schedule the last set of hearings in Battleford, where some sixty Indians were in custody by early Au-gust.[64] This change of venue made a mockery of the remaining trials. Still smarting from the so-called siege, Battleford residents expected—even demanded—the severest possible punishment.[65] And Judge Charles Rouleau was called upon to dispense this crude justice. It was an unfortunate twist of fate. A year earlier, Hayter Reed had privately criticized Rouleau for giving Kahweechatwaymat, the warrior who had assaulted John Craig during the Poundmaker thirst dance, a one-week sentence. "Rouleau has been but a short time in the country," a disappointed Reed had written Dewdney, "and not . . . yet grasped the Indian question."[66] But events in Battleford that spring had remedied this "shortcoming." Not only had Rouleau fled to Swift Current fearing for his life, but his home, including his valued collection of legal books, had been destroyed by fire just before the arrival of Otter's column. And when he resumed his duties at

Judge Charles Rouleau, who had fled Battleford in late March 1885, seemed to believe that no punishment was too severe for the Indians. *Saskatchewan Archives Board R-B3762*

Battleford, it was with a kind of blinkered vengeance. Protesting that General Middleton had been far too kind, he bluntly told Dewdney, "It is high time . . . Indians should be taught a severe lesson."[67] He would be the one to do so, especially since he doubled as judge and jury at most of the trials and the defendants were without legal counsel.

The first prisoner, led in irons into criminal court on the morning of 22 September, was Wandering Spirit, described by the *Saskatchewan Herald* as "one of the greatest murderers that ever walked on two legs in America."[68] He was lucky to be alive. Shortly after his surrender at Fort Pitt, Big Bear's war chief had tried to commit suicide by plunging a knife into his chest, puncturing his left lung.[69] Over the next two months, while he recuperated slowly in the Battleford gaol, Wandering Spirit seems to have resigned himself to his fate—even allowing himself to be baptised and given a Christian name.[70] His much-anticipated appearance for murdering Agent Quinn proved anticlimactic. As soon as the indictment had been entered and translated, the man whose very stare had struck terror in hearts quietly pleaded guilty. It was over in a matter of minutes. So too were the hearings for Itka and Man Without Blood, the Assiniboine warriors accused of killing farm instructor James Payne and farmer Barney Tremont, respectively. Brought before Rouleau on 5 October, they both pleaded guilty and were sentenced to join Wandering Spirit on the scaffold on 27 November.

The other murder trials were just as speedy—even when the defendants pleaded not guilty. There was no attempt to understand why or how the slayings had occurred; it was simply a matter of assigning guilt and doling out the punishment. On 1 October, for example, Round the Sky elected to be tried by Rouleau for killing Father Fafard at Frog Lake. Three other Cree who were there that fateful morning testified that the defendant had delivered the coup de grâce. After Round the Sky had heard the evidence against him, he declined to cross-examine the witnesses, claiming instead that they had told the truth.[71] Rouleau then promptly sentenced him to hang. Bad Arrow and Miserable Man were treated the same way two days later, when they too refused to challenge the Crown's witnesses. Nor did a lack of evidence act as a deterrent to the judge's decisions. On 9 October, Little Bear was convicted of the murder of George Dill, even though he claimed that he had intentionally missed his target; he had been seen riding after the trader on his horse and firing in his direction.[72] In all, eleven Indians were condemned to death in a two-and-a-half-week period.

Rouleau's treatment of the other Indian prisoners, especially those from Big Bear's band, was equally ruthless. He seemed to believe that no punishment was too severe for the Cree—even if the length of sentence contradicted standard practice. The Idol, one of

Miserable Man (third from right) had turned himself in at Battleford in the hope that the white man's justice system would deal leniently with him; he was sentenced to death. *National Archives of Canada C17374*

Lucky Man's councillors, received six years for stealing an Indian department horse, while God's Otter, who had a mare from Fort Pitt in his possession, was given four. Three of the men who had placed their names on the Cut Knife letter to Riel, meanwhile, were sentenced to two years. It did not matter that several witnesses reported that the letter was composed at the insistence of Riel's emissaries.[73] Rouleau's harshest punishment, however, was reserved for those who had committed arson, reflecting the personal outrage that he and others had felt about the burning of Battleford. On 24 September, Four Sky Thunder, who had decided not to flee to the United States with Imasees, was sentenced to an incredible fourteen years for torching the Roman Catholic church at Frog Lake. Toussaint Calling Bull and Little Wolf were somewhat more fortunate, receiving only ten years for setting fire to a government building and stable, respectively. One can only wonder how Poundmaker, Big Bear, One Arrow, and the other Indian defendants might have fared if all of the trials had been held at Battleford.

By the fall of 1885, then, the Macdonald government had made great advances in its campaign to subdue the Plains Cree. Choosing to ignore repeated Indian protestations of loyalty—not to mention numerous acts of allegiance—Ottawa deliberately portrayed the rebellion as the work of the Métis traitor Riel and his brutal Indian henchmen. They were common allies in an evil cause, rebels who had to be punished—not only for bringing the Saskatchewan country to the brink of a full-scale war, but for breaking their treaty promises and turning against the very government that sustained them. Ottawa's response was swift and methodical. While Indian Affairs officials secretly gathered information on the conduct of western bands in preparation for the imposition of new repressive policies, the courts were used to intimidate the Indian population in one of the most shameful episodes of Canadian legal history. Not only were influential leaders, such as Poundmaker and Big Bear, imprisoned for crimes they did not commit, but scores of other Indians received unusually severe sentences with little justification except for their race. It was as if Ottawa had declared war on the First Nations—a war it was determined to win, whatever the cost. As he was about to be led away in chains, Big Bear eloquently summed up the sorry situation of his people. "I always thought it paid to do all the good I could. Now my heart is on the ground."[74]

chapter eleven

Snaring Rabbits

W HEN LOUIS RIEL dropped to his death—
some might argue, martyrdom—on 16 November 1885, most Canadians considered
it the final act in the North-West Rebellion. The Métis leader had
started the armed showdown with his declaration of a provisional
government at Batoche in the late spring, and it symbolically ended
with his hanging almost exactly eight months later. The popular
fascination with Riel and his fate, however, has not extended to the
eight warriors who were publicly executed at Battleford eleven days
later, or the dozens of other Indians, including three Cree chiefs, who
languished in prison. Nor did Ottawa's retribution stop there. In
order to bring the First Nations under its absolute control and
supposedly prevent another uprising, the Indian Affairs department
adopted a program of coercion and interference that negated the
spirit and purpose of the treaties. Centuries-old traditions and practices were to be stamped out in the interests of forced assimilation
and civilization. The department also took deliberate steps to ensure
its objectives by instituting a policy of rewards and punishments:
those bands and individuals considered loyal were recognized, while
those who supposedly had been unfaithful to the Crown were denied
annuity payments, and in a few cases, even their reserves. Sadly, this
government retribution—and the great suffering that accompanied

it—was wholly unjustified. The Indians had stood staunchly by the Queen during the rebellion, and yet in the aftermath, the Canadian government had treated them as outlaws in their own country. It was a betrayal of the worst kind.

The Macdonald administration's plan to subdue the Plains Cree, and in the process crush the treaty rights movement, was first given expression in early July 1885. While camped at Fort Pitt, awaiting the surrender of the Plains and Woods Cree, General Middleton issued a set of instructions to his soldiers regarding the treatment of incoming Indians.[1] Although Middleton had signed the orders, they were clearly the handiwork of Assistant Indian Commissioner Hayter Reed. Reed had accompanied the general to Pitt to be present when the fleeing Indians returned from the north and, more important, to see that the department's ideas were put in place.[2] Their intent was brutally clear—abject subordination. All guns, ammunition, horses, cattle, carts, wagons, harnesses, and even treaty medals were to be taken from the Cree. Shotguns, once branded on the stock, would be returned to the owners on the understanding that the guns were now the Queen's property and could be confiscated at any time; those Indians, meanwhile, who were found with a rifle or handgun in the future were "liable to be shot on sight."[3] All males, including chiefs and councillors, were also required to register, and their future movements made fully known. Finally, no rations were to be distributed, except to those willing to work for them. "[H]aving revolted," Reed coolly reasoned, "no doubt they have seen their way clear to earning a livelihood without aid from the Queen."[4]

Reed expanded upon these directives once he returned to Regina in anticipation of the upcoming trials. On 13 July, he submitted a draft memo to Commissioner Edgar Dewdney, in which he set forth fifteen hard-hitting recommendations for the "future management of Indians"[5]—not just those implicated in the rebellion. Dewdney evidently endorsed the document in principle, for he was given a longer, more palatable version one week later. No amount of editorial refining, however, could blunt the thrust of the proposals. Reed first zeroed in on the pending Indian trials and suggested that all who could be charged with a particular crime should "be dealt with in as severe a manner as the law will allow";[6] no one, especially prominent leaders, was to be exempt. He then recommended abolishing the existing tribal system and ousting rebel chiefs and councillors so that Indian Affairs employees could deal with band members on an individual basis. He also urged—on the grounds that the treaties had been "entirely abrogated by the rebellion"[7]—that annuity payments to rebel groups be suspended and that any future payments be seen as a gift, not a right. There would also be no more handouts. If Reed had his way, all Indians would have to work for any food and provisions not specified in the treaties. Nor would the disloyal be able to leave their reserves without first securing a permit from the local Indian department official; in fact, to ensure that they stayed put, horses were to be confiscated and sold for cattle and other necessities. "This action," in Reed's words, "would cripple them for future rebellious movements."[8]

Most of the other recommendations in the memo dealt with particular bands. Reed suggested, for example, that the One Arrow band be stripped of its reserve and amalgamated with Beardy's, while Big Bear's followers be broken up and scattered. He also encouraged the Macdonald government to recognize loyal bands, such as Ahtahkakoop and Mistawasis, by providing them with presents. His most bizarre and shocking proposal was recommendation eight: "The leaders of the Teton Sioux who fought against the troops should be hanged, and the rest sent out of the country."[9] Reed had confused Whitecap's band, who were Santee or Eastern Sioux, with the Teton Sioux from the Upper Missouri. It was an outstanding gaffe for someone in Reed's position and underscored his profound ignorance of the Indian situation. It also revealed how nasty Reed could be, especially since Whitecap's band had wanted no part in the rebellion.

Reed's recommendations constituted one of the most far-reaching initiatives in the history of Indian-government relations in Canada; they advocated an entirely new relationship with the First Nations—on the government's terms. Most disturbing, though, is that the proposals became, in effect, the working policy of the Indian Affairs department and its senior officers. Commissioner Dewdney found the measures "very desirable,"[10] and though he believed that some of the recommendations were unworkable or unrealistic, he was entirely sympathetic with the document's intent and was eager to see the ideas pursued. Nor was he alone in his thinking. There was no shortage of advice on how to handle the Indians. John Rae, the Battleford Indian agent who had refused to meet with Poundmaker, regarded leniency as a sign of weakness and proposed that any chief or headman who had been involved in the fighting be shot; otherwise, the government would be asking for more trouble in the future.[11] T.G. Jackson, a settler in the Fort Qu'Appelle district, warned that farmers would leave the region unless the military completely disarmed the Indians; only then, Jackson predicted, would there be a lasting peace.[12] Even the local clergy had suggestions. Drawing upon over thirty years experience in the North-West, mostly spent in present-day Alberta, Oblate priest Albert Lacombe put forward his own list of recommendations that were remarkably similar to the sentiments expressed in Reed's memo. He proposed that Indians be deprived of their arms and horses and be forced to stay on their reserves and work on their farms. "Consider the Indians in all and everywhere at least for many years as real minors," Lacombe remarked at one point, sounding much like Reed. "Consequently they are not at liberty and are under the tutelage of the Government."[13]

Dewdney submitted Reed's recommendations, along with his own brief, marginal comments, to the prime minister on 1 August, the day after Riel was sentenced to death. He told Macdonald, in a matter-of-fact style, that "considerable changes would seem necessary"[14] in light of the recent unrest. It was not until some three weeks later, however, that Ottawa came to appreciate the apparent magnitude of the Indian involvement, when Dewdney provided a table listing the behaviour of nearly eighty bands during the rebellion.[15] It was an extraordinary document—both in terms of the number of bands considered disloyal, and how Reed had determined the classification. The assessment was more a reflection of the author's attitude and agenda than of reality. He identified twenty-eight bands as rebellious—not surprisingly, the bulk of them in the Carlton, Battleford, and Pitt agencies. Curiously, he described Beardy's band as "all disloyal," yet the chief had not been arraigned on charges as had his Willow Cree neighbour, One Arrow. On the other hand, Reed designated the Dakota band at Moose Woods as loyal, even though Chief Whitecap was awaiting trial in the Regina gaol for treason-felony. Several other bands accused of disloyalty, moreover, had been reported absent during the fighting and hence in violation of Dewdney's 6 May proclamation that ordered all Indians to remain quietly on their reserves or be treated as rebels. That many of these bands had fled their homes in fear of the Canadian troops or come together for collective security as in the Frog Lake and File Hills areas did not enter into Reed's thinking. He was also prone to sweeping conclusions. Thunderchild and Sweetgrass, for example, were condemned simply because they were part of the Battleford agency and likely participants in the siege of the fort and the battle at Cut Knife. That their designation as disloyal was later reversed only confirmed the hastily contrived nature of the list.[16]

The Macdonald government used Reed's list to reward loyal individuals, particularly chiefs. Dewdney had promised during the troubles that any leader who kept his people peaceful would receive special recognition, and he was anxious to keep his word, especially since the trials of the Indian leaders were underway.[17] Ottawa agreed, and on 29 August, less than two weeks after Poundmaker's conviction, Lawrence Vankoughnet, the deputy superintendent general of Indian Affairs, instructed Dewdney to look into the benefits of granting the Blackfoot chiefs and other loyal leaders a special medal.[18] Reed, in the meantime, had returned to the North Saskatchewan country to restore order at the agency offices, as well as to investigate which individuals should be singled out for some kind of reward. It was evident from two letters he sent to Dewdney at the end of August that he could not resist implementing some of his measures, even though they were still under consideration in Ottawa. On 29 August, Reed reported from Battleford that he had taken away all the Indians' ponies and branded them department property and that the police were chasing away anyone in town without a pass. Two days later, he bragged that he had cut the ration list down to forty souls. Reed

Chief Thunderchild wearing the special medal that was presented to him for his allegiance during the rebellion. Hayter Reed initially identified his band as disloyal. *National Archives of Canada PA28839*

justified these steps as the department's only alternative in the wake of the troubles. "Now is the time to strain every nerve and be constantly on the jump," he wrote Dewdney, "so as to prevent these Indians reverting back into their old state."[19] In the same letter, though, he made it clear that the local bands "bow to the inevitable and it would take very much indeed to get them to rise again were it even within their power."[20]

Although there was no official response from the prime minister's office to the Reed recommendations by the end of the first series of Indian trials, the government was closely watching events in the West. On 3 September, almost three weeks before the Battleford trials were scheduled to get underway, Dewdney wired Macdonald that "any Indians sentenced to be hanged should be executed where tried. Object to hanging on reserves. Might lead to desertion of reserves. Indians very superstitious."[21] The prime minister immediately relayed this information to the governor general, Lord Lansdowne, who was somewhat intrigued by Dewdney's explanation but supported the recommendation. In the same letter, Lansdowne told Sir John that he was making a determined effort to refrain from commenting on the Riel case;[22] his sense of vice-regal detachment apparently did not apply to the Indian defendants who were yet to come to trial.

Reed, for his part, welcomed the idea of a public execution and asked Dewdney on 6 September to send to Battleford any Indians who were sentenced to death during the second series of Regina trials so that they could be executed at the same time. The assistant Indian commissioner insisted that "the punishment be public as I am desirous of having the Indians witness it—no sound thrashing having been given them I think a sight of this sort will cause them to meditate for many a day and besides have ocular demonstration of the fact."[23] He would get his wish.

Once the trials were over, Ottawa returned to the matter of how to recognize loyal Indians. By this point, the provision of rewards seemed to be aimed more at soothing Indian sensibilities in the aftermath of the trials and preventing a potential backlash. This certainly appeared to be the case with the Blackfoot. At Crowfoot's request, Poundmaker's hair was not cut in prison. The government also considered sending the Blackfoot chief to England to visit the Queen.[24] This treatment contrasted starkly with Ottawa's plans for the Cree.

In the aftermath of the Indian trials, Ottawa was worried about the reaction of the Blackfoot, in particular Chief Crowfoot. *National Archives of Canada C1871*

On 28 October, Prime Minister Macdonald, as the senior Indian official in the country, replied to the "management of Indians" recommendations through his assistant, Vankoughnet. The response was overwhelmingly positive, as seen by the prime minister's repeated notation, "approved," followed by his initials, on an earlier briefing document that Vankoughnet had prepared for his consideration.[25] Macdonald agreed that the tribal system should be abolished where possible, that annuity payments to rebel bands and individuals be suspended, that able-bodied Indians be required to work for any provisions, and that guns and horses be turned in on a voluntary basis. He also sanctioned the abolition of Big Bear's band, one of the largest Plains Cree groups at one time. Particularly revealing, however, were those instances where Macdonald, at Vankoughnet's urging, took Reed's suggestions one step further. For example, he directed Dewdney to treat any Indian who had been implicated in the troubles as a rebel, even if the courts had found otherwise. He also ordered, despite qualms about its legality, that the proposed pass system be applied as soon as possible to all Indians, including those who had been loyal.[26] This heavy-handed response was perhaps understandable, if not forgivable, had Macdonald been depending upon Dewdney and Reed for information and advice. But the prime minister knew better. In an earlier exchange with Lansdowne, he had referred to the uprising as a form of domestic trouble that did not deserve to be elevated to the rank of rebellion.

The governor general bristled at the comment and chastised Macdonald. "We cannot now reduce it to the rank of a common riot. If the movement had been at once stamped out by the NWM Police the case would have been different, but we were within a breath of an Indian war."[27] A somewhat unrepentant Sir John replied in his defence, "We have certainly made it assume large proportions in the public eye. This has been done however for our own purposes, and I think wisely done."[28]

These purposes included the mass execution of the eight men found guilty of murder at the Battleford trials. Nothing was going to stand in the way of seeing justice take its rightful course. Whereas Riel's hanging was delayed by three appeals before it was finally carried out in Regina on the morning of 16 November, the speed with which the Indian executions proceeded was a model of government efficiency. By the end of October, copies of the trial documents from the Battleford murder cases had been forwarded to Ottawa. They were reviewed by the minister of Justice, John Thompson, and then delivered to the governor general, with the government's recommendation that the sentences be carried out. On 3 November, Lansdowne signed the orders authorizing all eleven executions. The secretary of state immediately communicated this decision to Commissioner Dewdney, who in turn requested that the hangings be a public spectacle.[29] Macdonald concurred. One week before the event, he mused in a confidential letter to the Indian commissioner, "The executions . . . ought to convince the Red Man that the White Man governs."[30]

The condemned were initially held in a log stable that had been converted into a makeshift gaol. Double guards nervously paced outside day and night, fearing that some of the Indians from one of the outlying reserves might attempt a rescue. The prisoners certainly were not going anywhere; immobilized by ball and chain, they passed their days squatted, with a blanket pulled over their shoulders, deep in thought.[31] Father A.H. Bigonesse, the parish priest, attended daily to the men in a determined effort to convert them before their deaths. The two Assiniboine warriors, Itka and Waywahnitch, eventually agreed to be baptised,[32] but only after they learned of Riel's execution. In an interview with the *Saskatchewan Herald*, Bigonesse reported that news of the Métis leader's death induced a marked change in the prisoners' demeanour, and they quietly resigned themselves to their fate—all except Little Bear, who continued to protest his innocence.[33] He became visibly more upset when the condemned received word that Louison Mongrain, the convicted assassin of NWMP Corporal Cowan at Fort Pitt, had been reprieved. Dressyman and Charlebois, who had killed the old, deranged woman in the Frog Lake camp, also had their sentences commuted a few days later. The Macdonald government had decided, upon further reflection, that the two men were bound by tribal practice and that their crime did not compare to the murders committed by the others.[34]

Poundmaker (centre) with some of the Indians who were later executed at Battleford on 27 November 1885. *Saskatchewan Archives Board R-B2061*

At least two reporters received permission to speak to the condemned men. As with the trials a month earlier, the journalists made little attempt to understand the bleak circumstances that had driven the Cree and Assiniboine to take lives. Wandering Spirit spoke freely to his interviewers. When asked why the Cree had taken up arms, he reminisced about his days as a great warrior, fighting the Blackfoot, and how he had tried to be friendly with the whites. He admitted that he did not want his people to repeat what had happened that spring and conceded that he deserved to hang for his acts. He also assured his interviewers that he was not afraid to die and had accepted Christianity. But mindful of his traditional beliefs about the afterlife, he sought assurances that his shackles would be removed before his burial. Miserable Man, on being questioned about the unrest, said that he had heard from Big Bear's son, Imasees, that Riel had told the chiefs at the 1884 Duck Lake council that he planned to start a rebellion when the leaves came out and that he expected the Cree to take part in it. Worried that he would die slowly at the end of the rope, he asked to be shot. He then requested a pair of shoes with thick soles for the long walk over the sand hills between this world and the next. The only other prisoner willing to speak was Little Bear. Still adamant about his innocence, he wanted the reporters to tell the authorities that the Creator had told him that he could not be hanged.

Outside, the mood among the gathering Indians was subdued, if not solemn. A few, like Chief Thunderchild, said that the sentences were just and that all the fools who had taken part in the troubles should be forced to witness the executions. Others wondered, in fairness, why the soldiers who had killed Indians were not being hanged. Someone apparently decided to take matters into his own hands and fired two shots at a sentry the night before the executions.[35]

The final few days inside the barracks were punctuated with the sounds of hammers and saws at work on the gallows. The original plan was to hang two men at a time, but then it was increased to four, and finally, all eight at once. These repeated modifications to the scaffold did not bother hangman Robert Hodson, who had a personal stake in the executions. The former cook for the McLean family at Fort Pitt, he had been one of Wandering Spirit's prisoners and endured several weeks of ridicule for his peculiar appearance—short and pudgy with glasses and a pockmarked complexion. "They appeared to regard him as some kind of grub," recalled fellow captive William Cameron four decades later, "and . . . they would have liked to kill him out of mere idle curiosity to see him squirm."[36] It was now Hodson's turn to see the Indians twist and writhe, and he oversaw the construction of a massive gallows, twenty feet by eight feet, about ten feet off the ground, and with a railing around the trap door. It was successfully tested before local officials the day prior to the execution by dropping weights from all the ropes at once. Hodson's talents would not go unrewarded; he was appointed dominion hangman the following year.[37]

Friday 27 November was a cold, grey day that constantly threatened snow. The condemned, having been transferred to the guardhouse a few days before, were officially told at seven that the court's sentence was to be carried out. They spent the next half-hour saying their goodbyes and thanking the police for their kindness over the last few days; their greatest concern was for the future welfare of their families, and they asked that the government take care of them. Hodson then got busy with the preparations. While Itka chanted his death song to show that he was not afraid to die, Hodson removed the shackles that the men had dragged about for months and tied their hands behind their backs. The prisoners were also fitted with a black cap and a veil that probably seemed sloppy atop their closely shaved heads. Led by deputy sheriff, A.P. Forget, who carried the death warrants in his hands, and accompanied by Fathers Cochin and Bigonesse, the eight stepped out into the cold morning air at about 8:15 and were escorted between two rows of police to the scaffold steps. Their appearance was greeted with an uneasy silence. One hundred and fifty armed policemen, commanded by Major Crozier of the Duck Lake fiasco, ringed three sides of the gallows. Curious townspeople huddled in small groups off to the side, while a large number of Indian families, mostly from the Moosomin, Thunderchild, and Sweetgrass reserves, occupied the square in front of the gallows.[38]

Miserable Man was the first to ascend the stairs. He had decided at the last moment against fleeing to the United States with Imasees and turned himself in at Battleford hoping that the white man's justice system would treat him leniently; now, he was facing death for killing carpenter Charles Gouin at Frog Lake. Next came Bad Arrow, Gouin's other convicted murderer, and Round the Sky, who had finished off an already dying Father Fafard. They were followed by Wandering Spirit, the man who had started the bloody carnage that fateful April morning when subagent Tom Quinn refused one request too many. The Indian faced his death stoically, the anger, bitterness, and frustration that had once consumed his every waking moment now spent. Iron Body and Little Bear came next. Both had been convicted of killing trader George Dill, as he tried to escaped the melee. The question of who fired the fatal shot was secondary to punishing those who were there during the carnage, especially when several other participants were beyond the reach of the law in American territory. The Assiniboines came last: the older Itka, who had settled a personal grudge with farm instructor James Payne, and Man Without Blood, who could not back down from a dare from his warrior friends and killed an unpopular local rancher. Surprisingly, there are no known photographs of the scene, let alone the eight together.

Positioned in a single line, above the trap door, facing outward, the men were each firmly strapped at the ankles by Hodson. They were then asked, through interpreter William McKay, the local HBC trader, whether they had any final words. Miserable Man spoke first, conceding the justness of the sentence and cautioning the Indian onlookers to avoid trouble in the future. Wandering Spirit was equally repentant and regretted that so many had to die for following his example—he dearly wished that his own death would suffice. Itka, on the other hand, remained proudly defiant. He railed against their treatment at the hands of a foreign government and called on the Indian witnesses to never forget how the white man had treated them.[39] He then resumed his death chant, the voices of the others joining in, while Hodson went from man to man, lowering the veil over their faces and adjusting the nooses. The two priests offered final words and began to pray. This was Hodson's signal. He withdrew the bolt, and the eight bodies dropped in unison through the open trap to a sickening jolt. The immense gallows strained with the sudden weight, but barely shook; six died instantly, while the other two gasped briefly. All were still within seconds.[40]

After the limp bodies had hung for about fifteen minutes, Dr. A.W. Rolph, the assistant NWMP surgeon, pronounced the men dead. The bodies were then cut down and dropped into waiting coffins

Indian families from the surrounding reserves were brought to the Battleford barracks to witness the mass execution. *James Smith*

below the scaffold; the man who had been hired to handle the men's burial did not want to touch them![41] Once the coroner's jury, headed by P.G. Laurie, confirmed that the death warrants had been satisfied, the bodies were buried in a common grave behind the fort at the base of a sandy ravine on the North Saskatchewan River. Late that afternoon, a small knot of Indian women were spotted weeping at the Roman Catholic cemetery—in the ridiculous belief, according to the local paper, that the men would be placed in the same graveyard with victims of the rebellion.[42] Over the years, because of erosion, some of the bones of the dead became exposed, and officials decided in late 1954 to cap the mass burial site with a concrete slab.[43] Battleford had a long memory.

The *Saskatchewan Herald* looked upon the executions as the close of a terrible period in the region's history. "It is devoutly to be hoped," P.G. Laurie reflected three days later, "that the Indians at large will be duly impressed with the certainty with which punishment has overtaken their deluded fellows."[44] Other Canadian newspapers shared these sentiments, including *The Week*, which had earlier sympathized with Poundmaker's plight. "The execution of the Indians could not have been avoided," it argued in a short editorial, "if a dangerous licence to crime was not to be given."[45] Dewdney was elated. "Battleford hangings went off well not a hitch—eight all at once," he boasted to the prime minister. "Moosomin our good Indian said thats [sic] the way we snare rabbits."[46] Dewdney's cockiness, however, had been tempered by an uneasiness about the Indian reaction. That is why he issued special presents to the Blood Indians, and possibly other groups, in the week leading up to the executions.[47] And it is also why a heavily armed police patrol scoured the countryside beyond Battleford, while the artillery above the fort was primed the day before the event.[48]

As for the Indians assembled in front of the gallows, they watched in quiet horror as the men dropped to their doom and then silently moved off once the bodies had been placed in the coffins. Nothing was said or done. They simply returned to their reserves, trying to put behind them the shock of the executions. But to this day, the executions have remained a numbing event, comparable to an old scar on the soul of a people. Elder Paul Chicken of the Sweetgrass reserve recalled how the Indians of the area lived in morbid fear of being picked up and tried before "Hanging Judge Rouleau."[49] Dressyman's grandson, meanwhile, related how his reprieved grand-

The mass grave site at the base of a sandy ravine on the North Saskatchewan River was capped with a concrete slab in 1954. *RCMP Museum*

father and several other men were forced to watch the executions and threatened with a similar fate if there was any more trouble. "My grandfather was there, he saw them hung, he watched it all," he recounted. "They didn't like the hanging . . . the law overdone it."[50] Don Chatsis, a descendant of one of the Cut Knife warriors, said that he often heard the elders speak of the bravery of the condemned men, how they all sang on the platform in the face of death. He also speculated that the police refused to release the bodies for a traditional burial because the government did not want the men glorified as braves. "So they were forbidden to have anything to do with them. That's why they buried them right there in a mass grave," Chatsis said. "It would have defeated the whole purpose of the hanging if they let these people [bodies] go."[51]

The Battleford trials and executions accelerated the exodus of Indians to the relative safety of the United States. Initially, only about one hundred Cree fled to Montana in the early summer with Imasees, Lucky Man, and Little Poplar. But once it became apparent that the Canadian government was determined to punish anyone suspected of being involved in the rebellion, the urge to leave the North-West grew stronger. The implementation of Hayter Reed's recommendations made things even worse. In a sense, the Indians were pushed into exile—a phenomenon that Reed discovered in late August, when a survey of five Cree bands in the Battleford district found that close to seventy families were gone; thirty families alone were missing from the rolls of the Sweetgrass reserve, one of the bands that had originally been charged with disloyalty, but subsequently exonerated.[52] Less than two months later, Grizzly Bear's Head abandoned his reserve and headed south with about one hundred Assiniboine, including many from the Lean Man and Mosquito bands.[53] Dewdney tried to stem this flow by announcing in early November that there would be a general amnesty for all Indians, except those still wanted for the Frog Lake murders. But by the time the governor general formally approved the pardon the following summer, several hundred Canadian Indians had sought asylum in Montana.[54]

Most of the refugees found only deprivation and death. At first, the U.S. army tried to send the Cree back across the border and in late 1885 rounded up some twenty-four lodges at Rocky Point, along the Missouri River, and another seventeen lodges near Fort Belknap.[55] Items found in their possession, such as silverware and ladies clothing, clearly linked the group to the looting of Fort Pitt. But when the army sought federal permission to deport the Cree, it was denied—apparently on the grounds that Canada had set a precedent by granting asylum to the Sioux after the battle of the Little Big Horn in 1876.[56] Over the next decade, the Cree wandered in search of a new home, when not trying to survive. Some found work in the Fort Assiniboine and Belknap areas and eked out a miserable existence doing odd jobs for the military or begging for rations. Another large group camped on the Milk River and reportedly survived on the carcasses of coyotes poisoned by nearby ranching companies. Imasees, now known as Little Bear by the Americans, first tried to find a place for his followers on the Crow reservation, but soldiers turned them back. He then attempted to settle on the Flathead reservation but that too fell through. The band ended up suffering through two wretched winters on Willow Creek; the nightmare years of the early 1880s seemed to be repeating themselves. So many people were freezing or starving to death that President Cleveland authorized the War Department to provide emergency relief.[57] By this point, the Cree had acquired a local reputation "as scavengers, for they eat everything from a mouse to a dead horse, and they are not very particular about how long it has been dead."[58]

The group that Grizzly Bear's Head took across the line fared somewhat better because there were other bands of Assiniboine already living in northern Montana. Many had kinship ties with their American counterparts that could be traced back several generations.

JUSTICE STILL UNSATISFIED.

Sir John.—Well, madam, Riel is gone ; I hope you are quite satisfied.
Justice.—Not quite ; you have hanged the EFFECT of the Rebellion ; now I want to find and punish the CAUSE.

Some Canadian newspapers questioned the government's role in the rebellion—but not the treatment of the Indians. *Toronto* Grip, *1 November 1885*

Although Indian officials initially chased the newcomers off the reservations, the Assiniboine managed to elude authorities and blend in with the local population, eventually being taken on the reserve rolls. Their testimony at the time of enrolment was quite fascinating, for it often included mention of a family history in Canada that was deliberately vague in details. A somewhat evasive Rattle Snake, the son of Lean Man, for example, repeatedly claimed during his 1921 application hearing that he could not remember or was too young at the time.[59] It would also appear that White Buffalo, one of the warriors present at the Tremont killing and who was briefly taken into custody,[60] assumed a new identity in the United States as "White"; he died in 1936 at age eighty-four at Wolf Point on the Fort Peck Reservation.[61]

In 1896, in response to growing complaints from Montana ranchers, the U.S. State Department and the Canadian Indian Commissioner reached an agreement to return the homeless Cree to their former reserves in Saskatchewan. The American authorities assumed that the 1886 amnesty proclamation would apply to the over five hundred deported Indians. But when Little Bear and Lucky Man arrived in Lethbridge by train in late June, the local mounted police arrested them for the Frog Lake murders. One month later, when the pair appeared in a Regina court, the charges were dismissed for lack of evidence because the sole witness, the Indian widow of Tom Quinn, refused to identify them. The incident convinced many of the returnees that they were still not safe from persecution in Canada, and several of them returned to Montana by the end of the year. Little Bear, meanwhile, travelled to the Hobbema area with about one hundred followers to take possession of the former Bobtail reserve (renamed Montana) that had been set aside for his band. He quickly became disillusioned when he was unable to collect treaty money dating back to 1884, and after a futile attempt to join the Onion Lake reserve, he returned to Montana. There, he wandered in exile until 1916, when an act of Congress finally granted him a reserve on the abandoned Fort Assiniboine military reserve to share with another homeless band, a group of Chippewas led by Rocky Boy (Stonechild).[62] The historic ties with Canada, however, continue today in a pattern of regular travel by First Nations people between Montana, Battleford, Onion Lake, and Hobbema.

For those bands that remained in Canada after the rebellion, the situation was equally bleak, especially if the reserve had been designated disloyal. Chiefs and councillors of so-called rebel bands were deposed, and the positions left vacant to undermine Indian autonomy. Many of these groups also suffered through five years without annuity payments, including the Cold Lake Chipewyan, whose only crime was being duped into joining Wandering Spirit's camp during the troubles.[63] The Chacastapasin and Young Chipewyan bands, on the other hand, were eventually stripped of their reserves in 1897 on the grounds that they had joined the rebels and then fled to the United States; they had never occupied the land before the rebellion, but officials ignored this in favour of portraying them as rebels who had been off their reserves and thereby in violation of Dewdney's May 1885 edict.[64]

One of the most tragic stories was that of the One Arrow band. In mid-January 1886, a mounted police inspector sent to investigate rumours of starvation in the Duck Lake area found instances of acute deprivation in the Métis communities, but nothing prepared him for the horrifying scene on the One Arrow reserve. When the band refused to move to Beardy's, as recommended in Reed's report, and give up their land, they were left to cope on their own—with bows and arrows and little else. "Their state . . . would be impossible to exaggerate," the policeman wrote his supervisor, "they are miserable beyond description . . . poorly clothed and huddled in their huts like sheep in a pen . . . Last summer they lived on gophers and this winter on rabbits . . . they can't go far because they have no clothes because of the severe weather."[65] He went on to describe how the wife of the imprisoned chief would often have to walk the ten miles to Duck Lake in severe weather to get a few pounds of flour for her sick daughter. He also reported that the local agent and farm instructor had not visited the reserve in almost a year and how a few old horse blankets had been welcomed like priceless gifts. This act of kindness elicited a stern reprimand from Dewdney, who resented the interference and bluntly told the mounted police commissioner that rebel Indians were to be treated as such.[66] An Indian department inspector visited the reserve only a few days after the inspector, and in a letter full of complaints about record-setting low temperatures, conceded that the band was in a "bad state."[67]

Commissioner Dewdney was anxious to limit and regulate access to provisions and supplies in the aftermath of the rebellion, whether it be tobacco, sugar, or old horse blankets, because he saw it as an effective way to control the Indians. Much as a person would train a dog, loyal and obedient chiefs and bands would receive gifts and other recognition, while the uncooperative received the equivalent of a good cuff. After a few years, this system of rewards and punishments would convince the recalcitrant to behave or bring them to their knees. Either way, Dewdney won, and he was determined to push ahead with this plan once the executions were over. He consequently opposed a suggestion from General Middleton, in response to rumours that winter of another Indian uprising, that a flying column be sent through the Saskatchewan country in the spring of 1886. He was convinced that a show of force was not the way to proceed—it would simply demoralize the Cree or, worse, cause panic and encourage more to flee. The only way to get the Indians to work, in Dewdney's mind, was through his subtle, though more insidious, plan.[68]

In late January 1886, the Regina office finally provided Macdonald with a detailed, itemized list of rewards for loyal chiefs and bands that amounted to over eleven thousand dollars. Chiefs Mistawasis and Ahtahkakoop, for example, were each to receive fifty dollars, one gun, twenty sheep, and two oxen, while their bands were to be given an additional twenty sheep and five cows. Piapot, on the other hand, was singled out for remaining aloof from the troubles and setting an example for his band; it earned him two oxen. In the covering letter that accompanied the list, Reed justified the cost of the rewards by arguing that many of the agricultural items had been held back from the bands at the time of the treaties and that the Indians could now be trusted with the care of cattle and other livestock. He also indicated—in complete contradiction to what had been said publicly— that so many Indians had remained loyal during the troubles that only those "worthy of some marked recognition"[69] could be rewarded. The Indian department's most symbolic gesture was a proposed tour of eastern Canada by a handful of representative Cree and Blackfoot leaders that would include a meeting with the prime minister and governor general. Dewdney hoped this event would strengthen the bonds between loyal chiefs and the government and act as a deterrent to future unrest.[70]

Dewdney and Reed were able to act with such impunity after the rebellion because they had the blessing of Macdonald and his hard-line assistant, Vankoughnet. The Canadian West had failed to attract the great number of immigrants that had been enthusiastically pre-dicted only a decade earlier, and in laying the blame for this stalled

The Macdonald government invited Blackfoot leaders to Ottawa in the aftermath of the rebellion. *National Archives of Canada PA45666*

Poundmaker surrounded by a group of visiting French journalists at Stony Mountain Penitentiary. *Glenbow Archives NA-448*

settlement, it was easy to point to the First Nations as an obstacle. This did not mean that the Macdonald administration escaped criticism for its handling of western affairs, in particular its Indian policy. In the House of Commons in April 1886, Liberal Malcolm Cameron provided a devastating critique of the department, its officers, and its methods that was subsequently printed and distributed in pamphlet form. He charged that a deliberate policy of neglect, dishonesty, and starvation had driven the Indians to revolt. An annoyed Macdonald countered that it was Riel who had roused the First Nations and that they had no legitimate reason to revolt. Then, in what would become a standard defence of federal Indian policy over the next few decades, the prime minister laid the blame squarely on the Indians themselves and their slovenly ways—an argument that the government put forward in its own publication on the topic.[71] "It is a peculiarity of their race," Dewdney observed in his annual report for 1886, "to be extremely susceptible to influence, to care little for the morrow if the day satisfies their wants."[72] This kind of subterfuge suggested that Ottawa had not only been just, but had met its commitments to the Indians and then some. It also conveniently implied that the Indians were the problem, not the policy, and that the coercion and interference being advocated by Dewdney and Reed were necessary to bring about meaningful change. Sadly, both sides in the debate over the government's treatment of the Indians blithely argued that they had actively and willingly participated in the uprising.

By the first anniversary of the rebellion's end, Ottawa had completely transformed its relationship with the First Nations of western Canada; it had imprisoned scores of Indians, executed eight warriors, and introduced repressive measures that were unprecedented in their scope and severity. In short, the Canadian government held the upper hand and exercised its power over the Indians with a ruthlessness and absoluteness more in keeping with a totalitarian state. It would brook no dissent. Ottawa's decision to begin releasing the Indian prisoners from Stony Mountain Penitentiary in the late winter of 1886 underlined its confidence in the strength and rightfulness of its position. But even here, Indian Affairs officials were manipulative and self-serving. In February 1886, the prime minister decided to use the Crowfoot–Poundmaker relationship to the government's advantage and secretly instructed Dewdney to get the Blackfoot chief to make a special plea for Poundmaker's release—which, of course, would be granted. Poundmaker's freedom, however, was short-lived. A broken man when he was released on 4 March, the forty-six-year-old chief died exactly four months later, from tuberculosis, while visiting Crowfoot; he was buried at Blackfoot Crossing.[73] A gravely ill One Arrow, meanwhile, was taken to Winnipeg's St. Boniface hospital on 8 April, but it was too late to send him home, and he spent his final days at the archbishop's residence, where he was baptised and given the name Marc. Just before One Arrow's death on Easter Sunday 25 April, Hayter Reed tried to get the Willow Cree chief to send word to his band that they should move to Beardy's; it would be several months before his people discovered what had happened to him.[74] Big Bear's release came on 27 January 1887, but only because he was suffering from debilitating fainting spells and the government did not want him to perish in prison.[75] Not having a reserve of his own, the frail chief took up residence on Little Pine, where he died quietly in his sleep less than a year later on 17 January 1888.

Alexander Morris had expected a different outcome. In reflecting on the treaty process almost a decade earlier, he had asked, "What is to be the future of the Indian population of the North-West?" The treaty commissioner offered two possible futures. The first was "a hopeful one," in which "these faithful allies of the Crown" would enjoy a "happy, prosperous, and self-sustaining" life. "I have every confidence," he asserted boldly, "in the desire and ability of the

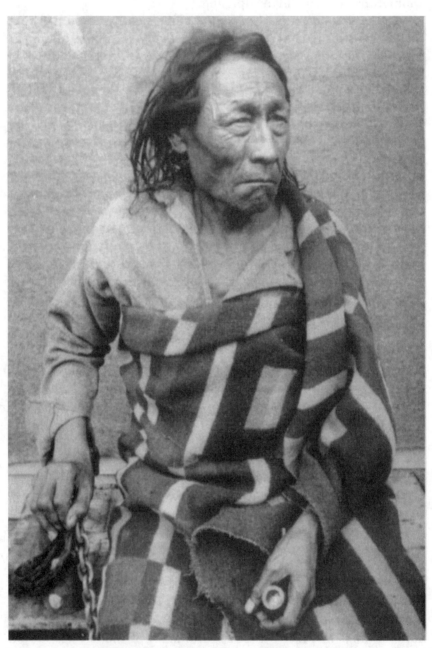

Big Bear was released from prison in January 1887 because he was ill and the government did not want him to die in captivity. *National Archives of Canada C1873*

present administration, as of any succeeding one, to carry out the provisions of the treaties, and to extend a helping hand to this helpless population." The other future was a dead end—the disappearance of the First Nations people. Morris considered this outcome unthinkable, especially since Canada was duty-bound to "the red men of the North-West, and thereby to herself." But the sorry experience of the Cree and their leaders suggested otherwise. In the aftermath of the rebellion, it appeared that the Indians were doomed to melt away "as snow before the sun."[76]

Keeping Faith

AGENT, YOU REMEMBER THE TIME I promised I would go on my Reserve, I also said that I and my young men's fighting days were over. I stick to those words."[1] That's how Chief Kahkewistahaw admonished Agent Allan McDonald at an emergency council meeting of the Crooked Lake reserves held in the wake of the armed clash at Duck Lake. It was not an isolated pledge. On 22 April 1885, two days before the Fish Creek skirmish, Pasquah and Muscowpetung sent an impassioned appeal to Prime Minister Macdonald: "We have good thoughts in our hearts . . . don't think anything disloyal of us, it hurts us, we depend upon promises made by Great Mother to us because of us keeping faith."[2] Their neighbour, Chief Piapot, who had a reputation in government circles for being intractable, was equally forthright. "I promise you as I have promised our Governor," he assured Macdonald in early May, "that I will never fight against the white man."[3] These were honourable words from honourable men— leaders who were fiercely committed to upholding the sanctity of the treaties they had signed with the Canadian government. And Macdonald responded in statesmanlike fashion. "You can inform them," he wired Indian Commissioner Dewdney the same day that Batoche fell, "that the Government will do everything that it properly can to forward their interests and improve the conditions of the red man.

All treaty promises will be faithfully carried out and the loyalty of the Chiefs is fully appreciated."[4]

Macdonald never kept his word. Several weeks before the last shot of the rebellion was fired, the Canadian government chose to deliberately portray the Indians as willing accomplices of the Métis. The chiefs' vows of loyalty were forgotten, and the actions of the bands presented in the worst possible light. They were rebels of convenience, and like all rebels, they had to be punished. Indian Affairs saw to it that they were.

The restrictive measures that followed, together with the mass execution of eight men and the false imprisonment of three leaders, left a lasting legacy with the First Nations people. Twenty-eight bands still carry the stigma of having broken their sacred agreements with the Crown. The official record, meanwhile, leaves the unmistakable impression that the Indians participated fully in the fighting and, in some instances, took the lead. How else can one explain the large number of Indian convictions for rebellion crimes?

There are also lingering consequences at the band level. The One Arrow First Nation never received official notification of its former leader's death, and it has only recently discovered the whereabouts of his unmarked grave in Winnipeg's St. Boniface cemetery. One Arrow's people want to bring his remains home for burial. The people of nearby Beardy's reserve, on the other hand, continue to wonder what became of the treaty medal their chief turned over to General Middleton as a sign of good faith. Its return has special meaning; Beardy believed that once the band had been cleared of disloyalty, the medal would be given back. One hundred miles to the west, at a special ceremony atop Cut Knife Hill, community leaders recently petitioned the federal Justice minister to exonerate Poundmaker of any wrongdoing.[5] It is a formidable request; no one in Canadian history has ever been pardoned posthumously. Still farther west, around Onion Lake and Hobbema, an attempt is underway to trace the modern-day descendants of the former members of Big Bear's band. Those involved in the genealogical project believe that the famous chief's band should be reconstituted and formally recognized—therein fulfilling a century-old prophecy.

One of the biggest stumbling blocks to the resolution of these and other problems is the persistent myth that the Indians and Métis acted in concert during the North-West Rebellion. Contrary to popular belief, the Indians of western Canada did not look to Louis Riel for

Poundmaker's grave site at the top of Cut Knife Hill, Poundmaker First Nation reserve.

leadership; nor were they unable to think and act for themselves during the difficult transitional period following the disappearance of the buffalo. The Cree had developed their own strategy for dealing with the Canadian government and its tight-fisted implementation of the treaties, and this strategy did not include open rebellion. They were determined to honour the agreements they had made in the presence of the Creator and use diplomatic means to bring about their favourable revision. Consequently, once Riel formed his provisional government and pushed the region into war, only a small group of Indians became directly involved, while the vast majority consciously chose not to participate—despite the urging of Métis agents. In fact, many of those who were dragged into the conflict, such as Poundmaker and Big Bear, counselled restraint and did all they could within their limited power to promote peace.

This version of events is not new. It can be found in the rebellion trials' transcripts, the official records of the Indian Affairs department, and the personal papers of John A. Macdonald and Edgar Dewdney. But these are obscure sources, and Canadians have largely overlooked or ignored the government's duplicitous role in the rebellion. The prime minister's portrait, for example, is curiously absent from the ministers' gallery in the Indian Affairs building in Hull, even though Macdonald was the country's most senior Indian official for most of the 1880s.

It has fallen to elders to set the record straight. They have quietly maintained for years that the Indians did not violate the treaties, that there was no Indian rebellion, and that the Indians were not rebels. The story of how the Indians kept faith and remained loyal to the Queen during a time of national crisis has been passed from one generation to the next. It is now up to the Canadian government to finally acknowledge this fact, in keeping with the reciprocal spirit underlying the treaties. As one Indian elder remarked, to insist on telling the story of 1885 from the official government perspective alone is akin to the man who believes that the sun comes up just when he opens his eyes.

Treaty Six

A RTICLES OF A TREATY made and concluded near Carlton, on the twenty-third day of August, and on the twenty-eighth day of said month, respectively, and near Fort Pitt on the ninth day of September, in the year of Our Lord one thousand eight hundred and seventy-six, between her most Gracious Majesty the Queen of Great Britain and Ireland, by her Commissioners, the Honorable Alexander Morris, Lieutenant-Governor of the Province of Manitoba and the North-West Territories, and the Honorable James McKay and the Honorable William Joseph Christie, of the one part, and the Plain and the Wood Cree Tribes of Indians, and the other Tribes of Indians, inhabitants of the country within the limits hereinafter defined and described, by their Chiefs, chosen and named as hereinafter mentioned, of the other part.

Whereas the Indians inhabiting the said country have, pursuant to an appointment made by the said Commissioners, been convened at meetings at Fort Carlton, Fort Pitt and Battle River, to deliberate upon certain matters of interest to Her Most Gracious Majesty, of the one part, and the said Indians of the other;

And whereas the said Indians have been notified and informed by Her Majesty's said Commissioners that it is the desire of Her Majesty to open up for settlement, immigration and such other purposes as to Her Majesty may seem meet, a tract of country, bounded and described as hereinafter mentioned, and to obtain the consent thereto of her Indian subjects inhabiting the said tract, and to make a treaty and arrange with them, so that there may be peace and good will between them and Her Majesty, and that they may know and be assured of what allowance they are to count upon and receive from Her Majesty's bounty and benevolence;

And whereas the Indians of the said tract, duly convened in council as aforesaid, and being requested by Her Majesty's Commissioners to name certain Chiefs and head men, who should be authorized, on their behalf, to conduct such negotiations and sign any treaty to be founded thereon, and to become responsible to Her Majesty for the faithful performance by their respective bands of such obligations as shall be assumed by them, the said Indians have thereupon named for that purpose, that is to say:—representing the Indians who make the treaty at Carlton, the several Chiefs and Councillors who have subscribed hereto, and representing the Indians who make the treaty at Fort Pitt, the several Chiefs and Councillors who have subscribed hereto;

And thereupon, in open council, the different bands having presented their Chiefs to the said Commissioners as the Chiefs and head men, for the purposes aforesaid, of the respective bands of Indians inhabiting the district hereinafter described;

And whereas the said Commissioners then and there received and acknowledged the persons so represented, as Chiefs and head men, for the purposes aforesaid, of the respective bands of Indians inhabiting the said district hereinafter described;

And whereas the said Commissioners have proceeded to negotiate a treaty with the said Indians, and the same has been finally agreed upon and concluded as follows, that is to say:

The Plain and Wood Cree Tribes of Indians, and all the other Indians inhabiting the district hereinafter described and defined, do hereby cede, release, surrender and yield up to the Government of the Dominion of Canada for Her Majesty the Queen and her successors forever, all their rights, titles and privileges whatsoever, to the lands included within the following limits, that is to say:

Commencing at the mouth of the river emptying into the north-west angle of Cumberland Lake, thence westerly up the said river to the source, thence on a straight line in a westerly direction to the head of Green Lake, thence northerly to the elbow in the Beaver River, thence down the said river northerly to a point twenty miles from the said elbow; thence in a westerly direction, keeping on a line generally parallel with the said Beaver River (above the elbow), and about twenty miles distance therefrom, to the source of the said river; thence northerly to the north-easterly point of the south shore of Red Deer Lake, continuing westerly along the said shore to the western limit thereof, and thence due west to the Athabaska River, thence up the said river, against the stream, to the Jasper House, in the Rocky Mountains; thence on a course south-eastwardly, following the easterly range of the Mountains, to the source of the main branch of the Red

Deer River; thence down the said river, with the stream, to the junction therewith of the outlet of the river, being the outlet of the Buffalo Lake; thence due east twenty miles; thence on a straight line south-eastwardly to the mouth of the said Red Deer River on the South Branch of the Saskatchewan River; thence eastwardly and northwardly, following on the boundaries of the tracts conceded by the several Treaties numbered Four and Five, to the place of beginning;

And also all their rights, titles and privileges whatsoever, to all other lands, wherever situated, in the North-West Territories, or in any other Province or portion of Her Majesty's Dominions, situated and being within the Dominion of Canada;

The tract comprised within the lines above described, embracing an area of one hundred and twenty-one thousand square miles, be the same more or less;

To have and to hold the same to Her Majesty the Queen and her successors forever;

And Her Majesty the Queen hereby agrees and undertakes to lay aside reserves for farming lands, due respect being had to lands at present cultivated by the said Indians, and other reserves for the benefit of the said Indians, to be administered and dealt with for them by Her Majesty's Government of the Dominion of Canada, provided all such reserves shall not exceed in all one square mile for each family of five, or in that proportion for larger or smaller families, in manner following, that is to say:—

That the Chief Superintendent of Indian Affairs shall depute and send a suitable person to determine and set apart the reserves for each band, after consulting with the Indians thereof as to the locality which may be found to be most suitable for them;

Provided, however, that Her Majesty reserves the right to deal with any settlers within the bounds of any lands reserved for any band as she shall deem fit, and also that the aforesaid reserves of land or any interest therein may be sold or otherwise disposed of by Her Majesty's Government for the use and benefit of the said Indians entitled thereto, with their consent first had and obtained; and with a view to show the satisfaction of Her Majesty with the behaviour and good conduct of her Indians, she hereby, through her Commissioners, makes them a present of twelve dollars for each man, woman and child belonging to the bands here represented, in extinguishment of all claims heretofore preferred;

And further, Her Majesty agrees to maintain schools for instruction in such reserves hereby made, as to her Government of the Dominion of Canada may seem advisable, whenever the Indians of the reserve shall desire it;

Her Majesty further agrees with her said Indians that within the boundary of Indian reserves, until otherwise determined by her Government of the Dominion of Canada, no intoxicating liquor shall be allowed to be introduced or sold, and all laws now in force or hereafter to be enacted to preserve her Indian subjects inhabiting the reserves or living elsewhere within her North-West Territories from the evil influence of the use of intoxicating liquors, shall be strictly enforced;

Her Majesty further agrees with her said Indians that they, the said Indians, shall have right to pursue their avocations of hunting and fishing throughout the tract surrendered as hereinbefore described, subject to such regulations as may from time to time be made by her Government of her Dominion of Canada, and saving and excepting such tracts as may from time to time be required or taken up for settlement, mining, lumbering or other purposes by her said Government of the Dominion of Canada, or by any of the subjects thereof, duly authorized therefore, by the said Government;

It is further agreed between Her Majesty and her said Indians, that such sections of the reserves above indicated as may at any time be required for public works or buildings of what nature soever, may be appropriated for that purpose by Her Majesty's Government of the Dominion of Canada, due compensation being made for the value of any improvements thereon;

And further, that Her Majesty's Commissioners shall, as soon as possible after the execution of this treaty, cause to be taken, an accurate census of all the Indians inhabiting the tract above described, distributing them in families, and shall in every year ensuring the date hereof, at some period in each year, to be duly notified to the Indians, and at a place or places to be appointed for that purpose, within the territories ceded, pay to each Indian person the sum of five dollars per head yearly;

It is further agreed between Her Majesty and the said Indians that the sum of fifteen hundred dollars per annum shall be yearly and every year expended by Her Majesty in the purchase of ammunition and twine for nets for the use of the said Indians, in manner following, that is to say:—In the reasonable discretion as regards the distribution thereof, among the Indians inhabiting the several reserves, or otherwise included herein, of Her Majesty's Indian Agent having the supervision of this treaty;

It is further agreed between Her Majesty and the said Indians that the following articles shall be supplied to any band of the said Indians who are now cultivating the soil, or who shall hereafter commence to cultivate the land, that is to say:—four hoes for every family actually cultivating, also two spades per family as aforesaid; one plough for every three families as aforesaid, one harrow for every three families as aforesaid; two scythes, and one whetstone and two hayforks and two reaping-hooks for every family as aforesaid; and also two axes, and also one cross-cut saw, and also one hand-saw, one pit-saw, the necessary files, one grindstone and one auger for each band; and also for each Chief, for the use of his band, one chest of ordinary carpenter's tools; also for each band, enough of wheat, barley, potatoes and oats to plant the land actually broken up for cultivation by such band; also for each band, four oxen, one bull and six cows, also one boar and two sows, and one handmill when any band shall raise sufficient grain therefor; all the aforesaid articles to be given *once for all* for the encouragement of the practice of agriculture among the Indians;

It is further agreed between Her Majesty and the said Indians, that each Chief, duly recognized as such, shall receive an annual salary of twenty-five dollars per annum; and each subordinate officer, not exceeding four for each band, shall receive fifteen dollars per annum; and each such Chief and subordinate officer as aforesaid, shall also receive, once every three years, a suitable suit of clothing, and each Chief shall receive, in recognition of the closing of the treaty, a suitable flag and medal, and also, as soon as convenient, one horse, harness and waggon;

That in the event hereafter of the Indians comprised within this treaty being overtaken by any pestilence, or by a general famine, the Queen, on being satisfied and certified thereof by her Indian Agent or Agents, will grant to the Indians assistance of such character and to such extent as her Chief Superintendent of Indian Affairs shall deem necessary and sufficient to relieve the Indians from the calamity that shall have befallen them;

That during the next three years, after two or more of the reserves hereby agreed to be set apart to the Indians, shall have been agreed upon and surveyed, there shall be granted to the Indians included under the Chiefs adhering to the treaty at Carlton, each spring, the sum of one thousand dollars to be expended for them by Her Majesty's Indian Agents, in the purchase of provisions for the use of such of the band as are actually settled on the reserves and are engaged in cultivating the soil, to assist them in such cultivation;

That a medicine chest shall be kept at the House of each Indian Agent for the use and benefit of the Indians, at the discretion of such Agent;

That with regard to the Indians included under the Chiefs adhering to the treaty at Fort Pitt, and to those under Chiefs within the treaty limits who may hereafter give their adhesion hereto (exclusively, however, of the Indians of the Carlton Region) there shall, during three years, after two or more reserves shall have been agreed upon and surveyed, be distributed each spring among the bands cultivating the soil on such reserves, by Her Majesty's Chief Indian Agent for this treaty in his discretion, a sum not exceeding one thousand dollars, in the purchase of provisions for the use of such members of the band as are actually settled on the reserves and engaged in the cultivation of the soil, to assist and encourage them in such cultivation;

That, in lieu of waggons, if they desire it, and declare their option to that effect, there shall be given to each of the Chiefs adhering hereto, at Fort Pitt or elsewhere hereafter (exclusively of those in the Carlton district) in recognition of this treaty, so soon as the same can be conveniently transported, two carts, with iron bushings and tires;

And the undersigned chiefs, on their behalf, and on behalf of all other Indians inhabiting the tract within ceded, do hereby solemnly promise and engage to strictly observe this treaty, and also to conduct and behave themselves as good and loyal subjects of Her Majesty the Queen;

They promise and engage that they will in all respects obey and abide by the law, and they will maintain peace and good order between each other, and also between themselves and other tribes of Indians, and between themselves and others of Her Majesty's subjects, whether Indians or whites, now inhabiting or hereafter to inhabit any part of the said ceded tracts, and that they will not molest the person or property of any inhabitant of such ceded tracts, or the property of Her Majesty the Queen, or interfere with or trouble any person passing or travelling through the said tracts or any part thereof; and that they will aid and assist the officers of Her Majesty in bringing to justice and punishment any Indian offending against the stipulations of this treaty, or infringing the laws in force in the country so ceded.

In witness whereof, Her Majesty's said Commissioners and the said Indian Chiefs have hereunto subscribed and set their hands, at or near Fort Carlton, on the day and year aforesaid, and near Fort Pitt on the day above aforesaid.

(Signed)

> Alexander Morris,
> Lieut.-Governor, N.-W.T.

> James McKay,
> W.J. Christie,
> Indian Commissioners.

Mist-ow-as-is,	His x mark.
Ah-tuk-uk-koop,	x
Head Chiefs of the Carlton Indians.	

| Pee-yahn-kah-nihk-oo-sit, | x |
| Ah-yah-tus-kum-ik-im-um, | x |

Kee-too-wa-han,   x
Cha-kas-ta-pay-sin,   x
John Smith,   x
James Smith,   x
Chip-ee-way-an,   x
        Chiefs.

[Source: A. Morris, *The Treaties of Canada with the Indians of Manitoba and the North-West Territories* (Saskatoon 1991), 351–56.]

Notice

W HEREAS, the troubles in the North have necessitated the bringing of large bodies of troops into the country to suppress the troubles, and punish those causing them, and when these troops meet any Indians off their Reserves they may be unable to tell whether they are hostile or friendly, and may attack them;

And Whereas, runners are constantly being sent by Riel throughout the country spreading lies and false reports, trying to induce different bands of Indians to join him, by threats and otherwise;

And Whereas, it is the intention of the troops to arrest and punish such runners wherever the same may be found, and it will be necessary for them, in order to accomplish this, to arrest all Indians, or any suspicious persons whom they may see, in order to ascertain whether or not they are runners from Riel;

And Whereas, it is expedient that all good and loyal Indians should know how to act under the present circumstances so as to secure their own safety and the good will of the Government;

Now, this is to give notice that all good and loyal Indians should remain quietly on their Reserves where they will be perfectly safe and receive the protection of the soldiers; and that any Indian being off his Reserve without special permission in writing from some authorized person, is liable to be arrested on suspicion of being a rebel, and punished as such.

Any Loyal Indian who gives such information as will lead to the arrest and conviction of any such runner from Riel, or any hostile bands of Indians, will receive a reward of Fifty Dollars ($50.00).

E. Dewdney,
Indian Commissioner.

Regina, 6th May, 1885.

[Source: *National Archives of Canada*, Government Archives Division, Indian Affairs, RG 10, v. 3584, f. 1130.]

Hayter Reed on the Future Management of Indians

Memorandum for the Honourable the Indian Commissioner relative to the future management of Indians

1. All Indians who have not during the late troubles been disloyal or troublesome should be treated as heretofore; as they have not disturbed our treaty relations, and our treatment in the past has been productive of progress and good results.

2. As the rebellious Indians expected to have been treated with severity as soon as overpowered, a reaction of feeling must be guarded against. They were led to believe that they would be shot down, and harshly treated. Though humanity of course forbids this, unless severe examples are made of the more prominent participators in the rebellion much difficulty will be met with in their future management, and future turbulence may be feared. It is therefore suggested that all leading Indian rebels whom it is found possible to convict of particular crimes, such as instigating and citing to treason, felony, arson, larceny, murder, etc., be dealt with in as severe a manner as the law will allow and that no offences of their most prominent men be overlooked.

3. That other offenders, both Halfbreed and Indian, who have been guilty of such serious offences as those above mentioned should be punished for their crimes in order to deter them from rebellious movements in future.

4. That the tribal system should be abolished in so far as is compatible with the treaty, i.e., in all cases in which the treaty has been broken by rebel

tribes; by doing away with chiefs and councillors, depriving them of medals and other appurtenances of their offices. Our instructors and employees will not then be hampered by Indian consultations and interferences, but will administer direct orders and instructions to individuals; besides by this action and careful repression of those that become prominent amongst them by counselling, medicine dances, and so on, a further obstacle will be thrown in the way of future united rebellious movements.

5. No annuity money should be now paid any bands that rebelled, or any individuals that left well disposed bands and joined the insurgents. As the Treaty expressly stipulated for peace and good will, as well as an observance of law and order, it has been entirely abrogated by the rebellion. Besides this fact, such suggestion is made because in the past the annuity money which should have been expended wholly in necessaries has to a great extent been wasted upon articles more or less useless and in purchasing necessaries at exorbitant prices, entailing upon the Department a greater expenditure in providing articles of clothing, food and implements, not called for by the terms of the Treaty, than need have been entailed if the whole of the annuity money had been well and economically applied to the purchase of such necessaries. All future grants should be regarded as concessions of favour, *not of right*, and the rebel Indians be made to understand that they have forfeited every claim as "matter of right."

6. Disarm all rebels, but to those rebel Indians north of the North Saskatchewan who have heretofore mainly existed by hunting, return shotguns (retaining the rifles) branding them as I.D. property and keeping lists of those to whom arms are lent. Those to whom arms are thus supplied if left to their own resources—under careful supervision— would suffer great hardship and doubtlessly be benefitted by experiencing the fact that they cannot live after their old methods. They would soon incline to settlement and be less likely to again risk losing the chance of settling down.

7. No rebel Indians should be allowed off the reserves without a pass signed by an I.D. official. The danger of complications with whitemen will thus be lessened, and by preserving a knowledge of individual movements any inclination to petty depredations may be checked by the facility of apprehending those who committed the first of such offences.

8. The leaders of the Teton Sioux who fought against the troops should be hanged, and the rest be sent out of the country, as there are certain of the settlers who are greatly inclined to shoot them on sight; and the settlements are more in fear of such marauders as these than of anything else.

9. Big Bear's Band should either be broken up and scattered amongst other bands or be given a reserve adjacent to that at Onion Lake. The action in this regard could be decided better when it is known, after their surrender, the number that will have to be dealt with. If the band is kept intact and settled as suggested the Instructor stationed at Onion Lake would be sufficient for the two bands.

10. One Arrow's band should be joined with that of Beardy and Okemasis and their present reserve be surrendered. Chacastapasin's band should be broken up and its reserve surrendered; the band being treated as suggested with One Arrow's. Neither of these bands are large enough to render it desirable to maintain instructors permanently with them, and as they are constituted of bad and lazy Indians nothing can be done without constant supervision for them. The action suggested therefore would have been wise in any case, their rebellion justifies its pursuit.

11. All halfbreeds, members of rebel bands, although not shewn to have taken any active part in the rebellion, should have their names erased from the paysheets, and if this suggestion is not approved of, by directing that all belonging to any bands should reside on the reserves. Most of these halfbreeds would desire to be released from the terms of the treaty. It is desirable however that the communication between such people and the Indians be entirely severed as it is never productive of aught but bad results.

12. There are one or two Canadians, not possessed of Indian blood, on the paysheets; these should be struck off.

13. James Seenum's band especially should receive substantial recognition of its loyalty, and all Indians like Mistawasis and Ahtahkakoop and other bands that have held aloof from the rebellion should receive some mark of the government's appreciation of their conduct. If such a mark is conferred carefully it will at once confirm them in their loyalty and assist in ensuring it in future, whilst increasing the contrast between their treatment and that of those who have acted differently; without leading them to believe that it is for the purchase of good behaviour, an effect to be guarded against.

14. Agents should be particularly strict in seeing that each and every Indian now works for every pound of provision given to him, and I would urge that so soon as possible directions be given to treat Indians that receive assistance in provisions and clothing in excess of treaty stipulations, as coming under the Masters and Servants Act, until such time as they become self-dependent. Unwilling ones can then be made to give value for what they receive, a policy heretofore most difficult to carry out.

15. Horses of rebel Indians should be confiscated, sold, and cattle or other necessaries be purchased with the proceeds of such sale. This action would cripple them for future rebellious movements; and they do not require ponies if made to stop on reserves, and adhere to agricultural pursuits. They would be retained on reserves too, with greater ease, if the means of travelling expeditiously, are taken from them. In view of the desirability of keeping them from wandering, where confiscation is impossible, endeavours might be made to induce a voluntary exchange of ponies for cattle, etc.

Hayter Reed
Asst. Com.

Regina
July 20th/85

[Source: *Glenbow Archives*, Edgar Dewdney papers, box 4, f. 66, 1414–20.]

Hayter Reed's List of Band Behaviour during Rebellion

No. of Reserve	Band	Remarks

Birtle Agency

No. of Reserve	Band	Remarks
57	Enoch, Sioux, Bird Tail Creek	—
58	Young Chief, Wadbudiska, Little Crow, Sioux Assiniboine and Oak Rivers	I do not think that these Sioux should be in any way rewarded for their loyalty, as this country is an asylum for them, and they fully understood the fruits of disloyalty
59	No chief, Sioux, Old Lake	—
60	Ka dominie, Sioux, Turtle Mountain	—
61	Kee-see-koo-wenin, Salteaux, Riding Mountain	Loyal
62	Way way se cappo, Salteaux, Bird Tail	A few became impudent
63	The Gambler, Salteaux, Silver Creek	Loyal—Two men of this Band raided a house, were caught, tried and imprisoned.
64	Coté, Salteaux, Crow Stand, near Pelly	Loyal

65	The Key, Salteaux and Swampy, Fort Pelly	Loyal
66	Kee-see-Kouse, Salteaux and Swampy, Fort Pelly	Loyal
67	South Quill, Salteaux, Rolling River	Loyal
68	Pheasant Rump, Assiniboine, Moose Mountains	Loyal
69	Ocean Man, Assiniboine and Cree, Moose Mountains	Loyal
70	White Bear, Assiniboine and Cree, Moose Mountains	Loyal

Crooked Lakes Agency

71	Ka-ke-she-way, or Loud Voice, Assiniboine and Cree, Round Lake	Four men from this Band reported to have been North during the Rebellion, names known. Only one appears paid with his Band in 1884.
72	Ka-ke-wis-ta-kaw, Cree and Assiniboine, Round Lake	Five of this Band reported to have been North during the Rebellion, names known, only two paid in /84 with their chief.
73	Cowesess, or Little Child, Assiniboine and Cree, Crooked Lakes	Loyal with one or two exceptions.
73a	Ouchaness, or Little Bone, Assiniboine and Cree, Leech Lake	Some of these Indians raided farms, and stole some horses; they are awaiting trial.
74	Sakimay, or Mosquito, Assiniboine and Cree, Crooked Lakes	Loyal
76	The-man-who-took-the-coat, Assiniboine, Indian Head. This Band includes remnant of Long Lodges'	Very Loyal
81	Pee-pee-kee-sis, Salteaux and Cree, File Hills	+One of this Band reported North during Rebellion. Name known. Not on paysheets.
82	Okanese, Salteaux and Cree, File Hills	File Hill Indians generally behaved very bad, killed a large number
83	Star Blanket,	a large number of their cattle, and it is

	Salteaux and Cree File Hills	believed did some raiding. They received more rations than any Indians in the South.
84	Little Black Bear, Salteaux and Cree, File Hills	Two of this Band reported North during Rebellion; names known, not paid in /84 with their chief.

Muscowpetungs's Agency

75	Pia-pot, Cree, Qu'Appelle Valley	Six of this Band reported in the North during Rebellion, none of whom were paid in /84 with their Chief—names known.
78	Standing Buffalo, Sioux, Qu'Appelle Lakes	Very Loyal
79	Pasquah, Salteaux and Cree, Qu'Appelle Lakes	Loyal
80	Muscowpetung, Salteaux and Cree, Qu'Appelle Valley	A few of these Indians joined some Leech Lake Indians, and committed some depredations. These are being arrested.

Touchwood Hills Agency

85	Mus-cow-e-quahn, Salteaux and Cree, Little Touchwood Hills	Loyal—although several urgent appeals were made by Riel to them to join, as papers found at Batoche prove.
86	George Gordon, Salteaux and Cree, Little Touchwood Hills	Loyal
87	Day Star, Salteaux and Cree, Touchwood Hills	Two of this Band reported North during the Rebellion—names known—with this exception Loyal, neither of them paid with their chief in /84.
88	Kah-wah-kah-toose, or Poor Man, Salteaux and Cree, Touchwood Hills	Loyal but very unsettled
89	Yellow Quill, Salteaux and Cree, Fishing Lake	Know nothing definite of them. Papers found at Batoche, state they were ready to join the movement.
90	at Nut Lake	

Carlton Agency

94	White Cap, Sioux, Moose Woods	A few remained loyal but are not deserving of special recognition.
95	One Arrow, Cree, 5 miles south of South Saskatchewan	All disloyal
96	Okemasis, Cree, Duck Lake	Ditto
97	Beardy, Cree, Duck Lake	Ditto
98	Chekastaypaysin, Cree, South Saskatchewan	A few of these men I think were loyal, but are not deserving of any special recognition.
99	John Smith, Swampy and Cree, South Saskatchewan	This Band remained loyal, but there is no person in it who one could single out for special recognition, still I think it should receive some mark of favour.
100	James Smith, Swampy and Cree, Fort à la Corne	Ditto
101	William Twatt, Swampy and Cree, Sturgeon Lake, north of Prince Albert	Ditto
102	Petequakey, Swampy and Cree, Muskeg Lake	Disloyal after check received by the troops at Fish Creek, and must be treated as Rebel
103	Mis-tah-wasis, Swampy and Cree, Snake Lake	The loyalty of this chief and his Band was particularly marked, and should receive a most substantial recognition.
104	Ah-tah-kah-koop, Swampy and Cree, Sandy Lake	Ditto. I think I can reward these two Chiefs by giving them light waggons and horses, intended for other Chiefs pursuant to Treaty Stipulations, but which will not now be given.
105	Ko pah ha wa kenum, or Flying Dust, Swampy and Cree, Meadow Lakes	These Indians looted the Green Lake H.B.Cos. posts.

| 106 | Kenemotayo,
Swampy and Cree,
Assiniboine Lake | These Indians looted the Green Lake
H.B.Cos. posts. |

Battleford Agency

107	Young Chippeweyan, Cree	Disloyal
108	Red Pheasant, Cree, Eagle Hills	Some two or three Indians including the chief of this Band who although found in the rebel ranks are loyal. The Chief's brother "Baptiste" saved Applegarth's life.
109	Mosquito, Stony, Eagle Hills	Disloyal
110	Bear's Head, Stony, Eagle Hills	Disloyal
111	Lean Man, Stony, Eagle Hills	Disloyal
112	Moosoomin, Cree, Jack Fish Creek	Should be rewarded, a few members took part in cattle stealing, but not as armed rebels.
113	Sweet Grass, Cree, Battle River	Disloyal. The Chief was one of the most loyal.
113a	Strike-him-on-the-back, Cree, Battle River	Disloyal
114	Poundmaker, Cree, Battle River	Disloyal
115	Thunder Child and Napahase, Battle River	Disloyal
116	Little Pine, Cree, Battleford	Disloyal
117	Lucky Man, Cree, Battleford	Disloyal

Fort Pitt Agency

| 118 | Big Bear,
Cree, Fort Pitt | Disloyal |
| 119 | Seekaskootch,
Cree, Onion Lake | Disloyal. Chief killed at Frenchman's Hill. |

120	Wemisticooseawasis, Cree, Stony Lake	Disloyal
121	Ooneepowohayo, Cree, Frog Lake	Disloyal
122	Puskeahkewenin, Cree, Frog Lake	Disloyal
123	Keeheewin, Cree, Moose Lake	Disloyal
124	Kinoosayo, Chippeweyan, Cold Lake	Disloyal

Victoria Agency

125	Late Little Hunter's BD, Cree, Saddle Lake	Disloyal
126	Muskegwatic, Cree, Washatenow Creek	Disloyal
127	Blue Quill, Cree, Egg Lake	Loyal
128	Seenum, Cree, Whitefish Lake	Chief and some of his men should be rewarded. Official reports show the Loyal position they took.
129	Peeaysees, Cree, Lac la Biche	Disloyal
130	Antoine, Chippeweyans, Hearts Lake	Disloyal
131	Kaquamum, Cree, Beaver Lake	Disloyal

Edmonton Agency

132	Michel, Cree, Sturgeon River	Unsettled and should not receive any acknowledgement, but there may be some individual instances in this and other Edmonton Bands similar to this where rewards should be given.
133	Alexis, Stony, Lac Ste. Annes	Ditto
134	Alexander, Stony, Lac la Nonne	Ditto

| 135 | Enoch Lapotac, Cree, N. Edmonton | Ditto |
| 136 | Pass-pass-chase, Cree, Edmonton | Ditto |

Peace Hills Agency

137	Ermineskin, Cree, Bear's Hill	Same remark applied to Michel No. 132 applies here.
138	Sampson Cree Bear's Hill	A good many of these very unsettled and some raiding done,—a few individual cases will have to be dealt with severely.
139	Bobtail, Cree, Battle River	—
140	Muddy Bull, Cree, Pigeon Lake	Loyal
141	Chepoostequahn, or Sharphead, Stony, Peace Hills	Loyal

Blackfoot Crossing Agency

142	Stonies, Chiefs Jacob,	The whole of these Indians remained Loyal. I don't know of an individual case of joining the Rebels.
143	Bear's Paw, Chimiquy, Morleyville	
145	Sarcees, Bull's Head, Calgary	Ditto
146	Blackfeet, Crowfoot, and Old Sun, North and South of Bow River	Ditto

Blood Reserve Agency

| 147 | Piegans, Chief Eagle Tail, Old Man's River | The whole of these Indians remained Loyal. I don't know of an individual case of joining the Rebels. |
| 148 | Bloods, Red Crow, Pelly River | Ditto |

[Source: *National Archives of Canada*, Government Archives Division, Indian Affairs, RG 10, v. 3710, f. 19550-3, E. Dewdney to J.A. Macdonald, 21 August 1885.]

Indian Convictions

Defendant	Offence	Trial Venue	Conviction Date	Sentence
Tahkokan	Larceny	Battleford	June 27	2 years
Natoose	Horse Stealing	Battleford	June 29	6 years
Chesenus	Larceny	Battleford	June 29	6 years
Mistatimawas	Assault & Larceny	Battleford	June 29	6 years
Charles Pooyak	Horse Stealing	Battleford	June 29	6 years
Papequositauce	Stealing Cattle	Battleford	July 22	6 years
Seahkatamo	Stealing Cattle	Battleford	July 22	6 years
Weasaskewen	Stealing Cattle	Battleford	July 22	6 years
Big Belly	Arson	Battleford	July 22	6 years
White Face	Horse Stealing	Battleford	July 22	6 years
One Arrow	Treason-Felony	Regina	Aug. 14	3 years
Poundmaker	Treason-Felony	Regina	Aug. 19	3 years
A-ya-ta-ka-me-ka-pe-tung	Felony	Regina	Sept. 5	3 years
Aw-pis-ke-nen	Felony	Regina	Sept. 5	3 years
Was-pos-o-yan	Felony	Regina	Sept. 5	2 years
Big Bear	Treason-Felony	Regina	Sept. 10	3 years

Defendant	Offence	Trial Venue	Conviction Date	Sentence
Nan-e-sue	Treason-Felony	Regina	Sept. 16	2 years
Mis-cha-chaq-e-mish	Treason-Felony	Regina	Sept. 16	2 years
Kah-sah-ko-wa-tit	Treason-Felony	Regina	Sept. 16	2 years
Koos-top-e-quob	Treason-Felony	Regina	Sept. 16	2 years
Nah-pace-is	Treason-Felony	Regina	Sept. 16	2 years
Kah-ke-we-pah-tow	Treason-Felony	Regina	Sept. 16	2 years
Oos-ka-ta-task	Treason-Felony	Regina	Sept. 16	2 years
Ah-tim-yoo	Treason-Felony	Regina	Sept. 16	2 years
Ah-tom-iss-com-co-ah-wah-see	Treason-Felony	Regina	Sept. 16	2 years
The Hole	Treason-Felony	Regina	Sept. 17	6 months
Red Eagle	Treason-Felony	Regina	Sept. 17	3 years
Poor Crow	Treason-Felony	Regina	Sept. 17	3 years
Red Bean	Treason-Felony	Regina	Sept. 17	3 years
Left Hand	Treason-Felony	Regina	Sept. 17	3 years
Wandering Spirit	Murder	Battleford	Sept. 24	Death
Four Sky Thunder	Arson	Battleford	Sept. 24	14 years
Toussaint Calling Bull	Arson	Battleford	Sept. 24	10 years
Little Wolf	Arson	Battleford	Sept. 24	10 years
God's Otter	Horse Stealing	Battleford	Sept. 24	4 years
Old Man	Horse Stealing	Battleford	Sept. 24	6 years
Idol	Horse Stealing	Battleford	Sept. 24	6 years
Erect Man	Horse Stealing	Battleford	Sept. 24	2 years
Little Runner	Horse Stealing	Battleford	Sept. 24	4 years
Mountain Man	Stealing Cattle	Battleford	Sept. 25	6 months
Charles Ducharmes (alias Charlebois)	Murder	Battleford	Sept. 25	Death—reprieved

Defendant	Offence	Trial Venue	Conviction Date	Sentence
Dressy Man	Murder	Battleford	Sept. 25	Death— reprieved
Bright Eyes	Murder	Battleford	Sept. 25	20 years (Man- slaughter)
Louison Mongrain	Murder	Battleford	Sept. 25	Death— reprieved
Round the Sky	Murder	Battleford	Oct. 1	Death
Bad Arrow	Murder	Battleford	Oct. 3	Death
Miserable Man	Murder	Battleford	Oct. 3	Death
Itka	Murder	Battleford	Oct. 5	Death
Man Without Blood	Murder	Battleford	Oct. 5	Death
Mus-sin-ass	Treason-Felony	Battleford	Oct. 8	2 years
Oo-pin-ou-way-win	Treason-Felony	Battleford	Oct. 8	2 years
Pee-yay-cheew	Treason-Felony	Battleford	Oct. 8	2 years
Iron Body	Murder	Battleford	Oct. 9	Death
Little Bear	Murder	Battleford	Oct. 9	Death
Wahpiah	Treason-Felony	Battleford	Oct. 21	6 years

The above list does not include several Indians who were sentenced to less than six months.

[Source: Canada. *Sessional Papers*, 1886, n. 8, "Report of the Commissioner of the North-West Mounted Police, 1885," appendix O.]

note on sources

L OYAL TILL DEATH is based on a diverse collection of primary materials. This list is not meant to
be comprehensive, but simply highlights some of
the more important sources for the study. Readers interested in particular
or detailed references should consult the chapter notes.

Two sets of interviews were utilized: a small number collected on
behalf of the Saskatchewan Indian Federated College in 1984-85; and a
larger collection undertaken for the purposes of this study between 1992
and 1994. Although the oral history accounts were often lacking in specific
detail and therefore of limited use, the interviews provided invaluable
insight into Indian attitudes and motivations in 1885. This material was
supplemented by several unpublished reserve histories that were prepared for the Federation of Saskatchewan Indians in the 1980s.

A number of government sources were also consulted: the volumi-
nous records of the Department of Indian Affairs (National Archives of
Canada, Government Archives Division, Record Group 10); the rebellion
trials material assembled by the Justice department (RG 13); and early
historic sites files for rebellion events (Parks Canada, RG 84). Equally
invaluable were the trial transcripts for Louis Riel's capital case (Canada.
Sessional Papers, 1886, n. 43, including the appendix of Batoche documents) and the hearings of the Indian and Métis defendants (n. 52).

A good deal of Indian material is found in the papers of Prime
Minister John A. Macdonald—not a surprising discovery since Macdonald
was the senior Indian bureaucrat in Canada from 1878 to 1887. This
material is nicely complemented by the papers of Edgar Dewdney (both
in Ottawa and Calgary), who doubled as Indian commissioner and lieutenant governor for the North-West Territories.

There are also a number of seemingly obscure sources at various
western Canadian archival institutions that provided some rewarding new
information: Canadian Pacific Railway rebellion telegrams, and Alberta
Indian agency records at the Glenbow Museum and Archives; trader W.J.
McLean's reminiscences of events in the Fort Pitt area, and transcripts of

the 1886 Rebellion Claims Commission hearings at Prince Albert at the Hudson's Bay Company Archives; anthropologist David Mandelbaum's historical field notebooks, Thomas Clarke's 1885 Battleford diary, and the Campbell Innes papers (Canadian North-West Historical Society) at the Saskatoon branch of the Saskatchewan Archives Board; the Oblate collection at the Provincial Archives of Alberta; and the two-volume Cloutier account at the Archives de l'Archevêché de Saint-Boniface.

Finally, the Battleford-based *Saskatchewan Herald* provides a detailed, though at times biased, chronicle of events in the region.

Notes

1. *National Archives of Canada* [NAC], Manuscript Division, J.A. Macdonald papers, v. 283, 129919, C. Tupper to J.A. Macdonald, 30 April 1885.
2. A.L. Haydon, *Riders of the Plains* (Edmonton 1971), 155–56.
3. R. Connor, *The Patrol of the Sun Dance Trail* (Toronto 1914), 12.
4. G.F.G. Stanley, *The Birth of Western Canada: A History of the Riel Rebellions* (London 1936), 364, 378.
5. *The Birth of Western Canada* has recently been reissued by University of Toronto Press in the Reprints in Canadian History series with a new laudatory introduction by Thomas Flanagan.
6. In 1983, John Tobias argued in the pages of the *Canadian Historical Review* that the Canadian government deliberately interpreted the isolated incidents of Indian violence as acts of rebellion in order to derail a growing Indian movement for renegotiation of the treaties and to make the government's policy of coercion more effective. J.L. Tobias, "Canada's Subjugation of the Plains Cree, 1879–1885," *Canadian Historical Review*, v. 64, n. 4, 1983, 519–48. Tobias's subjugation argument was supported by a number of related studies. Hugh Dempsey, Big Bear's biographer, described how the powerful Cree chief was interested in a peaceful resolution of Indian grievances and that the spontaneous action of younger, frustrated warriors in early April 1885 effectively ended his political career. H.A. Dempsey, *Big Bear: The End of Freedom* (Vancouver 1984). Gerald Friesen, author of the award-winning *The Canadian Prairies*, observed that there was no Cree military movement in 1885—let alone an Indian and Métis uprising—and that Big Bear and Poundmaker remained "aloof" from Métis leader Louis Riel. G. Friesen, *The Canadian Prairies: A History* (Toronto 1984), 153. That same year, Bob Beal and Rod Macleod argued in *Prairie Fire: The 1885 North-West Rebellion* (Edmonton 1984), now the standard text on the rebellion, that Ottawa was determined to punish the Indians even though the Métis had started the agitation. At a 1985 Saskatoon confer-

ence commemorating the centennial of the rebellion, Blair Stonechild presented the results of his oral-history research program, in particular the Assiyiwin story, and demonstrated that the Duck Lake engagement was not a joint Indian-Métis ambush. B. Stonechild, "The Indian View of the 1885 Uprising," in F.L. Barron and J.B. Waldram, eds., *1885 and After: Native Society in Transition* (Regina 1986). J.R. Miller in *Skyscrapers Hide the Heavens: A History of Indian-White Relations in Canada* (Toronto 1989) noted that there were still lingering tensions between the various Indian tribes in 1885, that any violence was limited and localized in nature, and that the majority of the bands did not participate. And in her examination of Indian agricultural policy in western Canada, *Lost Harvests*, Sarah Carter not only noted that most Indians honoured their treaty pledge not to take up arms, but also drew attention to the "often overlooked" fact that Indians were "equally uneasy and apprehensive" in 1885. S. Carter, *Lost Harvests: Prairie Indian Reserve Farmers and Government Policy* (Montreal 1990), 128.

7. See, for example, the spate of new university texts. R.C. Brown, ed., *The Illustrated History of Canada* (Toronto 1991), 356; J.M. Bumsted, *The Peoples of Canada: A Post-Confederation History* (Toronto 1992), 26; D.N. Sprague, *Post-Confederation History: The Structure of Canadian History Since 1867* (Scarborough 1990), 63-64; A. Finkel et al, *History of the Canadian Peoples, v. II: 1867 to the Present* (Toronto 1993), 49; R.D. Francis et al, *Destinies: Canadian History Since Confederation* (Toronto 1992), 83-84.

8. On 8 March 1885, Justice Minister John Thompson told the House of Commons that forty-four Indians were convicted of various rebellion-related crimes. The annual report of the North-West Mounted Police for 1885, however, indicates that fifty-five Indians were sentenced to six months or longer for so-called rebellion crimes (see appendix five). Canada. House of Commons, *Debates*, 8 March 1886, 61; *Sessional Papers*, 1886, n. 8, "Report of the Commissioner of the North-West Mounted Police, 1885," appendix O.

9. This signage is currently under review or has been revised. Heritage Canada officials are concerned with correcting past, one-sided accounts of the events of 1885 and are updating site interpretations, as well as involving the First Nations communities.

10. Regina *Leader-Post*, 28 June 1977, 25 August 1977.

11. *Saskatchewan Indian Federated College [SIFC]*, John B. Tootoosis interview, Poundmaker reserve, 30 November 1984.

12. *Ibid.*, Florence Paul interview, One Arrow reserve, 15 February 1985.

13. The first set of interviews was collected by Wilfred Tootoosis of the Poundmaker reserve in 1984-85 for the Saskatchewan Indian Federated College; excerpts from these interviews were used in Blair Stonechild, "Saskatchewan Indians and the Resistance of 1885: Two Case Studies,"

Saskatchewan Education curriculum resource book, 1986. A more ambitious interview program, generously funded by Parks Canada, was undertaken between 1992 and 1994 for the purposes of this study. The interview work was conducted by aboriginal research assistants from ten Saskatchewan reserves and had the prior support and endorsement of the chief and/or council. The elders were presented with a traditional gift and then told about the project and the kind of information being sought. Over fifty interviews were collected.

14. Much of the information contained in government and political records about Indian behaviour during the rebellion was largely ignored up until the last generation when a new group of scholars did some excellent work in the area. Prime Minister John A. Macdonald, for example, served as superintendent general of Indian Affairs for nine years (1878-1887), and yet Donald Creighton's award-winning biography, written at a time when aboriginal history was not treated as part of Canadian history, says virtually nothing about this aspect of his career.

15. Miller, *Skyscrapers*, 188.

Accepting the Queen's Hand (pages 5-26)

1. J.L. Tobias, "Canada's Subjugation of the Plains Cree, 1879-1885," in J.R. Miller, ed., *Sweet Promises: A Reader in Indian-White Relations in Canada* (Toronto 1991), 212-14.

2. A. Morris, *The Treaties of Canada with the Indians of Manitoba and the North-West Territories* (Saskatoon 1991), 173.

3. See J.R. Miller, *Skyscrapers Hide the Heavens: A History of Indian-White Relations in Canada* (Toronto 1989), chapters 4-5.

4. R. Macleod, *The North-West Mounted Police and Law Enforcement* (Toronto 1976), 3.

5. Morris, *Treaties*, 296-97.

6. S. Sliwa, "Treaty Day for the Willow Cree," *Saskatchewan History*, v. 47, n. 1, spring 1995, 5.

7. *Ibid.*, 4-5. For a good discussion of this notion of reciprocity, see Jean Friesen, "Magnificent Gifts: The Treaties of Canada with the Indians of the Northwest 1869-76," *Transactions of the Royal Society of Canada*, series 5, v. 1, 1986, 41-51.

8. See A.J. Ray, *Indians in the Fur Trade: Their Role as Hunters, Trappers and Middlemen in the Lands Southwest of Hudson Bay, 1660-1870* (Toronto 1974).

9. Quoted in Sliwa, "Treaty Day," 4.

10. *Glenbow Archives*, Richard Hardisty papers, W. McKay to R. Hardisty, 28 August 1874. This reference was kindly provided by J.R. Miller.

11. Sliwa, "Treaty Day," 6-8.

12. P. Erasmus, *Buffalo Days and Nights* (Calgary 1974), 245.

13. Morris, *Treaties*, 181, 187.

14. *Ibid.*, 176; See also Sliwa, "Treaty Day," 3-4, 7.

15. *Saskatchewan Archives Board* [*SAB*], David Mandelbaum papers, R875, notebooks and transcripts, III-IV, 1934, f. 8a (2 of 3 folders), Joe Wolf interview, 21 July 1934, 7-9.

16. Erasmus, *Buffalo Days*, 238.

17. *Ibid.*, 239.

18. For a description of the nature and significance of the pipe-stem bundle, see D. Mandelbaum, *The Plains Cree* (Regina 1979), 258-60.

19. Morris, *Treaties*, 198.

20. Erasmus, *Buffalo Days*, 240-43. Apart from agreeing to pay Erasmus for his work translating at the negotiations, Erasmus was offered and accepted employment with the Department of Indian Affairs at White-fish Lake.

21. Morris, *Treaties*, 199.

22. *Ibid.*, 202.

23. Erasmus, *Buffalo Days*, 244.

24. Morris, *Treaties*, 205.

25. *Ibid.*, 208.

26. *Ibid.*

27. Erasmus, *Buffalo Days*, 247.

28. *Ibid.*, 249.

29. *Ibid.*, 249-50.

30. *Ibid.*, 250.

31. Morris, *Treaties*, 210-11.

32. *Ibid.*, 211.

33. *Ibid.*, 212-13.

34. *Ibid.*, 213.

35. *Ibid.*, 215-16.

36. *Ibid.*, 219-20.

37. *Ibid.*, 212.

38. Erasmus, *Buffalo Days*, 254.

39. 1,746 individuals: 13 chiefs, 44 headmen, 262 men, 473 women, 473 boys, and 481 girls. Morris, *Treaties*, 224.

40. Sliwa, "Treaty Day," 7; Morris, *Treaties*, 187-88, 225.

41. Morris, *Treaties*, 226.

42. Sliwa, "Treaty Day," 7-10.

43. Morris, *Treaties*, 188.

44. *Ibid.*, 183, 189, 229.

45. Erasmus, *Buffalo Days*, 259.

46. Morris, *Treaties*, 231.

47. *Ibid.*, 190.

48. Erasmus, *Buffalo Days*, 260.

49. Morris, *Treaties*, 237.
50. *Ibid.*, 238.
51. *Ibid.*, 239.
52. *Ibid.*, 240.
53. H.A. Dempsey, *Big Bear: The End of Freedom* (Vancouver 1984), 74.
54. Morris, *Treaties*, 240.
55. *Ibid.*, 241.
56. *Ibid.*, 242.
57. Dempsey, *Big Bear*, 77-78; Mandelbaum papers, notebooks and transcripts, V-VII, 1934, f. 8a (3 of 3 folders), Penes interview, 2 August 1934, 47-48. Sweetgrass was evidently buried at Frog Lake.

Feed Them or Fight Them (pages 27-45)

1. The Canadian government's attempt to subjugate the Indians of western Canada and the reasons for this policy are explained at length in J.L. Tobias, "Canada's Subjugation of the Plains Cree, 1879-1885," in J.R. Miller, ed., *Sweet Promises: A Reader in Indian-White Relations in Canada* (Toronto 1991), 212-40.
2. J. Friesen, "Magnificent Gifts: The Treaties of Canada with the Indians of the Northwest 1869-76," *Transactions of the Royal Society of Canada*, series 5, v. 1, 1986, 41-51. This idea is also discussed in S. Sliwa, "Treaty Day for the Willow Cree," *Saskatchewan History*, v. 47, n. 1, spring 1995, 9-10.
3. For the importance of establishing reserve farming before the buffalo disappeared, see S. Carter, *Lost Harvests: Prairie Indian Reserve Farmers and Government Policy* (Montreal 1990), 57-58.
4. J. Hines, *The Red Indians of the Plains: Thirty Years Missionary Experience in Saskatchewan* (Toronto 1916), 152.
5. J.L. Tobias, "History of the Mistawasis Band, 1870-1925," unpublished report, 10.
6. M.B. Todd, "Report on the Treaty Land Entitlement of the Beardy-Okemasis Band," unpublished report, 1980, 4-5.
7. B. Beal and R. Macleod, *Prairie Fire: The 1885 North-West Rebellion* (Edmonton 1984), 39-45.
8. *Ibid.*, 8.
9. Quoted in *Saskatchewan Herald*, 23 September 1878.
10. Todd, "Beardy-Okemasis Band," 8-12.
11. *National Archives of Canada* [NAC], Government Archives Division, Parks Canada, RG 84, v. 1383, f. HS-10-3-11, H. Tatro, "Duck Lake Detachment of the North-West Mounted Police," 13 April 1961.
12. J.L. Tobias, "Kamiyistowesit" (Beardy), in F. Halpenny, ed., *Dictionary of Canadian Biography*, v. 11 (Toronto 1982), 458-59.
13. *Saskatchewan Herald*, 9 February 1880.

14. E. Ahenakew, *Voices of the Plains Cree* (Regina 1995), 115.
15. Canada. *Sessional Papers*, 1881, n. 14, "Annual Report of the Department of Indian Affairs," 84.
16. See D. Owram, *Promise of Eden: The Canadian Expansionist Movement and the Idea of the West* (Toronto 1980).
17. Carter, *Lost Harvests*, 50-51.
18. *Ibid.*, 67.
19. *Ibid.*, 67-69.
20. *Ibid.*, 68-69.
21. Quoted in *Ibid.*, 70.
22. Quoted in *Ibid.*
23. *Ibid.*, 71-72.
24. N. Dyck, *What is the Indian "Problem"?: Tutelage and Resistance in Canadian Indian Administration* (St. John's 1991), 59-60.
25. *Ibid.*, 60.
26. Carter, *Lost Harvests*, 79-84.
27. *Ibid.*, 104.
28. *Ibid.*, 84-95.
29. E.B. Titley, "Hayter Reed and Indian Administration in the West," in R. Macleod, *Swords and Ploughshares* (Edmonton 1993), 113.
30. *NAC*, Manuscript Division, H. Reed papers, v. 18, H. Reed to T.M. Daly, 1893.
31. Canada. *Sessional Papers*, 1881, n. 14, "Annual Report of the Department of Indian Affairs," 83.
32. K.J. Tyler, "The History of the Mosquito, Grizzly Bear's Head, and Lean Man Bands, 1878-1920," unpublished interim report, 7-8.
33. Carter, *Lost Harvests*, 99.
34. Montreal *Gazette*, 29 September 1879.
35. Quoted in Carter, *Lost Harvests*, 117.
36. *Ibid.*, 88-89, 99-100.
37. S. Sliwa, "Standing the Test of Time: A History of Beardy's/Okemasis Reserve, 1876-1951," unpublished M.A. thesis, Trent University, 1993, 65-66.
38. Titley, "Hayter Reed," 112.
39. *Saskatchewan Herald*, 22 March 1880.
40. H.A. Dempsey, *Big Bear: The End of Freedom* (Vancouver 1984), 85.
41. *Ibid.*, 78, 89.
42. Quoted in *Ibid.*, 90.
43. Tobias, "Canada's Subjugation," 216.
44. Quoted in Dempsey, *Big Bear*, 107.
45. T. Flanagan, *Louis "David" Riel: "Prophet of the New World"* (Toronto 1979), 101-9; M. Siggins, *Riel: A Life of Revolution* (Toronto 1995), 293-96.
46. Flanagan, *Louis "David" Riel*, 107-8.
47. Chicicum, a member of Beardy's band, fell under Riel's influence in

Montana and subsequently served as one of his special emissaries in 1885. See chapter eight.

48. Quoted in Dempsey, *Big Bear*, 94.
49. W.B. Cameron, *Blood Red the Sun* (Calgary 1950), 36.
50. Tobias, "Canada's Subjugation," 218.
51. *Glenbow Archives*, Edgar Dewdney papers, box 4, f. 56, 1176-77, D.L. Macpherson to E. Dewdney, 22 August 1881.
52. Tobias, "Canada's Subjugation," 218.
53. *NAC*, Government Archives Division, Indian Affairs, RG 10, v. 3768, "Report to the Minister of the Interior on the Governor General's Tour," 4 November 1881.
54. *Ibid.*
55. *Ibid.*
56. N. Sluman, *Poundmaker* (Toronto 1967), 128-37.
57. *Saskatchewan Herald*, 30 September 1882.
58. Quoted in Dempsey, *Big Bear*, 102.
59. *Ibid.*, 100-5.
60. Quoted in *Ibid.*, 109.
61. *Ibid.*

Anything Short of War (pages 46-64)

1. Reproduced in *Edmonton Bulletin*, 3 February 1883.
2. See *Guide to Canadian Ministries Since Confederation* (Ottawa 1982), 13-16.
3. S. Gwyn, *The Private Capital: Ambition and Love in the Age of Macdonald and Laurier* (Toronto 1986), 128.
4. J.L. Tobias, "Piapot Band During the Period 1870-1958," unpublished interim report, 6-8.
5. J.L. Tobias, "Canada's Subjugation of the Plains Cree, 1879-1885," in J.R. Miller, ed., *Sweet Promises: A Reader in Indian-White Relations in Canada* (Toronto 1991), 219.
6. Besides withholding rations, the police arrested any Indians caught transporting a stolen horse into Canada and sentenced them to time in Stony Mountain Penitentiary. B. Hubner, "Horse Stealing and the Borderline: The NWMP and the Control of Indian Movement, 1874-1900," *Prairie Forum*, v. 20, n. 2, fall 1995, 290-91.
7. Tobias, "Piapot Band," 12-13.
8. *Glenbow Archives* [GA], Edgar Dewdney papers, box 3, f. 45, 741-42, F. White to E. Dewdney, 17 October 1882.
9. Tobias, "Canada's Subjugation," 219-20.
10. *Ibid.*, 220.
11. Quoted in H.A. Dempsey, *Big Bear: The End of Freedom* (Vancouver 1984), 116.
12. B. Beal and R. Macleod, *Prairie Fire: The 1885 North-West Rebellion*

(Edmonton 1984), 77-78.

13. Quoted in D.C. Barnett, *Poundmaker* (Don Mills 1976), 15.

14. Grizzly Bear's Head was also known as Powder Necklace, while Lean Man was sometimes called Thin Man.

15. *Saskatchewan Herald*, 20 January 1883.

16. K.J. Tyler, "The History of the Mosquito, Grizzly Bear's Head, and Lean Man Bands, 1878-1920," unpublished interim report, 2-4.

17. Canada. House of Commons, *Debates*, 9 May 1883, 1106

18. Canada. *Sessional Papers*, 1884, n. 6, "Auditor-General's Report for the Year ended 30th June, 1883," 1.

19. *Ibid.*, 332.

20. N.E. Dyck, "The Administration of Federal Indian Aid in the North-West Territories, 1879-1885," unpublished M.A. thesis, University of Saskatchewan, 1970, 40.

21. "Auditor-General's Report for 1883," 345.

22. Dyck, "Administration of Federal Indian Aid," 39, 42.

23. *GA*, Dewdney papers, box 2, f. 36, 471-72, J.A. Macdonald to E. Dewdney, 17 November 1883.

24. Dempsey, *Big Bear*, 120-21.

25. S. Carter, *Lost Harvests: Prairie Indian Reserve Farmers and Government Policy* (Montreal 1990), 119-20.

26. Quoted in I. Andrews, "Indian Protest Against Starvation: The Yellow Calf Incident of 1884," *Saskatchewan History*, v. 28, n. 2, spring 1975, 46.

27. *Ibid.*, 48. In the 1880s, the average death rate on the Battleford reserves was 58 per 1,000 population; File Hills 62 per 1,000; and Crooked Lakes 56.4 per 1,000. By comparison, the death rate in Winnipeg in 1890 was 15.7 per 1,000. M. Lux, "Beyond the 'Biological Invasion' Theory of History: Disease and Native Peoples on the Canadian Prairies, 1880-1920," unpublished paper presented before Canadian Historical Association, Montreal, 1995. Blair Stonechild has calculated an annual 10 percent decline in the Indian population for the period 1880-85. Blair Stonechild, "The Indian Role in the North-West Rebellion of 1885," unpublished M.A. thesis, University of Regina, 102 (table 4).

28. *National Archives of Canada* [*NAC*], Government Archives Division, Indian Affairs, RG 10, v. 3745, f. 29656, pt. 1, O.C. Edwards to J.A. Macdonald, 13 May 1884.

29. Tobias, "Piapot Band," 15-22.

30. Dempsey, *Big Bear*, 123-25.

31. *Ibid.*, 123.

32. Quoted in *Ibid.*, 126.

33. *Ibid.*, 127.

34. *Ibid.*, 128-34.

35. *GA*, Dewdney papers, box 4, f. 69, 1493-96, L.N. Crozier to F. White, 27 July 1884.

36. See T. Flanagan, *Louis "David" Riel: "Prophet of the New World"* (Toronto 1979).

37. Canada. *Sessional Papers*, 1886, n. 43, "The Queen v. Louis Riel," appendix (43h), 2.

38. NAC, Manuscript Division, J.A. Macdonald papers, v. 107, 42831, E. Dewdney to J.A. Macdonald, 26 July 1884.

39. GA, Dewdney papers, box 4, f. 69, 1493-96, L.N. Crozier to F. White, 27 July 1884.

40. NAC, Macdonald papers, v. 107, 42831-33, J.A. Macrae to E. Dewdney, 29 July 1884.

41. S. Sliwa, "Standing the Test of Time: A History of Beardy's/Okemasis Reserve, 1876-1951," unpublished M.A. thesis, Trent University, 1993, 65-69.

42. Tobias, "Canada's Subjugation," 224-25.

43. NAC, RG 10, v. 3697, f. 15423, J.A. Macrae to E. Dewdney, 25 August 1884.

44. *Ibid.*, Macdonald papers, v. 107, 42872-77, H. Reed to E. Dewdney, 25 August 1884.

45. Dempsey, *Big Bear*, 140-41.

46. E. Ahenakew, *Voices of the Plains Cree* (Regina 1995), 114 (n. 24).

47. *Saskatchewan Herald*, 6 September 1884.

48. NAC, Macdonald papers, v. 107, 42807-14, J.M. Rae to J.A. Macdonald, 5 July 1884.

49. GA, Dewdney papers, box 4, f. 6, C.B. Rouleau to E. Dewdney, 5 September 1884.

50. NAC, Macdonald papers, v. 107, 42872-77, H. Reed to E. Dewdney, 25 August 1884; GA, Dewdney papers, box 4, f. 54, 1111-16, E. Dewdney to L. Vankoughnet, 12 December 1884.

51. Tobias, "Canada's Subjugation," 221-26.

52. Quoted in Dempsey, *Big Bear*, 126.

53. These measures were formalized in the 1884 Indian Amendment Act and the Indian Advancement Act, D. De Brou and B. Waiser, *Documenting Canada: A History of Modern Canada in Documents* (Saskatoon 1992), 135-40.

54. Tobias, "Canada's Subjugation," 227.

55. GA, Dewdney papers, box 3, f. 47, 797-98, J.A. Macdonald to F. White, 15 September 1884.

56. Tobias, "Canada's Subjugation," 227.

57. NAC, RG 10, v. 3701, f. 17,169, P. Ballendine to E. Dewdney, 20 November 1884.

58. GA, Dewdney papers, box 3, f. 47, 802-3, L.N. Crozier to F. White, 14 November 1884.

59. NAC, Macdonald papers, v. 107, 42945-46, W. Pearce to A.M. Burgess, 22 September 1884.

60. J.L. Tobias, "A Brief History of Little Pine/Lucky Man Bands, 1870-

1910," interim report, n.d., 21-23; *NAC*, Macdonald papers, v. 107, 43003-7, H. Reed to E. Dewdney, 24 January 1885.

61. *NAC*, RG 10, v. 3697, f. 15,423, H. Reed to J.A. Macdonald, 23 January 1885.

62. *GA*, Dewdney papers, box 2, f. 38, 546-47, J.A. Macdonald to E. Dewdney, 23 February 1885.

63. Tobias, "Canada's Subjugation," 226-27; Dempsey, *Big Bear*, 142-49.

Everything to Lose (pages 65-84)

1. *Saskatchewan Indian Federated College* [*SIFC*], Harry Michael interview, Beardy-Okemasis reserve, 13 March 1985; Assiyiwin was a twin; the other child died at birth. Harry Angus interview, Thunderchild reserve, 5 April 1985.

2. Canada. *Sessional Papers*, 1886, n. 43, "The Queen v. Louis Riel," 51.

3. *Ibid.*, appendix (43h), 47-48.

4. Many of the South Branch Métis, although bearing French names, were unilingual Cree or Ojibwa-Cree speakers. D. Lee, "The Métis Militant Rebels of 1885," *Canadian Ethnic Studies*, v. 21, n. 3, 1989, 10-12. See also D. Payment, *"The Free People–Otipemisiwak": Batoche, Saskatchewan, 1870-1930* (Ottawa 1990).

5. *SIFC*, Samuel Seeseequasis interview, Beardy-Okemasis reserve, 7 March 1985.

6. *Ibid.*, H. Michael interview.

7. B. Beal and R. Macleod, *Prairie Fire: The 1885 North-West Rebellion* (Edmonton 1984), 154.

8. *SIFC*, S. Seeseequasis interview.

9. *Ibid.*, H. Michael interview. The presence of a partially blind Indian is also mentioned in the Cloutier account. *Archives de l'Archevêché de Saint-Boniface*, Fonds Taché, "Compte rendu de l'abbé G. Cloutier," 1886, v. 2. 28; Robert Jefferson, *Fifty Years on the Saskatchewan* (Battleford 1929), 114; T. Flanagan, ed., *The Collected Writings of Louis Riel, v. 3* (Edmonton 1985), 75 (Assiyiwin is mistakenly identified as a member of the One Arrow band).

10. *SIFC*, H. Michael interview.

11. The Macleod *Gazette*, on 28 March 1885, for example, spoke in the gravest tones of the union of Métis and Indian forces. The most influential expression of the Indian-Métis conspiracy idea has been G.F.G. Stanley, *The Birth of Western Canada: A History of the Riel Rebellions* (London 1936).

12. *Glenbow Archives* [GA], Edgar Dewdney papers, box 4, f. 66, 1398-1401, H. Reed to E. Dewdney, 4 September 1884.

13. *National Archives of Canada* [NAC], Government Archives Division, Indian Affairs, RG 10, v. 3548, f. 749, P. Ballendine to H. Reed, 8 November 1884.

14. J.L. Tobias, "Canada's Subjugation of the Plains Cree, 1879-1885," in J.R. Miller, ed., *Sweet Promises: A Reader in Indian-White Relations in Canada* (Toronto 1991), 225-26.

15. *NAC*, Manuscript Division, John A. Macdonald papers, v. 107, 43001, E. Dewdney to J.A. Macdonald, 14 February 1885.

16. *GA*, Dewdney papers, box 4, f. 66, 1406-9, D.H. Macdowall to E. Dewdney, 14 January 1885.

17. Quoted in D. Light, *Footprints in the Dust* (North Battleford 1987), 128.

18. Quoted in Beal and Macleod, *Prairie Fire*, 138.

19. D.N. Sprague, *Canada and the Métis, 1869-1885* (Waterloo 1988), 173.

20. Quoted in Beal and Macleod, *Prairie Fire*, 139.

21. On 18 March 1885, the day Irvine's force left Regina, the men had lunch on the Piapot reserve and then camped for the night on the Muscowpetung reserve. Two days later, they camped next to the Poor Man and Day Star reserves in the Touchwood Hills. Light, *Footprints*, 138, 145.

22. Quoted in Beal and Macleod, *Prairie Fire*, 139.

23. Quoted in Light, *Footprints*, 141.

24. *GA*, Dewdney papers, box 4, f. 67, 1428, L. Crozier to E. Dewdney, 18 March 1885.

25. *NAC*, RG 10, v. 3709, f. 19,550-51, J.B. Lash to E. Dewdney, 17 March 1885.

26. The capture of Lash and Tompkins is often cited as the first act of the North-West Rebellion.

27. K.J. Tyler, "Kapeyakwaskonam" (One Arrow), in F. Halpenny, ed., *Dictionary of Canadian Biography*, v. 11 (Toronto 1982), 461.

28. *Saskatchewan Archives Board [SAB]*, David Mandelbaum papers, notebooks and transcripts, I-II, 1934, f. 8a, Duck Lake Agency, 18 July 1934, 174-78.

29. *NAC*, v. 3682, f. 12628, A.W. Ponton to E. Dewdney, 31 December 1884.

30. Canada. *Sessional Papers*, 1886, n. 52, "Rebellion Trials," 32.

31. Lee, "Métis Militant Rebels," 12.

32. After the rebellion, Dumas fled to the United States with Gabriel Dumont and joined the Buffalo Bill show. G. Woodcock, *Gabriel Dumont: The Métis Chief and His Lost World* (Edmonton 1975), 226, 231.

33. *NAC*, Macdonald papers, v. 212, 90617-21, C.W. Herchmer to E. Dewdney, 10 February 1886.

34. *SIFC*, Florence Paul interview, One Arrow reserve, 15 February 1985.

35. "Rebellion Trials," 11.

36. J.B. Dawson, *The Relationship of the Catholic Clergy to Métis Society in the Canadian North-West, 1845-1885: With Particular Reference to the South Saskatchewan District* (Ottawa 1979), 238-39.

37. J.L. Tobias, "Kamiyistowesit" (Beardy), in Halpenny, ed., *Dictionary of Canadian Biography*, v. 11, 458-59.

38. Philomene Gamble interview, Edwin Mandes interview, n.d.; Albert Seeseequasis interview, Beardy-Okemasis reserve, March 1994.

39. "There were only a few Indians who supported Riel . . . My grandfather was always careful not to mention the names of those who assisted the Métis." *SIFC*, H. Michael interview; Alice Peeteeuce interview, Beardy-Okemasis reserve, March 1994.
40. Flanagan, ed., *Collected Writings*, v. 2, 232-34.
41. Lee, "Métis Militant Rebels," 11.
42. *NAC*, Macdonald papers, v. 107, 42872-77, H. Reed to E. Dewdney, 25 August 1884.
43. *Ibid.*, v. 212, 90617-21, C.W. Herchmer to E. Dewdney, 10 February 1886.
44. *SIFC*, S. Seeseequasis interview.
45. *Ibid.*, A. Seeseequasis interview.
46. *NAC*, Macdonald papers, v. 107, 43030-33, E. Dewdney to J.A. Macdonald, 25 March 1885.
47. *Ibid.*, v. 290, 133047-51, L. Vankoughnet to J.A. Macdonald, 31 March 1885.
48. *NAC*, RG 10, v. 3668, f. 10,644, J.A. Macdonald to Privy Council, 18 January 1884.
49. *GA*, Dewdney papers, box 2, f. 38, 553-56, J.A. Macdonald to E. Dewdney, 29 March 1885.
50. Quoted in Beal and Macleod, *Prairie Fire*, 122.
51. Reproduced in Flanagan, ed., *Collected Writings*, v. 2, 272.
52. *Ibid.*, 240.
53. T. Flanagan, *Louis "David" Riel: "Prophet of the New World"* (Toronto 1979), 107-9.
54. *Ibid.*, 133-34.
55. *Ibid.*, 127-29. Maggie Siggins also discusses Riel's new theology throughout her biography, *Riel: A Life of Revolution* (Toronto 1995).
56. R. Wiebe and B. Beal, eds., *War in the West: Voices of the 1885 Rebellion* (Toronto 1985), 87.
57. Reproduced in Flanagan, ed., *Collected Writings*, v. 3, 60.
58. Canada. *Sessional Papers*, 1886, n. 52, "Rebellion Trials," 18.
59. *Ibid.*, appendix (43h), 46.
60. Flanagan, ed., *Collected Writings*, v. 3, 67-68.
61. Reproduced in *Ibid.*, 69 (Chers parents et amis, nous vous conseillons de faire attention, Tenez-vous prêt à tout. Prenez avec vous les sauvages. Ramassez-les de tous coté . . . Murmurez, gondez et menacez. Soulevez les sauvages. Mettez aussi la Police du Fort Pitt et du Fort Bataille dans l'impossibilité . . . Ayez confiance en Jésus-christ. Mettez-vous sous la protection de la Sainte Vierge.)
62. Beal and Macleod, *Prairie Fire*, 162; Light, *Footprints*, 183.
63. Reproduced in Flanagan, ed., *Collected Writings*, v. 3, 77.
64. *Ibid.*, 76.
65. *SAB*, Mandelbaum papers, notebooks and transcripts, I-II, 1934, f. 8a, 157, 164. Sounding with Flying Wings was also known as Keetoowahan

(sometimes spelled Keeteewayhow or Uktuwehau); Payment, *Free People*, appendix c, 329; A. Morris, *The Treaties of Canada with the Indians of Manitoba and the North-West Territories* (Saskatoon 1991), 356.

66. Lee, "Métis Militant Rebels," 11.
67. *Hudson's Bay Company Archives* [HBCA], E.9/29, "Evidence Collected at the 1886 Rebellion Claims Commission Hearing at Prince Albert," George Robertson testimony, 15–17.
68. Solomon Johnstone interview, Mistawasis reserve, *Kataayuk* (Saskatoon n.d.), mimeographed collection of interview transcripts, Saskatchewan Indian Cultural College.
69. *Ibid.*
70. *Ibid.*; See also J. Tobias, "History of the Mistawasis Band, 1870–1925," unpublished report, 18–19.
71. *HBCA*, "Claims Commission," C.N. Garson testimony, 5.
72. *NAC*, RG 10, v. 3584, f. 1130, pt. 3A, L. Couture to A. McDonald, 20 March 1885.
73. *Ibid.*, A. McDonald to E. Dewdney, 31 March 1885.
74. *Ibid.*, A. McBeath to A. McDonald, 28 March 1885.
75. *GA*, Dewdney papers, box 4, f. 67, 1446, T.C. Down to A.E. Forget, 24 March 1885.
76. *Ibid.*, CPR telegrams, E. Dewdney to J.M. Egan, 26 March 1885.
77. *NAC*, RG 10, v. 3584, f. 1130, pt. 3A, H. Keith to A. McDonald, 31 March 1885.
78. *Ibid.*, A. McDonald to E. Dewdney, 8 April 1885.

Unnecessary Nervousness (pages 85–105)

1. B. Waiser, "The North-West Mounted Police in 1874–1889: A Statistical Study," *Parks Canada Research Bulletin*, n. 117, November 1979, 13–14. Regina replaced Battleford as the territorial capital in 1883.
2. Red Pheasant, Mosquito, Grizzly Bear's Head, Sweetgrass, Strike-Him-on-the-Back, Thunderchild, Moosomin, Poundmaker, and Little Pine.
3. Canada. *Sessional Papers*, 1886, n. 52, "Rebellion Trials," 297–98.
4. *Ibid.*, 301–2.
5. *Saskatchewan Herald*, 14 June 1884.
6. R. Jefferson, *Fifty Years on the Saskatchewan* (Battleford 1928), 129.
7. *Saskatchewan Indian Federated College*, [SIFC], Alex Sapp interview, Little Pine reserve, 17 August 1982. According to the story, the Sweetgrass council already knew what had happened at Duck Lake by the time Riel's messengers arrived.
8. *Ibid.*
9. "Rebellion Trials," 310.
10. Jefferson, *Fifty Years*, 125.
11. "Rebellion Trials," 312.

12. *Glenbow Archives [GA]*, Edgar Dewdney papers, box 4, f. 57, 1224-25, L. Crozier to E. Dewdney, 30 January 1885.
13. "Battleford During the Rebellion of 1885," *Saskatchewan History*, v. 38, n. 2, spring 1985, 109-10, 20-29 March 1885.
14. Canada. *Sessional Papers*, 1880, n. 4, "Annual Report of the Department of Indian Affairs for 1879," 96.
15. *Saskatchewan Herald*, 9 January 1885.
16. *Saskatchewan Archives Board [SAB]*, Thomas Clarke papers, 1885 diary, 24 March 1885.
17. GA, 1885 CPR telegrams, P.G. Laurie to Winnipeg *Times*, 28 March 1885.
18. *SAB*, Clarke papers, 1885 diary, 29 March 1885.
19. "Rebellion Trials," 301-2.
20. *Ibid.*, 297-98.
21. GA, Dewdney papers, box 4, f. 66, 1398-1401, H. Reed to E. Dewdney, 4 September 1884.
22. *National Archives of Canada [NAC]*, Government Archives Division, Indian Affairs, RG 10, v. 3852, f. 949, J.M. Rae to E. Dewdney, 19 November 1884; P. Ballendine to H. Reed, 20 November 1884.
23. *Ibid*, Manuscript Division, E. Dewdney papers, v. 5, J.M. Rae to E. Dewdney, 29 March 1885.
24. *Ibid*, J.A. Macdonald papers, v. 107, 42829-90, J.M. Rae to E. Dewdney, 29 July 1884.
25. *Ibid.*, 42993-94, E. Dewdney to J.A. Macdonald, 13 February 1885.
26. "Rebellion Trials," 299.
27. *Ibid.*, 296-98.
28. Dobbs would later be killed at the Cut Knife battle.
29. *Hudson's Bay Company Archives [HBCA]*, E.9/29, "Evidence Collected at the 1886 Rebellion Commission Claims Hearing at Prince Albert," W. McKay testimony, 49-50.
30. NAC, Dewdney papers, v. 5, 1879, J.M. Rae to E. Dewdney, 30 March 1885.
31. *Ibid.*
32. GA, 1885 CPR telegrams, E.W. Warner to J.M. Egan, 31 March 1885; "Battleford During the Rebellion," 110, 30 March 1885.
33. W.B. Cameron, "Clan McKay in the West," *The Beaver*, September 1944, 5.
34. G. Woodcock, *Gabriel Dumont: The Métis Chief and His Lost World* (Edmonton 1975), 187; T. Flanagan, ed., *The Collected Writings of Louis Riel*, v. 3 (Edmonton 1985), 70; Jefferson, *Fifty Years*, 123, 134; D. Light, *Footprints in the Dust* (North Battleford 1987) 122-23.
35. NAC, Macdonald papers, v. 213, 90899-900, E. Dewdney to J.A. Macdonald, 22 November 1886.
36. *Ibid.*, v. 107, 43162-64, statement of William Lightfoot, 31 May 1885; "Rebellion Trials," 306-7.

37. *NAC*, Macdonald papers, v. 213, 90899–900, E. Dewdney to J.A. Macdonald, 22 November 1886.

38. *Ibid.*, 43156–57, statement of Heymozah, 31 May 1885.

39. Light, *Footprints*, 173.

40. K.J. Tyler, "The History of the Mosquito, Grizzly Bear's Head, and Lean Man Bands, 1878–1920," unpublished interim report, 1–2.

41. Itka was also known as Crooked Legs or "One-Who-Turns-a-Blanket-Inside-Out."

42. *SIFC*, John B. Tootoosis interview, Poundmaker reserve, 30 November 1984. Another version of the story suggests that Itka went to Payne for food for his sick daughter and that when he was refused he came back later and shot him.

43. Light, *Footprints*, 173.

44. *NAC*, Macdonald papers, v. 107, 43162–64, statement of William Lightfoot, 31 May 1885.

45. Light, *Footprints*, 275.

46. "Rebellion Trials," 296.

47. Jefferson, *Fifty Years*, 128.

48. "Battleford During the Rebellion," 110, 31 March, 4 April 1885.

49. *NAC*, Macdonald papers, v. 107, 43162–64, statement of William Lightfoot, 31 May 1885.

50. Poundmaker was originally a member of the Red Pheasant band but left and took up his own reserve because of a disagreement with former Red Pheasant chief Wuttunee.

51. Light, *Footprints*, 188; *GA*, 1885 CPR telegrams, A.E. Fenton to J.M. Egan, 6 April 1885.

52. W. Hildebrandt, *Views from Fort Battleford: Constructed Visions of an Anglo-Canadian West* (Regina 1994), 85.

53. *Saskatchewan Herald*, 12 October 1885.

54. Light, *Footprints*, 190–91.

55. *SAB*, Clarke papers, 1885 diary, 31 March 1885.

56. D. Morton and R. Roy, eds., *Telegrams of the North-West Campaign, 1885* (Toronto 1972), 64, W. Morris to F. White, 31 March 1885.

57. *Ibid.*, 46, J.M. Rae to E. Dewdney, 30 March 1885.

58. *GA*, 1885 CPR telegrams, J.M. Rae to E. Dewdney, 31 March 1885.

59. *SAB*, Clarke papers, 1885 diary, 31 March 1885.

60. Jefferson, *Fifty Years*, 128.

61. On 13 March 1885, the *Saskatchewan Herald* reported that Red Pheasant was near death.

62. "Rebellion Trials," 309, 312.

63. For a description of the Rattler Society, see Light, *Footprints*, 353.

64. *NAC*, Government Archives Division, Parks Canada, RG 84, v. 1057, f. BA28, pt. 1, A.J.H. Richardson memorandum, 18 April 1957.

65. "Rebellion Trials," 296.

66. *GA*, 1885 CPR telegrams, W. McKay to HBC Commissioner, 1 April 1885.
67. "Battleford During the Rebellion," 111-12, 1-8 April 1885.
68. This interpretation seemed confirmed when Riel's note calling on the Indians of the area to neutralize the fort later fell into government hands.

Spring of Blood (pages 106-25)

1. Quote attributed to Father Lestanc in *Saskatchewan Herald*, 24 March 1879. Edgar Dewdney also considered Big Bear to be the most influential Indian on the prairies in the early 1880s. N. Dyck, *What is the Indian "Problem"?: Tutelage and Resistance in Canadian Indian Administration* (St. John's 1991), 66.
2. Allen Ronaghen argues in "Who Was that 'Fine Young Man'? The Frog Lake Massacre Revisited" (*Saskatchewan History*, v. 47, n. 2, fall 1995, 13-19) that ten men were actually killed at Frog Lake—the tenth being the new schoolteacher at the mission, a Mr. Michaux.
3. *Glenbow Archives* [*GA*], Edgar Dewdney papers, box 4, f. 66, H. Reed to E. Dewdney, 4 September 1884.
4. *Ibid.*, f. 57, L.N. Crozier to E. Dewdney, 30 January 1885.
5. D. Light, *Footprints in the Dust* (North Battleford 1987), 75.
6. Quoted in W.B. Cameron, *The War Trail of Big Bear* (London 1927), 19.
7. H.A. Dempsey, *Big Bear: The End of Freedom* (Vancouver 1984), 123; Light, *Footprints*, 107.
8. *National Archives of Canada* [*NAC*], Government Archives Division, Indian Affairs, RG 10, v. 3755, f. 30973, H. Reed to E. Dewdney, 18 June 1881.
9. *Ibid.*, Parks Canada, RG 84, v. 1381, f. HS10-3-2, v. 1, George Stanley, "An Account of the Frog Lake Massacre," October 1926. This story was originally collected by A.E. Peterson in response to a request from Judge F.W. Howay of the Historic Sites and Monuments Board for information about the events of April 1885. It was one of the few instances where the board actively sought the Indian perspective on the North-West Rebellion. See also Dempsey, *Big Bear*, 160, 165.
10. Dempsey, *Big Bear*, 141-48.
11. *NAC*, Manuscript Division, John A. Macdonald papers, v. 213, 90963, A. André to E. Dewdney, 8 September 1884. Father André also recommended the appointment of Jean-Baptiste Boucher, a future member of Riel's Exovedate.
12. G. Charette, *Vanishing Spaces: Memoirs of Louis Goulet* (Winnipeg 1976), 113.
13. *Ibid.*, 113, 131; Light, *Footprints*, 165, 208; Cameron, *The War Trail of Big Bear*, 46.
14. *NAC*, RG 10, v. 3715, f. 21264, P. Ballendine to H. Reed, 16 February 1885.

15. *Hudson's Bay Company Archives* [*HBCA*], Rebellion Claims Commission hearings, J.K. Simpson testimony.
16. *NAC*, Macdonald papers, v. 107, 43110-18, E. Dewdney to J.A. Macdonald, 3 June 1885.
17. Dempsey, *Big Bear*, 153.
18. Light, *Footprints*, 192.
19. *Ibid.*, 133.
20. T. Gowanlock and T. Delaney, *Two Months in the Camp of Big Bear* (Parkdale 1885), 19.
21. Charette, *Vanishing Spaces*, 113.
22. Light, *Footprints*, 165.
23. Dempsey, *Big Bear*, 144-45.
24. *NAC*, RG 10, v. 3582, f. 949, H. Reed to J.A. Macdonald, 2 January 1885; L. Vankoughnet to H. Reed, 28 January 1885.
25. D. Morton and R. Roy, eds., *Telegrams of the North-West Campaign, 1885* (Toronto 1972), 70, J.M. Rae to L. Vankoughnet, 31 March 1885.
26. V. Lachance, "The Diary of Francis Dickens," *Queen's University Bulletin*, n. 59, May 1930, 14.
27. *Saskatchewan Indian Federated College* [*SIFC*], Fred Horse interview, Frog Lake reserve, 4 April 1985. An almost identical version of Kamistatin's story was recounted in October 1926 by John Horse (Duom), Fred's father. *NAC*, RG 84, v. 1381, f. HS10-3-2, v. 1, John Horse, "An Account of the Frog Lake Massacre," October 1926.
28. Nine of the Duck Lake dead were civilians.
29. *SIFC*, F. Horse interview.
30. Canada. *Sessional Papers*, 1886, n. 46, "Rebellion Trials," 213.
31. Dempsey, *Big Bear*, 153.
32. *SIFC*, F. Horse interview.
33. *Ibid.*
34. *Ibid.*
35. *Ibid.*
36. Stanley, "An Account of the Frog Lake Massacre."
37. Charette, *Vanishing Spaces*, 117.
38. Dempsey, *Big Bear*, 153-54.
39. *Ibid.*, 154-56.
40. *Ibid.*, 155-56; Charette, *Vanishing Spaces*, 120-21.
41. I. Little Bear, "My Own Story," *The Bonneyville Tribune*, v. 10, n. 4, 25 April 1958.
42. *SIFC*, F. Horse interview. Although some authors claim that Quinn went to the HBC store to secure Big Bear's permission to remain in the settlement (see, for example, Dempsey, *Big Bear*, 156-57), Kamistatin was there during Quinn's brief visit and said that the agent simply told Mrs. Simpson, the wife of the HBC store manager, that he had instructed all the prisoners to go to his house.

43. J. Horse, "An Account of the Frog Lake Massacre."
44. Little Bear, "My Own Story."
45. Morton and Roy, eds., *Telegrams*, 148, W.S. Morris to A.P. Caron, 9 April 1885.
46. Little Bear, "My Own Story."
47. *SIFC*, F. Horse interview.
48. "Rebellion Trials," 204.
49. *GA*, Dewdney papers, box 4, f. 66, H. Reed to E. Dewdney, 4 September 1884.
50. Stanley, "An Account of the Frog Lake Massacre."
51. *Ibid.*
52. *Ibid.*; Dempsey, *Big Bear*, 165.
53. Stanley, "An Account of the Frog Lake Massacre."
54. D. Christensen, "Selected Aspects of Fort Pitt's History," Saskatchewan Parks and Renewable Services, 1984, 99; Light, *Footprints*, 211; Seekaskootch carried with him a peace pipe from Big Bear that remains in the possession of the Mann family today. Dorothy Long telephone interview, 22 March 1996.
55. *Saskatchewan Archives Board* [*SAB*], Campbell Innes papers, A113, II(b)8, "Henry Halpin manuscript," 15.
56. Reproduced in T. Flanagan, ed., *The Collected Writings of Louis Riel*, v. *3* (Edmonton 1985), 77.
57. *SAB*, "Halpin manuscript," 31. At the Rebellion Claims Commission hearings in Prince Albert in 1886, Reverend Quinney testified that Dufresne, a mixed-blood who accompanied Wandering Spirit's war party to Pitt, had told him that Edmonton had been taken and that the Métis were coming to help Big Bear.
58. B. Beal and R. Macleod, *Prairie Fire: The 1885 North-West Rebellion* (Edmonton 1984), 103.
59. *HBCA*, MS 372(5707), W.J. McLean, "Reminiscences of the Tragic Events at Frog Lake and in the Fort Pitt District with Some of the Experiences of the Writer and His Family during the North West Rebellion of 1885," 8–11.
60. There is considerable confusion over the day on which the Cree arrived at Fort Pitt. These dates are taken from the account of prisoner Henry Halpin, who reported that the Cree started for Pitt on 13 April, and after spending the night at Onion Lake, reached the fort near sunset the next day. W.J. McLean, F.S. Simpson, and Rev. C. Quinney all reported that the Indians reached Pitt on 14 April in their testimony before the Rebellion Claims Commission hearings in Prince Albert in 1886.
61. Dempsey, *Big Bear*, 168–69.
62. Light, *Footprints*, 259.
63. *HBCA*, McLean, "Reminiscences," 1.

64. *Ibid.*, 10.

65. Dempsey, *Big Bear*, 170.

66. *HBCA*, Rebellion Claims Commission hearings, F.S. Simpson testimony.

67. *Ibid.*, 170–71.

68. Morton and Roy, eds., *Telegrams*, 344, F. Middleton to A.P. Caron, 13 June 1885.

69. Christensen, "Selected Aspects of Fort Pitt's History," 112.

70. *Ibid.*, 114.

71. *GA*, Dewdney papers, box 4, f. 71, 1529–31, J. Anderson to E. Dewdney, 8 December 1885.

72. "Rebellion Trials," 216.

73. *SAB*, "Halpin manuscript," 31.

Making History (pages 126–45)

1. In 1876, General G.A. Custer and the U.S. 7th Cavalry were wiped out at the battle of the Little Big Horn.

2. D. Morton, *The Last War Drum* (Toronto 1972), 56–58.

3. K. Foster, "Moose Jaw viewed war from sideline seat," *Western People*, 21 March 1985, 10.

4. S. Carter, *Lost Harvests: Prairie Indian Reserve Farmers and Government Policy* (Montreal 1990), 127–28.

5. Quoted in D. Light, *Footprints in the Dust* (North Battleford 1987), 219–20.

6. Morton, *Last War Drum*, 51, 58.

7. D. Morton and R. Roy, eds., *Telegrams of the North-West Campaign, 1885* (Toronto 1972), 154, F.D. Middleton to A.P. Caron, 10 April 1885.

8. *National Archives of Canada* [NAC], Government Archives Division, Indian Affairs, RG 10, v. 3584, f. 1130, pt. 3A, A. McDonald to E. Dewdney, 8 April 1885.

9. *Ibid.*, pt. 1, L. Herchmer to E. Dewdney, 30 March 1885.

10. *Ibid.*, 5 April 1885.

11. *Ibid.*, 8 April 1885.

12. Morton, *Last War Drum*, 58–59.

13. Quoted in *Ibid.*, 59.

14. On 9 April 1885, Inspector Morris warned that "Poundmaker's programme was to attack us three days ago"—in other words, the same day that Battleford first learned of the Frog Lake massacre. Morton and Roy, eds., *Telegrams*, 147, W. Morris to W. Irvine, 9 April 1885.

15. *Saskatchewan Archives Board* [SAB], Thomas Clarke papers, 1885 diary, 11 April 1885.

16. "Battleford During the Rebellion of 1885," *Saskatchewan History*, v. 38, n. 2, spring 1985, 112 (emphasis added).

17. Canada. *Sessional Papers*, 1886, n. 43, "Batoche papers," 39.

18. *NAC*, Government Archives Division, Justice, RG 13, series F-2, v. 807, 1094-96, Au Métis et aux Sauvages du Fort Bataille et des environs, 8 April 1885.

19. Canada. *Sessional Papers*, 1886, n. 52, "Rebellion Trials," 304-5.

20. Quoted in T. Flanagan, ed., *The Collected Writings of Louis Riel, v. 3* (Edmonton 1985), 386. (*"Vous donnerez à Tchekikam [Chicicum] ce qu'il vous demandera."*)

21. G. Woodcock, *Gabriel Dumont: The Métis Chief and His Lost World* (Edmonton 1975), 167.

22. D. Lee, "The Métis Militant Rebels of 1885," *Canadian Ethnic Studies*, v. 21, n. 3, 1989, 10.

23. *NAC*, RG 13, series F-2, v. 816, 2481-82, "List of Prominent Names," n.d.

24. The two emissaries reached the Poundmaker reserve on 12 or 13 April. *Ibid.*, v. 807, 1097-1100, "J.A. McRae memorandum," n.d.

25. Canada. *Sessional Papers*, 1886, n. 43, "The Queen v. Louis Riel," 228 (exhibit 9).

26. "Rebellion Trials," 276-77.

27. R. Jefferson, *Fifty Years on the Saskatchewan* (Battleford 1929), 137.

28. *Ibid.*, 320; *NAC*, RG 13, series F-2, v. 817, 2813-14, A. Nolin statement, n.d.

29. "Battleford During the Rebellion," 112, 14 April 1885.

30. Jefferson, *Fifty Years*, 135.

31. *Saskatchewan Indian Federated College* [*SIFC*], Alex Sapp interview, Little Pine reserve, 17 August 1982.

32. M.R. Stobie, *The Other Side of the Rebellion: The Remarkable Story of Charles Bremner and His Furs* (Edmonton 1986), 44-47.

33. Jefferson, *Fifty Years*, 138-39.

34. Don Chatsis interview, Prince Albert, 3 February 1994.

35. *Ontario Archives* [*OA*], acc. 12843, Charles W. Dunning diary, 22 April 1885.

36. *Ibid.*, 25 April 1885. Dunning reported that the troops did little sleeping upon their arrival in the Battleford area because they expected an Indian attack.

37. Light, *Footprints*, 191-92.

38. Ironically, the troops did some looting of their own. "I am sorry to say that [the] little [that] was left in our houses by the Indians," Indian Agent Rae complained, "has been carried away by the troops . . . they act towards us as if they were in the enemy's country and we were the enemy." *NAC*, J.A. Macdonald papers, v. 107, 43173-78, J.M. Rae to E. Dewdney, 15 June 1885.

39. *Saskatchewan Herald*, 23 April 1885.

40. *NAC*, Manuscript Division, Edgar Dewdney papers, v. 5, 1806, W.D. Otter to E. Dewdney, 26 April 1885.

41. Quoted in Morton, *Last War Drum*, 103.

42. Quoted in B. Beal and R. Macleod, *Prairie Fire: The 1885 North-West Rebellion* (Edmonton 1984), 243.

43. *Ibid.*

44. *Glenbow Archives* [GA], Dewdney papers, box 4, f. 66, 1412-13, F. Middleton to E. Dewdney, 3 May 1885.

45. Light, *Footprints*, 353-56.

46. "Rebellion Trials," 320.

47. *Ibid.*, 266-67, 279-81; Canada. *Sessional Papers*, 1886, n. 52a, "Rebellion Trials [Battleford]," 22-23.

48. Reproduced in "Rebellion Trials [Battleford]," 24.

49. *Ibid.*

50. "Rebellion Trials," 279.

51. *NAC*, RG 13, series F-2, v. 806, 902, Jaykikum [Chicicum] to L. Riel, 29 April 1885.

52. *OA*, Dunning diary, 29 April 1885.

53. For the story of Old Man Stone, see Light, *Footprints*, 358-62. At the sixtieth anniversary of the battle, Basil Favel, who took part in the defence of the camp, confirmed that old Jacob heard the troops coming. Art Kasokeo reported this as well in his interview. *SAB*, Campbell Innes papers, A113, II(B)4, "Cut Knife Hill," 26 July 1935, Basil Favel interview; Art Kasokeo interview, Poundmaker reserve, February 1994.

54. *SIFC*, John B. Tootoosis interview, Poundmaker reserve, 30 November 1984; A. Sapp interview.

55. Irene Fineday interview, Sweetgrass reserve, April 1994.

56. *NAC*, Government Archives Division, Parks Canada, RG 84, v. 1381, f. HS10-3-4, pt. 2, C.F. Winter to F.W. Howay, 19 May 1930.

57. Morton, *Last War Drum*, 105-6; Jefferson, *Fifty Years*, 146.

58. A. Sapp interview; I. Fineday interview; Jim Tootoosis interview, Poundmaker reserve, January 1994.

59. *SAB*, Innes papers, "Cut Knife Hill," 26 July 1935, Sapostokun interview.

60. Light, *Footprints*, 421.

61. Jefferson, *Fifty Years*, 142, 146; L. Cochin, *Reminiscences of Father Cochin in Translation* (Battleford 1927), 34; D. Chatsis interview; J. Tootoosis interview; Eli Bear interview, Little Pine reserve, February 1994.

62. John Cuthand, "Of Myth . . . Legend . . . and Fact," *Tomorrow File*, 20.

63. Stan Cuthand interview, Saskatoon, April 1994.

64. H.A. Kennedy, "Memories of '85," *Canadian Geographical Journal*, v. 70, n. 5, May 1965, 154.

65. Lennox Wuttunee interview, Red Pheasant reserve, September 1994.

66. Quoted in Light, *Footprints*, 412, 415.

67. The number of Indian dead at Cut Knife was reported to the minister of the Militia on 15 May as being 105. Morton and Roy, eds., *Telegrams*,

282-83, H.P. Dwight to A.P. Caron, 15 May 1885.

68. *NAC,* RG 84, v. 1381, f. HS10-3-4, pt. 1, W.D. Otter to J.B. Harkin, 30 October 1923.

69. *Ibid.,* RG 10, v. 3584, f. 1130, pt. 1A, H. Reed to E. Dewdney, 5 May 1885.

70. Jefferson, *Fifty Years,* 143.

71. *NAC,* Macdonald papers, v. 107, 43071-74, E. Dewdney to J.A. Macdonald, 7 May 1885.

A Rope about Their Necks (pages 146-69)

1. D. Morton, "Reflections on Old Fred: General Middleton and the North-West Campaign of 1885," *NeWest Review,* v. 10, n. 9, May 1985, 5-6.

2. Canada. *Sessional Papers,* 1886, n. 43, "The Queen v. Louis Riel," 51.

3. T. Flanagan, *Louis "David" Riel: "Prophet of the New World"* (Toronto 1979), 138.

4. *Ibid.,* 140.

5. W. Hildebrandt, *The Battle of Batoche: British Small Warfare and the Entrenched Métis* (Ottawa 1985), 89-92.

6. *Ibid.,* 16.

7. D. Payment, *"The Free People–Otipemisiwak": Batoche, Saskatchewan, 1870-1930* (Ottawa 1990), 33, 159.

8. B. Beal and R. Macleod, *Prairie Fire: The 1885 North-West Rebellion* (Edmonton 1984), 226.

9. *National Archives of Canada* [NAC], Government Archives Division, RG 10, v. 3584, f. 1130, pt. 1, L. Herchmer to E. Dewdney, 24 April 1885.

10. Andrew Ironside interview, Whitecap reserve, 24 March 1994; Melvina Eagle interview, Whitecap reserve, April 1994; P.D. Elias, *The Dakota of the Canadian Northwest: Lessons for Survival* (Winnipeg 1988), 172-74.

11. Canada. *Sessional Papers,* 1886, n. 52, "Rebellion Trials," 42-44, 46.

12. *Ibid.,* 46-51; A. Dietz, "Wapahaska: the early history of the Whitecap Band," *Saskatoon History Review,* February 1991, 43-44.

13. Although the Whitecap Dakota were considered "alien" Indians on Canadian soil and not included in any western treaty, they were granted a reserve in the Moose Woods area on the strength of their historic alliance with the Crown dating back to the American Revolution. Dietz, "Wapahaska," 39-41.

14. D. Lee, "The Métis Militant Rebels of 1885," *Canadian Ethnic Studies,* v. 21, n. 3, 1989, 3-5; D. Payment, *Free People,* 72.

15. "The Queen v. Louis Riel," appendix (43h), 38, 40.

16. *NAC,* RG 10, v. 3584, f. 1130, pt. 1, L. Herchmer to E. Dewdney, 5 April 1885.

17. A. Ironside interview; M. Eagle interview.

18. "Rebellion Trials," 36.

19. Beal and Macleod, *Prairie Fire,* 228.

20. "The Queen v. Louis Riel," appendix (43h), 44.
21. D. Morton, *The Last War Drum* (Toronto 1972), 59.
22. "The Queen v. Louis Riel," appendix (43h), 15–16.
23. Beal and Macleod, *Prairie Fire*, 228–29.
24. Archives de l'Archevêché de Saint-Boniface, Fonds Taché, "Compte rendu de l'abbé G. Cloutier," 1886, v. 2, 1; Beal and Macleod, *Prairie Fire*, 229–30.
25. H.A. Kennedy, "Memories of '85," *Canadian Geographical Journal*, v. 70, n. 5, May 1965, 160.
26. Beal and Macleod, *Prairie Fire*, 230–34; Morton, *Last War Drum*, 64–68.
27. Beal and Macleod, *Prairie Fire*, 234; "The Queen v. Louis Riel," appendix (43h), 27.
28. "Compte rendu de l'abbé G. Cloutier," 1886, v. 1, 2–9.
29. Elias, *Dakota of the Canadian Northwest*, 172–74.
30. Quoted in S. Carter, *Lost Harvests: Prairie Indian Reserve Farmers and Government Policy* (Montreal 1990), 150.
31. *NAC*, RG 10, v. 3584, f. 1130, E. Dewdney, "Notice," 6 May 1885.
32. *Ibid.*, John A. Macdonald papers, v. 107, 43071–74, E. Dewdney to J.A. Macdonald, 7 May 1885.
33. *Ibid.*, RG 10, v. 3584, E. Dewdney, "Notice," 6 May 1885.
34. The government toyed with the idea of a pass system in the early 1880s, but backed away when it was argued that such a policy constituted a breach of the western treaties. S. Carter, "Controlling Indian Movement: The Pass System," *NeWest Review*, v. 10, n. 9, May 1985, 8.
35. *NAC*, RG 10, v. 3584, f. 1130, pt. 3A, A. McDonald to E. Dewdney, 22 April 1885.
36. See, for example, *Ibid.*, v. 3710, f. 19, 550–53, A. McDonald to E. Dewdney, 28 May 1885.
37. J. Tobias, "Piapot Band During the Period 1870–1958," unpublished interim report, 23.
38. *NAC*, RG 10, v. 3584, f. 1130, pt. 3A, A. McDonald to E. Dewdney, 8 April 1885.
39. *Ibid.*, Pasquah and Muscowpetung to J.A. Macdonald, 21 April 1885.
40. *Ibid.*, v. 3709, f. 19, 550–52, Piapot to J.A. Macdonald, 30 April 1885.
41. *Ibid.*, A. McDonald to E. Dewdney, 26 April 1885; 27 April 1885.
42. *Ibid.*, 6 May 1885.
43. "Rebellion Trials," 263–65.
44. *NAC*, Macdonald papers, v. 107, 43071–74, E. Dewdney to J.A. Macdonald, 7 May 1885.
45. T. Flanagan, ed., *The Collected Writings of Louis Riel, v. 3* (Edmonton 1985), 401, 416.
46. There is considerable confusion over exactly who was sent to the Cut Knife camp. According to the minutes of the Exovedate, the seven men were: Isadore Parenteau, Joseph Arcand, Alexander Cayen (also known

as Cayieu or Keeteewayhow), Moise Carrière (called trois-pouces or Tripoos), Pierre Vandale, Charles Trottier, and John L. Crow (Dakota). "The Queen v. Louis Riel," appendix (43h), 45. During the subsequent trials, however, these and other names are mentioned. See "Rebellion Trials," 285, 319. Doug Light in *Footprints in the Dust* (North Battleford 1987) also provides different names (427).

47. "Rebellion Trials," 286.
48. *Ibid.*
49. *Ibid.*, 314; R. Jefferson, *Fifty Years on the Saskatchewan* (Battleford 1929), 147-48.
50. Hildebrandt, *Battle of Batoche*, 16-18; Payment, *Free People*, 72.
51. "Rebellion Trials," 1-13.
52. Quoted in Light, *Footprints*, 428.
53. "The Queen v. Louis Riel," appendix (43h), 45.
54. For a detailed, day-by-day analysis of the fight, see Hildebrandt, *Battle of Batoche*.
55. The exact number of Batoche dead varies greatly in the published accounts.
56. Dietz, "Wapahaska," 42; "Compte rendu de l'abbé G. Cloutier," 1886, v. 2, 36.
57. *Saskatchewan Indian Federated College* [*SIFC*], Samuel Seeseequasis interview, Beardy-Okemasis reserve, 7 March 1985.
58. *Ibid.*, Harry Michael interview, Beardy-Okemasis reserve, 13 March 1985. The medal was never given back and remains missing to this day.
59. D. Morton and R. Roy, eds., *Telegrams of the North-West Campaign, 1885* (Toronto 1972), 317, F. Middleton to A.P. Caron, 25 May 1885.
60. *NAC*, RG 10, v. 3584, f. 1130, pt. 1A, J.A. Macrae to E. Dewdney, 14 May 1885.
61. "Rebellion Trials," 303, 315-18.
62. L. Cochin, *Reminiscences of Father Cochin* (Battleford 1927), 35-36.
63. One of the men who delivered Poundmaker's letter of surrender was Alexander Cayen, the former mixed-blood chief of the Petequakey band and one of the agents Riel had sent to Cut Knife to bring the camp to Batoche. Light, *Footprints*, 463.
64. Quoted in *Ibid.*, 463.
65. Quoted in Cochin, *Reminiscences*, 61.
66. C.P. Mulvaney, *The History of the North-West Rebellion of 1885* (Toronto 1886), 384.
67. C.F. Winter, "The Surrender of Poundmaker," *The Cosmos*, v. 1, n. 10, October 1903, 84.
68. Mulvaney, *North-West Rebellion*, 386.
69. Winter, "The Surrender of Poundmaker," 84-86.
70. Mulvaney, *North-West Rebellion*, 393.
71. Cochin, *Reminiscences*, 38. See also M.R. Stobie, *The Other Side of*

Rebellion: The Remarkable Story of Charles Bremner and His Furs (Edmonton 1986), 64-65.

72. *NAC*, Macdonald papers, v. 107, 43071-74, E. Dewdney to J.A. Macdonald, 7 April 1885.

Too Many Scared People (pages 170-91)

1. One police scout counted 187 lodges near Frenchman's Butte. D. Christensen, "Selected Aspects of Fort Pitt's History," Saskatchewan Parks and Renewable Resources, 1984, 118.

2. *Ibid.*

3. *National Archives of Canada* [*NAC*], Manuscript Division, Hayter Reed papers, v. 18, f. Treaty Payments to Rebel Indians, L. Legoff to A.A.C. La Rivière, 31 March 1889. Father Legoff argued that the Chipewyan's situation was comparable to the Fort Pitt prisoners, in that both were induced to give themselves up out of fear. *Ibid.*, 17 April 1889.

4. H.A Dempsey, *Big Bear: The End of Freedom* (Vancouver 1984), 171-72.

5. *Hudson's Bay Company Archives* [*HBCA*], MS 372(5707), W.J. McLean, "Reminiscences of the Tragic Events at Frog Lake and in the Fort Pitt District with Some of the Experiences of the Writer and His Family during the North West Rebellion of 1885," 18-19.

6. *Ibid.*, 21-22, 28-29; Dempsey, *Big Bear*, 173.

7. Dempsey, *Big Bear*, 173.

8. E. Ahenakew, *Voices of the Plains Cree* (Regina 1995, 66); *HBCA*, McLean, "Reminiscences," 24-26.

9. B. Beal and R. Macleod, *Prairie Fire: The 1885 North-West Rebellion* (Edmonton 1984), 208.

10. G.F.G. Stanley, "Indian Raid at Lac la Biche," *Alberta History*, v. 24, n. 3, summer 1976, 25-27.

11. E. Rowand, "The Rebellion at Lac la Biche," *Alberta Historical Review*, v. 21, n. 3, summer 1973, 1-5; Dempsey, *Big Bear*, 166; Peter Shirt, a member of the Whitefish band, had had a dream a year earlier in which he saw death and trouble coming from the east (Frog Lake) and police coming from the west (Edmonton). See P. Erasmus, *Buffalo Days and Nights* (Calgary 1974), 271.

12. K.J. Tyler, "A Brief History of the Relations Between the Ministikwan Band and the Government of Canada, 1876-1916," unpublished report, 1-3.

13. *HBCA*, Rebellion Claims Commission hearings, 1886, J.N. Sinclair, "Green Lake Claim."

14. This analogy is taken from Beal and Macleod, *Prairie Fire*.

15. Quoted in D.H. Breen, "'Timber Tom' and the North-West Rebellion," *Alberta Historical Review*, v. 19, n. 3, summer 1971, 2.

16. *Provincial Archives of Alberta* [*PAA*], acc. 84.400, item 722, C. Scollen to V. Grandin, 20 April 1885.

17. *HBCA*, Rebellion Claims Commission hearings, 1886, T. Taylor testimony.

18. *NAC*, J.A. Macdonald papers, v. 107, 43062-66, C. Scollen to E. Dewdney, 12 April 1885; v. 107, 43066-67, C. Scollen to NWMP, Calgary, 15 April 1885.

19. *NAC*, RG 10, v. 3584, f. 1130, pt. 3A, Stonies in Council to E. Dewdney, 10 April 1885.

20. Quoted in Breen, "'Timber Tom,'" 3.

21. D. Morton and R. Roy, eds., *Telegrams of the North-West Campaign, 1885* (Toronto 1972), J. Cotton to A. Caron, 4 April 1885.

22. H. Dempsey, *Red Crow: Warrior Chief* (Saskatoon 1980), 152.

23. J. Dunn, *The Alberta Field Force of 1885* (Calgary 1994), 28-29; D. Light, *Footprints in the Dust* (North Battleford 1987), 265.

24. H. Dempsey, *Crowfoot* (Edmonton 1976), 192-93; H. Dempsey, "The Fearsome Fire Wagons" in H.A. Dempsey, ed., *The CPR West: The Iron Road and the Making of a Nation* (Vancouver 1984), 66-67.

25. Dunn, *Alberta Field Force*, 24.

26. *NAC*, Macdonald papers, v. 106, 42426, Crowfoot to J.A. Macdonald, 11 April 1885.

27. *Ibid.*, RG 10, v. 3709, f. 19,550-52, C. Denny to E. Dewdney, 1 May 1885.

28. *Glenbow Archives [GA]*, Blood Indian Agency, daily journal, 5 April to 17 April 1885.

29. Dunn, *Alberta Field Force*, 41.

30. Quoted in *Ibid.*, 269.

31. *NAC*, Macdonald papers, v. 107, 43075-77, E. Dewdney to J.A. Macdonald, 28 May 1885.

32. Quoted in D. Morton, *The Last War Drum* (Toronto 1972), 112.

33. *NAC*, RG 10, v. 3709, f. 19,550-52, C. Denny to E. Dewdney, 1 May 1885.

34. *GA*, Edgar Dewdney papers, box 4, f. 68, 1460-66, W.P. Sharpe to E. Dewdney, 9 April 1885; CPR telegrams, J.S. McDonald to J.M. Egan, 12 April 1885.

35. Quoted in Light, *Footprints*, 440.

36. *NAC*, RG 10, v. 3709, f. 19,550-52, S.B. Lucas to E. Dewdney, 30 April 1885.

37. *Ibid.*

38. *NAC*, Reed papers, v. 15, f. Rev. Father Scollen 1885, C. Scollen to E. Dewdney, 22 May 1885.

39. Dunn, *Alberta Field Force*, 90-93.

40. *NAC*, RG 10, v. 3710, f. 19,550-53, S.B. Lucas to E. Dewdney, 15 May 1885.

41. Breen, "'Timber Tom,'" 5-6.

42. Morton and Roy, eds., *Telegrams*, 270, H.P. Dwight to A.P. Caron, 12 May 1885.

43. Dunn, *Alberta Field Force*, 121-22.

44. *NAC*, Government Archives Division, Justice, RG 13, v. 806, 821-22, N. Delorme to beau-frère, 13 April 1885. John Pritchard had married Delorme's sister, Rose, in 1863. The wife of James K. Simpson, the local

HBC trader at Frog Lake, was apparently the sister of Gabriel Dumont.

45. W.J. McLean interview, Toronto *Mail*, 2 July 1885.

46. *HBCA*, McLean, "Reminiscences," 20-23.

47. Quoted in *Ibid.*, 26-27.

48. *Ibid.*, 27-28.

49. *Ibid.*, 29-30.

50. For a description of the thirst (or sun) dance and its purposes, see, K. Pettipas, *Severing the Ties that Bind: Government Repression of Indigenous Religious Ceremonies on the Prairies* (Winnipeg 1994), 53-61, 183-85.

51. Alex Stick interview, Loon Lake, 1885.

52. Amelia McLean, who was a prisoner in the camp, later suggested that Strange was able to surprise the Indians because they were so immersed in the thirst dance ceremony. A. Paget, *The People of the Plains* (Ryerson 1909), 40-41.

53. Dempsey, *Big Bear*, 175; *HBCA*, McLean, "Reminiscences," 33-34.

54. Dempsey, *Big Bear*, 175, n. 7; Dunn, *Alberta Field Force*, 153.

55. *NAC*, Government Archives Division, Parks Canada, RG 84, v. 1383, f. HS-10-3-9, pt. 1, Solomon Pritchard interview, September 1961. Pritchard's family had been held captive in the Frog Lake camp.

56. Strange preferred the name "Stand Off Coulee."

57. Dunn, *Alberta Field Force*, 159-67.

58. Kahweechatwaymat, the son of Lucky Man, was the same Indian who had assaulted farm instructor John Craig during the Little Pine thirst dance in July 1884.

59. Morton and Roy, eds., *Telegrams*, 333, F. Middleton to A.P. Caron, 6 June 1885. One member of Strange's force remarked that the battle should be "noted for the loss of good ammunition rather than the destruction of the enemy." J. Hicks, "With Hatton's Scouts in Pursuit of Big Bear," *Alberta Historical Review*, v. 18, n. 3, summer 1970, 19.

60. Quoted in Morton, *Last War Drum*, 123.

61. See, for example, *NAC*, Macdonald papers, v. 107, 43180-83, H. Reed to E. Dewdney, 23 June 1885.

62. Each cannon volley made two loud noises—one on discharge, the other on impact.

63. Dempsey, *Big Bear*, 176-77.

64. *Ibid.*

65. *HBCA*, McLean, "Reminiscences," 37-38; *NAC*, S. Pritchard interview.

66. Canada. *Sessional Papers*, 1886, n. 46, "Rebellion Trials," 182-83, 188.

67. One of their pursuers later remarked, "They did the very things to make us trouble, but stop and fight." Hicks, "With Hatton's Scouts," 19.

68. A. Stick interview.

69. Dempsey, *Big Bear*, 178.

70. A. Stick interview.

71. K.M. Yuill, "The Crossing of the Big Muskeg of Loon Lake, Saskatche-

wan, 1885," speech before North-West Field Association Reunion, Toronto, April 1935.

72. *HBCA*, McLean, "Reminiscences," 43.

73. *Ibid.*, 43-44.

74. W.A. Waiser, "Surveyors at War: A.O. Wheeler's Diary of the North–West Rebellion," *Saskatchewan History*, v. 38, n. 2, spring 1985, 49.

75. *Ontario Archives*, [*OA*], acc. 12843, Charles W. Dunning diary, 12 June 1885.

76. Waiser, "Surveyors at War," 50.

77. *NAC*, Macdonald papers, v. 107, 43180-83, H. Reed to E. Dewdney, 23 June 1885. See also 43173-78, J.M. Rae to E. Dewdney, 15 June 1885.

78. Morton and Roy, eds., *Telegrams*, 334, F. Middleton to A.P. Caron, 6 June 1885.

79. *Ibid.*, 344, F. Middleton to A.P. Caron, 13 June 1885.

80. *Ibid.*

81. *HBCA*, McLean, "Reminiscences," 45.

82. Dempsey, *Big Bear*, 179; *Saskatchewan Herald*, 6 July 1885.

83. *NAC*, Macdonald papers, v. 107, 43180-83, H. Reed to E. Dewdney, 23 June 1885.

Stabbing the Queen in the Behind (pages 192-213)

1. See, for example, Ansdell Macrae's report on the situation on the Battleford reserves in late May. *National Archives of Canada* [*NAC*], Government Archives Division, Indian Affairs, RG 10, v. 3584, f. 1130, pt. 1A, J.A. Macrae to E. Dewdney, 10 June 1885.

2. *NAC*, Manuscript Division, J.A. Macdonald papers, v. 107, 43075-77, E. Dewdney to J.A. Macdonald, 28 May 1885.

3. W.H. McKay, "Lucky Man's Flight," *Canadian Cattlemen*, December 1948.

4. *NAC*, Macdonald papers, v. 107, 43110-18, E. Dewdney to J.A. Macdonald, 3 June 1885.

5. J.L. Tobias, "Canada's Subjugation of the Plains Cree, 1879-1885" in J.R. Miller, ed., *Sweet Promises: A Reader in Indian-White Relations in Canada* (Toronto 1991), 231-32.

6. *Glenbow Archives* [*GA*], E. Dewdney papers, box 2, f. 38, 566-67, Edgar Dewdney to J.A. Macdonald, 16 June 1885; *NAC*, Macdonald papers, v. 107, 43166, Dewdney to Macdonald, 22 June 1885; 43171, 23 June 1885.

7. *NAC*, RG 10, v. 3584, f. 1130, E. Dewdney to L. Vankoughnet, 19 June 1885.

8. *Ibid.*, L. Vankoughnet to E. Dewdney, 3 July 1885.

9. *Ibid.*, pt. 1A, J.A. Macrae to E. Dewdney, 10 June 1885.

10. *Ibid.*, v. 3710, f. 19,550-53, A. McDonald to E. Dewdney, 29 May 1885.

11. D. Light, *Footprints in the Dust* (North Battleford 1987), 506.

12. S. Carter, *Lost Harvests: Prairie Indian Reserve Farmers and Government Policy* (Montreal 1990), 145.
13. See, for example, the list that Agent McDonald provided for his agency. *NAC*, RG 10, v. 3710, f. 19,350–51.
14. See D. Morton, *The Queen v Louis Riel* (Toronto 1974).
15. S.E. Bingaman, "The North-West Rebellion Trials," unpublished M.A. thesis, University of Regina, 1971, 3.
16. Only selected questions and answers were translated for the Indian defendants. See, for example, Canada. *Sessional Papers*, 1886, n. 52, "Rebellion Trials," 7.
17. *Ibid.*, 13.
18. Bingaman, "North-West Rebellion Trials," 7–8.
19. *NAC*, Macdonald papers, v. 290, 133119–20, L. Vankoughnet to J.A. Macdonald, 15 June 1885; 133121, A. Campbell to J.A. Macdonald, n.d.
20. Bingaman, "North-West Rebellion Trials," 30.
21. *Ibid.*, 110.
22. Quoted in J.R. Miller, *Skyscrapers Hide the Heavens: A History of Indian-White Relations in Canada* (Toronto 1989), 189.
23. B. Beal and R. Macleod, *Prairie Fire: The 1885 North-West Rebellion* (Edmonton 1984), 309.
24. "Rebellion Trials," 15.
25. *Ibid.*, 19.
26. *Ibid.*, 25.
27. *Ibid.*, 26–27.
28. *Ibid.*, 28.
29. *Ibid.*, 32–33.
30. *Ibid.*, 370.
31. *Ibid.*, 382.
32. *Ibid.*, 375.
33. *Ibid.*, 374.
34. *NAC*, RG 10, v. 3710, f. 19,350–53, J.A. Macrae to E. Dewdney, 14 May 1885.
35. *Ibid.*, Macdonald papers, v. 212, 90043, E. Dewdney to J.A. Macdonald, 16 February 1884.
36. Instead of fleeing to the United States with Gabriel Dumont, Michel Dumas, and Norbert Delorme, Jobin quietly returned to the Bellevue district (near Batoche) and died there in 1891. He was never brought to trial for his role in the rebellion.
37. "Rebellion Trials," 263–65.
38. *Ibid.*, 273.
39. *Ibid.*, 279–302.
40. *Ibid.*, 280. Jefferson knew what had happened in the Battleford area during the rebellion, but apparently decided not to speak up on Poundmaker's behalf to avoid getting in trouble with the Indian Affairs department.

41. *Ibid.*, 380.
42. *Ibid.*, 328.
43. *Ibid.*
44. *Ibid.*, 336.
45. *Ibid.*, 337.
46. *Saskatchewan Herald*, 24 August 1885.
47. *Ibid.*, 14 September 1885.
48. Lex, "Poundmaker's Trial," *The Week*, 10 September 1885, 645.
49. *Ibid.*, 646.
50. Quoted in Bingaman, "North-West Rebellion Trials," 43.
51. *Ibid.*, 36.
52. "Rebellion Trials," 175.
53. Light, *Footprints*, 521.
54. "Rebellion Trials," 218.
55. *Ibid.*, 231.
56. Quoted in W.B. Cameron, *The War Trail of Big Bear* (London 1927), 222-24.
57. See, for example, "Rebellion Trials," 249-51.
58. *Ibid.*, 338-41. The condemned Miserable Man apparently implicated Nault, but nothing was done. Bingaman, "North-West Rebellion Trials," 185.
59. D. Morton and R. Roy, eds., *Telegrams of the North-West Campaign, 1885* (Toronto 1972), 375, A.P. Caron to F. Middleton, 7 July 1885.
60. "Rebellion Trials," 45-50.
61. NAC, Government Archives Division, Justice, RG 13, series F-2, v. 820, 3388.
62. "Rebellion Trials," 51-52.
63. *Ibid.*, 60.
64. Bingaman, "North-West Rebellion Trials," 14.
65. See, for example, *Saskatchewan Herald*, 25 May 1885: "Good and loyal Indians are among the things of the past . . . there are none at present."; and 22 June 1885: " . . . the last remnant of this fiendish band [Poundmaker] should be wiped out of existence . . . put a price on their heads."
66. GA, Dewdney papers, box 4, f. 66, 1398-1401, H. Reed to E. Dewdney, 4 September 1884.
67. *Ibid*, 2508, C.B. Rouleau to E. Dewdney, 12 June 1885.
68. *Saskatchewan Herald*, 26 October 1885.
69. *Ibid.*, 20 July 1885.
70. Light, *Footprints*, 514.
71. Canada. *Sessional Papers*, 1886, n. 52a, "Battleford Trials," 6.
72. *Ibid.*, 8.
73. *Ibid.*, 22-23.
74. Quoted in Cameron, *War Trail*, 223.

Snaring Rabbits (pages 214-37)

1. *National Archives of Canada* [NAC], Manuscript Division, Hayter Reed papers, v. 14, f. Middleton, "Memo Relative to Indians who may surrender at Pitt," 3 July 1885.
2. *Ibid.*, J.A. Macdonald papers, v. 107, 43180-83, H. Reed to E. Dewdney, 23 June 1885.
3. *Ibid.*, Reed papers, Middleton memo, 3 July 1885.
4. *Ibid.*
5. *NAC*, Government Archives Division, Indian Affairs, RG 10, v. 3584, f. 1130, Hayter Reed, "Memorandum for the Honourable the Indian Commissioner relative to the future management of Indians," 13 July 1885.
6. *Glenbow Archives* [GA], Edgar Dewdney papers, H. Reed, "Memorandum for the Honble the Indian Commissioner relative to the future management of Indians," 20 July 1885.
7. *Ibid.*
8. *Ibid.*
9. *Ibid.*
10. *Ibid.*, marginal comments by Edgar Dewdney.
11. *NAC*, RG 10, v. 3584, f. 1130-1A, J. Rae to E. Dewdney, 18 May 1885.
12. *NAC*, Macdonald papers, v. 415, 201253-60, T.G. Jackson to J.A. Macdonald, 18 May 1885.
13. *Ibid.*, v. 107, 43240-42, A. Lacombe memorandum, n.d. (July 1885).
14. *Ibid.*, RG 10, v. 3710, f. 19,550-53, E. Dewdney to J.A. Macdonald, 1 August 1885.
15. *Ibid.*, E. Dewdney to J.A. Macdonald, 21 August 1885 (twenty-seven-page list of band behaviour during rebellion attached, see appendices).
16. Reed also accused the Flying Dust band of disloyalty, even though James Sinclair, the HBC agent at Green Lake, reported that the Indians had been loyal. *Ibid.*, v. 3585, f. 1130, J. Sinclair to J. Fortesque, 1 October 1888.
17. *Ibid.*, v. 3710, f. 19,550-53, E. Dewdney to J.A. Macdonald, 21 August 1885.
18. *Ibid.*, v. 3584, f. 1130, L. Vankoughnet to E. Dewdney, 29 August 1885.
19. *GA*, Dewdney papers, box 4, f. 57, 1232-39, H. Reed to E. Dewdney, 29 August 1885.
20. *Ibid.*
21. *NAC*, Macdonald papers, v. 212, 90330, E. Dewdney to J.A. Macdonald, 3 September 1885.
22. *Ibid.*, v. 174, 71811-14, Lansdowne to J.A. Macdonald, 4 September 1885.
23. *GA*, Dewdney papers, box 4, f. 57, H. Reed to E. Dewdney, 6 September 1885.
24. *Ibid.*, box 2, f. 38, 575-76, J. Maylan to J.A. Macdonald, 26 October 1885.

25. *NAC*, RG 10, v. 3710, f. 19,550-53, L. Vankoughnet to J.A. Macdonald, 17 August 1885 (Macdonald's comments are found in the margin along with his initials).
26. *Ibid.*, L. Vankoughnet to H. Reed, 28 October 1885 (this letter was written on behalf of Macdonald).
27. *Ibid.*, Macdonald papers, v. 106, 42559-62, Lansdowne to J.A. Macdonald, 31 August 1885.
28. *Ibid.*, v. 23, 271-72, J.A. Macdonald to Lansdowne, 3 September 1885.
29. For a chronology of the decisions leading up to the executions, see the capital case files in *NAC*, Government Archives Division, Justice, RG 13, v. 1421, f. 194A, 195A, 196A, 197A, 197A-1, 198A, 199A, 200A, and 203A; v. 1423, f. 206A and 207A.
30. *GA*, Dewdney papers, box 2, f. 38, 587-88, J.A. Macdonald to E. Dewdney, 20 November 1885.
31. W.B. Cameron, *The War Trail of Big Bear* (London 1927), 231-32.
32. D. Light, *Footprints in the Dust* (North Battleford 1987), 533. The new converts' godfather was Abraham Montour, who along with André Nault, had successfully avoided punishment for their activities in the Frog Lake area.
33. *Saskatchewan Herald*, 30 November 1885.
34. Mongrain's death sentence was commuted to life imprisonment because of the intervention of former hostage Amelia McLean, who stated in a sworn deposition that another Indian had reportedly shot Cowan at Fort Pitt and that Mongrain had protected the prisoners. *NAC*, RG 13, v. 1421, f. 200A, "Amelia McLean affidavit," 28 October 1885. For the Dressyman and Charlebois capital case files, see *Ibid.*, v. 1423, f. 206A and 207A.
35. Manitoba *Free Press*, 28 November 1885; *Saskatchewan Herald*, 30 November 1885.
36. Cameron, *War Trail*, 161.
37. Light, *Footprints*, 534.
38. Manitoba *Free Press*, 28 November 1885; *Saskatchewan Herald*, 30 November 1885.
39. *Ibid.*; Cameron, *War Trail*, 239.
40. *Ibid.*; In the United States's largest mass hanging, thirty-eight Sioux were executed at Fort Snelling, Minnesota, for their part in the 1862-63 uprising.
41. R. Jefferson, *Fifty Years on the Saskatchewan* (Battleford 1929), 153.
42. *Saskatchewan Herald*, 30 November 1885.
43. *NAC*, Government Archives Division, Parks Canada, RG 84, v. 1057, f. BA28, pt. 1, A.J.H. Richardson memo, 18 April 1957.
44. *Saskatchewan Herald*, 30 November 1885.
45. *The Week*, 3 December 1885, 9.
46. *GA*, Dewdney papers, box 2, f. 38, 589-90, E. Dewdney to J.A. Macdonald, 20 December 1885.

47. *GA*, M4792, Blood Indian Agency, daily journal, 21 and 24 November 1885.

48. *Saskatchewan Herald*, 30 November 1885.

49. Paul Chicken interview, Sweetgrass reserve, 11 June 1993.

50. Joe Dressyman interview, Red Pheasant reserve, 15 April 1993.

51. Don Chatsis interview, Prince Albert, 3 February 1994.

52. *NAC*, Macdonald papers, v. 212, 90322-26, H. Reed to E. Dewdney, 31 August 1885.

53. K. Tyler, "The History of the Mosquito, Grizzly Bear's Head, and Lean Man Bands, 1878-1920," unpublished interim report, 5.

54. Light, *Footprints*, 532; *The Canada Gazette*, v. 20, n. 3, 17 July 1886, 68.

55. L. Burt, "Nowhere Left to Go: Montana's Cree, Métis, and Chippewas and the Creation of the Rocky Boy Reservation," *Great Plains Quarterly*, v. 7, n. 3, summer 1987, 199.

56. J. Dempsey, "Little Bear's Band: Canadian or American Indians," *Alberta History*, v. 41, n. 4, autumn 1993, 3.

57. Burt, "Nowhere Left to Go," 200.

58. Quoted in *Ibid.*

59. Rattle Snake, Fort Belknap enrolment testimony, 1921. This document was kindly provided by Eva Walker of Montana, the great-great granddaughter of Lean Man.

60. Light, *Footprints*, 189, 514.

61. White probate file, allottee n. 1724, 28 March 1938, Fort Peck Agency, Bureau of Indian Affairs, Montana.

62. Burt, "Nowhere Left to Go," 202-7; Dempsey, "Little Bear's Band," 4-8. See also H.J. Peterson, "Imasees and His Band: Canadian Refugees after the North-West Rebellion," *The Western Canadian Journal of Anthropology*, v. 8, n. 1, 1978, 21-37.

63. *NAC*, Reed papers, v. 18, f. Treaty Payments to Rebel Indians, L. Legoff to A.A.C. La Rivière, 31 March 1889.

64. See, for example, T. Pyrch, "The Chacastapasin Surrender," unpublished interim report, 1973.

65. *NAC*, RG 10, v. 3585, f. 1130, pt. 8, Cuthbert to A.B. Perry, 20 January 1886.

66. *Ibid.*, Government Archives Division, Royal Canadian Mounted Police, RG 18, f. 796, E. Dewdney to A.G. Irvine, 1 February 1886.

67. *Ibid.*, Macdonald papers, v. 213, 90438-42, L. Herchmer to E. Dewdney, 21 January 1886.

68. *Ibid.*, v. 231, 90430-33, E. Dewdney to J.A. Macdonald, 26 January 1886.

69. *Ibid.*, RG 10, v. 3710, f. 19, 550-54, Hayter Reed to J.A. Macdonald, 25 January 1886.

70. *Ibid.*, Macdonald papers, v. 213, 90430-33, E. Dewdney to J.A. Macdonald, 26 January 1886.

71. S. Carter, *Lost Harvests: Prairie Indian Reserve Farmers and Government Policy* (Montreal 1990), 130-36.

72. Canada. *Sessional Papers*, 1186, n. 4, "Annual Report of the Department of Indian Affairs," 141.

73. *GA*, Dewdney papers, 596-97, J.A. Macdonald to E. Dewdney, 9 February 1886; *NAC*, Macdonald papers, v. 213, 90599-601, E. Dewdney to L. Vankoughnet, 23 February 1886; *NAC*, RG 10, v. 3757, f. 31106, M. Begg to E. Dewdney, 7 July 1886. Vankoughnet was adamantly opposed to Poundmaker's release and told Macdonald, "There has been an immense amount of sentimentality about this man owing to his fine appearance, but I believe him to be a consummate scoundrel." *NAC*, Macdonald papers, v. 213, 90427-29, L. Vankoughnet to J.A. Macdonald, 2 February 1886.

74. *NAC*, RG 10, v. 3584, f. 1130, pt. 8, A. Levesque to E. Dewdney, 8 April 1886 and 14 April 1886; v. 3598, f. 1141, H. Reed to E. Dewdney, 17 April 1886; *Le Manitoba*, 22 April 1886 and 29 April 1886. One Arrow apparently took his Christian name from Senator Marc Girard of Manitoba. *Saskatchewan Herald*, 17 May 1886.

75. The Macdonald government claimed to have released Big Bear as a favour to Chiefs Mistawasis and Ahtahkakoop (*NAC*, RG 10, v. 3584, f. 1130, pt. 8, E. Dewdney to Prince Albert Indian Agent, 5 March 1887), but a report from the prison doctor indicated that his condition was rapidly deteriorating and that he was likely to die in prison. Reed opposed the release on the grounds that the dispersed members of his former band had only started to adjust to their new locations (*NAC*, RG 10, v. 3774, f. 36486, H. Reed to J.A. Macdonald, 29 January 1886).

76. A. Morris, *The Treaties of Canada with the Indians of Manitoba and the North-West Territories* (Saskatoon 1991), 295-97.

Keeping Faith (pages 238-41)

1. *National Archives of Canada* [*NAC*], Government Archives Division, Indian Affairs, RG 10, v. 3709, f. 19, 550-51, A. McDonald to E. Dewdney, 8 April 1885.

2. *Ibid.*, Manuscript Division, J.A Macdonald papers, v. 106, 42437, Pasquah and Muscowpetung to J.A. Macdonald, 22 April 1885.

3. *Ibid.*, RG 10, v. 3709, f. 19,550-52, Piapot to J.A. Macdonald, 2 May 1885.

4. *Ibid.*, Macdonald papers, v. 106, 42468, J.A. Macdonald to E. Dewdney, 12 May 1885.

5. *The Globe and Mail*, 23 May 1994.

index

Blair Stonechild, a member of the Muscowpetung band in southern Saskatchewan, was born in Fort Qu'Appelle and raised in Lebret and Regina. He earned his B.A. at McGill University in Montreal, and an M.A. at the University of Regina. He has worked as an Indian land claims researcher for the Federation of Saskatchewan Indian Nations, and was the first instructor hired at the Saskatchewan Indian Federated College at the University of Regina in 1976. He went on to become head of the Department of Indian Studies and later dean of the college. He is currently executive director of planning and development at SIFC. Blair and his wife, Sylvia, and their three children live in Regina.

Bill Waiser earned a B.A. in history from Trent University, and obtained his M.A. and Ph.D. from the University of Saskatchewan. He worked as Yukon historian for the Canadian Parks Service before accepting a teaching position at the U. of S. in 1984. A full professor since 1990, he specializes in western and northern Canadian history and is currently head of the Department of History. Bill is the author of several books, including *The New Northwest: The Photographs of the Frank Crean Expeditions, 1908-1909* and *Saskatchewan's Playground: A*

History of Prince Albert National Park, which won a Canadian Parks Partnership National Award of Excellence and was recognized by the Canadian Historical Association as a "high quality book which makes a significant contribution to western Canada." He is also the author of the highly acclaimed *Park Prisoners: The Untold Story of Western Canada's National Parks, 1915-1946.* Bill lives in Saskatoon with his wife, Marley, and their three children.